Architecting Enterprise AI Strategies

From Vision to Scalable Execution

Dr. Rajnish Harjika

Apress®

Architecting Enterprise AI Strategies: From Vision to Scalable Execution

Rajnish Harjika
Dubai, Dubai, United Arab Emirates

ISBN-13 (pbk): 979-8-8688-2218-6 ISBN-13 (electronic): 979-8-8688-2219-3
https://doi.org/10.1007/979-8-8688-2219-3

Managing Director, Apress Media LLC: Welmoed Spahr
Acquisitions Editor: Aditee Mirashi
Editorial Assistant: Gryffin Winkler

Cover designed by eStudioCalamar

Cover image designed by kjpargeter on freepik

Distributed to the book trade worldwide by Springer Science+Business Media New York, 1 New York Plaza, New York, NY 10004. Phone 1-800-SPRINGER, fax (201) 348-4505, e-mail orders-ny@springer-sbm.com, or visit www.springeronline.com. Apress Media, LLC is a Delaware LLC and the sole member (owner) is Springer Science + Business Media Finance Inc (SSBM Finance Inc). SSBM Finance Inc is a **Delaware** corporation.

For information on translations, please e-mail booktranslations@springernature.com; for reprint, paperback, or audio rights, please e-mail bookpermissions@springernature.com.

Apress titles may be purchased in bulk for academic, corporate, or promotional use. eBook versions and licenses are also available for most titles. For more information, reference our Print and eBook Bulk Sales web page at http://www.apress.com/bulk-sales.

Any source code or other supplementary material referenced by the author in this book is available to readers on GitHub. For more detailed information, please visit https://www.apress.com/gp/services/source-code.

If disposing of this product, please recycle the paper

From the Author:

To my parents, especially my mother, Ms. Sulochna Harjika; my wife, Ms. Naveen Nav; and my friend and partner in crime, Mr. Furrukh Sohail. I would also like to express my gratitude to my former CEO, Mr. Gaurav Malhotra, and to my current CEO, Mr. Martin Pluecker of NovaPilot, for their trust and encouragement. Most importantly, I would like to thank Ms. Vanshika Gupta, the developmental editor and content architect, who worked with me to ensure that high-quality content was delivered.

From the Contributing Author:

To the butterfly that fluttered its wings and placed me as the medium through which this book came into existence, I bow to you with gratitude.
It was the early days of July 2025, and I had no idea that the moments that followed would change everything. In that same wind of chance, this opportunity found me to work on a subject that has become both humanity's greatest fascination and its deepest fear. I would like to thank Rajnish for giving me this opportunity, my parents, my brother Chaitanya, my Bono Ankita Dung Dung, Ritu Aunty, and everyone who believed in me for the support and strength they offered throughout this journey. In the end, no matter the chaos that surrounds you, there is always that one butterfly whose flight carries you through everything, even when it feels difficult to look beyond the chaos.

Table of Contents

About the Author

Rajnish Harjika is a seasoned technology leader with over two decades of global experience in enterprise architecture, AI/ML, and digital transformation, including extensive work in banking, healthcare, and smart city innovation. He has held pivotal leadership roles, such as Chief Enterprise Architect and Vice President of Technology, driving large-scale AI adoption and cloud modernization initiatives across North America, the Middle East, the UAE, and Southeast Asia. A recognized keynote speaker and published author, Harjika is known for uniting architectural depth with visionary leadership to guide organizations, from startups to global enterprises, toward responsible growth in the age of intelligence. He holds a PhD in strategic management with a focus on AI and generative AI and continues to help enterprises design ecosystems that are adaptive, secure, and capable of enduring transformation.

About the Contributing Author

Vanshika Gupta is a technology professional with a Bachelor of Technology in Information Technology, specializing in Artificial Intelligence. Her work reflects a deep engagement with emerging technologies and a growing focus in the domain of agentic AI. She brings together analytical thinking, design sensibility, and strategic vision, grounded in a clear understanding of how intelligent systems can be applied across industries. With a solid technical foundation and an enthusiasm for innovation, she approaches technology as both an engineer and a strategist. Through her professional initiatives, she continues to explore how technical precision and strategic foresight can come together to build solutions that create lasting value for enterprises and meaningful impact for people.

About the Technical Reviewer

Sanyam Jain is a globally recognized security engineering architect and cybersecurity thought leader, known for securing complex digital ecosystems and strengthening resilience across cloud-native environments. With expertise in cloud security, security operations, application security, compliance, and security automation, he helps enterprises and startups exceed their security goals through strategic foresight and technical excellence.

Embracing a DevSecOps-first approach, Sanyam designs secure architectures, embeds security in CI/CD pipelines, and automates compliance. His skills span threat detection, Kubernetes security, IAM, encryption, and network security across AWS, Azure, and Google Cloud. He is well-versed in frameworks such as ISO 27001, SOC 2, SOX, HITRUST, GDPR, HIPAA, PCI DSS, and NIST CSF, enabling secure-by-design implementations that meet audit requirements.

Sanyam's research has been featured in *Forbes, TechCrunch, ZDNet,* and other leading publications. He also serves as a judge for the Globee Awards and the Business Intelligence Group, an evaluator in the Smart India Hackathon, a mentor with NITI Aayog, and an advisor to startups and NGOs like the GDI Foundation.

A reviewer for O'Reilly, Apress, and BPB Publications, he has mentored thousands through Udacity and other learning platforms. Sanyam holds a master's degree in technology from BITS Pilani and is a Certified Kubernetes Administrator.

Acknowledgments

I extend my deepest gratitude to my parents for shaping the foundation of who I am. To my mother, **Ms. Sulochna Harjika**, whose unwavering belief in me has been a constant source of strength—this book carries your spirit on every page.

To my wife, **Naveen Nav**, thank you for supporting me far beyond the boundaries of this book. Your patience, encouragement, and love sustained me throughout this journey.

My heartfelt thanks also go to my sisters, whose presence and positivity have always lifted me, and to my best buddy and partner in crime, **Mr. Furrukh Sohail**, for standing by me through every high and low.

A special note of appreciation goes to **Ms. Vanshika Gupta**, my co-author. Thank you for your dedication, collaboration, and for helping turn this vision into reality.

This book exists because of all of you.

—Rajnish Harjika

Introduction

We begin this book with two convictions that shape everything that follows. They are neither distant theories nor polished slogans. They arise from observing how enterprises evolve, how they succeed, and how often they lose sight of the human purpose that once gave them meaning.

The **first conviction** affirms that enterprise architecture, or what we call EA thinking, belongs to everyone. Too often, it is framed as the domain of specialists, that is, the architect with diagrams or the executive with strategies. In truth, every decision in technology carries architectural weight. The student designing a modest application, the analyst shaping a dataset, and the manager requesting a new tool all participate in the design of the larger system. Each choice either strengthens the structure of the enterprise or isolates itself and weakens it over time. Innovation without architectural grounding burns briefly and disappears. Innovation built with foresight endures and grows. This book is therefore not addressed only to those who hold formal titles. It speaks to anyone who wishes to understand how their work contributes to the design of enterprise systems and how even the smallest actions influence outcomes far beyond their immediate scope.

The **second conviction** holds that artificial intelligence must deepen, not distort, our grasp of reality. We live in a moment when intelligence can be generated, replicated, and simulated so convincingly that the line between the authentic and the artificial begins to blur. The challenge of this moment rests in preserving moral strength, in keeping judgment clear, and in keeping purpose steady as intelligence expands its reach. When intelligence operates without human oversight, it produces reflection without reference and turns truth into imitation. When guided with such awareness, technology serves understanding and reveals truth with greater fidelity. To remain oriented, we return to what this book calls the Human Endpoint Principle: ***all systems exist to serve people***. This conviction finds resonance in the reflections of **Garry Kasparov**, the world chess champion who faced the earliest expressions of machine intelligence across the 64 squares of a chessboard. The match between human intuition and algorithmic reasoning marked one of the first moments when intellect in organic form met intellect in constructed form. What unfolded was more than a contest of moves; it was an encounter between two architectures of thought. The human mind, shaped by emotion, imagination, and memory, met a system that calculated through structure, precision, and pattern.

In later years, Kasparov reflected on that experience as a revelation of partnership. He described how the collaboration of human insight and machine analysis expanded both forms of intelligence. The game, once seen as a rivalry, evolved into a dialogue, an exchange in which humans learned from the patience of algorithms and algorithms gained purpose through human creativity. Chess became a metaphor for the emerging relationship between humanity and its own creation, a reminder that mastery is shared when design and imagination act together. Kasparov continued to emphasize that progress flourishes through this spirit of cooperation. The lessons of that early encounter continue to shape the age of artificial intelligence, revealing that the truest form of advancement arises when humanity and its machines learn to think together, each strengthening the other through awareness and purpose. The task before us, therefore, is to design systems that expand human agency while protecting the ground of reality from which meaning arises.

With these convictions, the arc of this book unfolds. We explore the global shift toward AI and distinguish promise from performance. We show how enterprise architecture forms the foundation of sustainable transformation. We examine the challenges faced by organizations of different scales and how data becomes the essential medium of intelligence. We move through questions of scale and platform design, follow real-world cases that reveal how AI reshapes industries, and turn to governance, ethics, and responsible practice. In the final chapters, we look outward to the cultural transformations that must accompany technological change if enterprises are to thrive in the ***Anno Artificialis Intelligenciae***, i.e., the age of artificial intelligence. This introduction stands as both a warning and an invitation. A warning that without architectural understanding, innovation remains fragile, and without human orientation, it loses purpose.

It is an invitation to approach intelligence as stewardship, to build it in a way that honors the people it serves. We continue with conviction: enterprise architecture as the discipline that aligns intelligence with purpose and humanity as the guiding principle that keeps its direction true.

CHAPTER 1

The Global Shift to AI: Hype vs. Reality

We can only see a short distance ahead, but we can see plenty there that needs to be done.

—Alan Mathison Turing (Computing Machinery and Intelligence, 1950)

Introduction

The story of artificial intelligence is often told as one of technological breakthroughs. For enterprises and for societies, however, the more pressing story is one of integration: how to fold intelligent systems into the messy realities of organizational life, human decision-making, and public trust. This chapter sets out those stakes. Although AI itself is not new, the circumstances surrounding its application today are unprecedented.

When Alan Turing posed the question ***"Can machines think?"*** in his 1950 paper "Computing Machinery and Intelligence" [1], he was less concerned with building machines that mimicked human thought than with testing the boundaries of what counted as "thinking." His "imitation game," later known as the Turing Test, offered a philosophical challenge: ***Could behavior alone, without reference to inner experience, be enough to grant intelligence?*** That thought experiment continues to influence how AI is evaluated, even in boardrooms.

Fast forward to today, and researchers like Geoffrey Hinton have argued for broader redefinitions. In his Analogy Machine Theory [2], Hinton suggests that human thought is fundamentally analogical rather than strictly logical. We draw connections, notice patterns, and infer relationships in ways that resist rigid rules. Machines built on similar principles may, paradoxically, feel less alien and more recognizably human in their

R. Harjika, *Architecting Enterprise AI Strategies*, https://doi.org/10.1007/979-8-8688-2219-3_1

reasoning. For enterprises, this shift is critical: AI systems are no longer just automating logic but approximating forms of creativity and judgment once thought to belong solely to people.

And yet, the tension remains. As *Communications of the ACM* (the flagship publication of the Association for Computing Machinery, the world's leading professional body for computing) observes in its reflections on the "human or machine" question [3], our daily lives are filled with blurred boundaries. A chatbot handling customer service, a recommendation engine influencing purchases, or an algorithm scanning for financial risk: each shows how human and machine contributions increasingly overlap. For enterprises, this overlap is both powerful and demanding. It extends the reach of automation but complicates accountability. ***Who takes responsibility when a machine-driven judgment produces unexpected consequences? How should leaders balance efficiency gains with ethical and reputational costs?***

These philosophical currents form the context for enterprise decision-making. As this book unfolds, we argue that understanding AI in the enterprise requires three layers of perspective:

- **Technological:** The architectures, data pipelines, and models that underpin AI systems
- **Organizational:** The structures, processes, and leadership practices that determine adoption success
- **Ethical and societal:** The guardrails, governance mechanisms, and environmental considerations that give AI legitimacy

We recognize that not all readers will meet this book with optimism, and rightfully so. For many, the prospect of job loss, the risks of bias and privacy breaches, or the immense energy costs of AI weigh heavily. These concerns deserve the same seriousness as the celebrated benefits of this technology. At the heart of every system we design lies an undeniable truth: the endpoint is always ***human***. Products and services do not exist for themselves; they exist to serve people. If we lose sight of this, if we design systems that serve the pursuit of superintelligence, competitive one-upmanship, or the race for the most powerful model rather than the needs of people, we risk creating technologies that overload rather than support and pressure rather than empower.

Who else qualifies to discuss the philosophical aspect of this better than the great Russian thinker Fyodor Dostoevsky? His work reminds us that genuine wisdom demands more than sheer intelligence; it requires the moral depth to act rightly.

It is this wisdom, rooted in the irreducible depth of the human spirit, that no algorithm can replicate. To forget this, in pursuit of profit or speed, would be to lose sight of what technology is meant to serve in the first place. This unspoken depth of the human spirit cannot be simulated. Because ***technology, in the absence of human context, is but a ghost: brilliant in form, hollow in purpose.***

This is why a central premise of this book is to engage skepticism as a compass rather than treat it as a negative instrument, because skepticism is not an enemy of progress. A central commitment of this book is to address these realities head-on. Chapters on ethics, governance, and environmental impact will outline frameworks enterprises can adopt to ensure that AI strengthens shareholder value only in ways that also build societal trust and sustainability. In doing so, enterprises move beyond mere adoption and step into leadership, bearing responsibility for shaping the regulatory and moral foundations of the AI age, since they hold the power to influence how these systems are deployed. Chapter 7 will expand this discussion through the broader lens of the technosocial impacts of AI, how these technologies ripple across society, shaping norms, expectations, and futures. These impacts are not abstract; they touch humans at both ends of the enterprise: the employees within organizations and the people they serve through their operations. With the endpoint always being human, enterprises must remain acutely aware of the technosocial consequences of their choices.

Technological advancement must continue; it always has, but its legitimacy rests on whether it serves humanity rather than threatens it. This is why skepticism matters. Many in the workforce hesitate to welcome AI because they sense a danger: that the very tools designed to ease their burden might instead erode what makes us human—our idiosyncrasies, dignity, agency, or livelihood. This does not mean they are against progress, but rather against losing what makes them human. Enterprises face the same hesitation. To ignore this premise is to endanger the very institutions AI is meant to strengthen. To build without that awareness is to build against ourselves. And if a system undermines humanity itself, then the question is not whether it can be built, but whether it should be.

For now, this introduction makes a modest claim: AI is neither a distant horizon nor a universal solution. It is a toolkit whose impact depends on the quality of its integration. Like Turing's test or Hinton's analogy machine, its promise lies in reshaping the conditions under which human and machine intelligence intersect, not in replacing human thought altogether. For enterprises, the opportunity lies in adopting AI responsibly and strategically, with a long-term view of consequences for both business and society.

1.1 The Evolution of AI: From the Turing Test to GPT Models

Artificial intelligence has always lived at the intersection of philosophy, mathematics, and engineering. To understand the state of AI today and its implications for enterprises, we need to appreciate its lineage. Before we proceed with how enterprises must incorporate AI, it is necessary to reflect on the very soul of the technology now being discussed at every turn. You have likely heard it in boardrooms or over coffee with a colleague: AI is framed as the "next big thing" for profitability and transformation. That may be true, but the pertinent questions are: ***What exactly is AI? Why does it suddenly feel ubiquitous, from billboards to job postings to self-check-in kiosks at your local takeaway counter? How did we reach the point where every organization is rushing to adopt it, often without a practical sense of why?***

To explain this, we divide the landscape into two timelines. Just as history is often segmented into Before Christ (B.C.) and Anno Domini (A.D.), our modern world increasingly feels split into Before AI and In the Age of AI, or what we term in this book, ***Anno Artificialis Intelligenciae (AAI)***. This phrase describes the years following the widespread integration of artificial intelligence into everyday systems and machines. What was once just a research buzzword has become embedded in daily life worldwide, from home automation to enterprise planning.

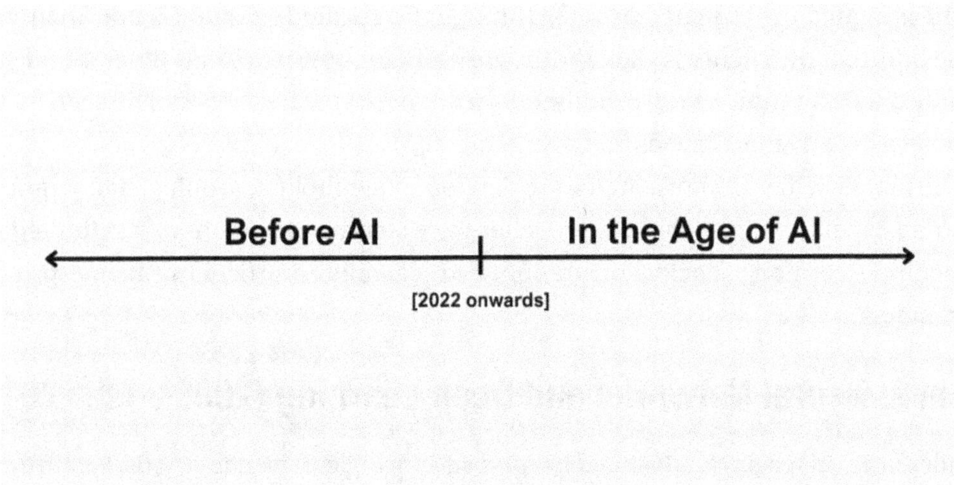

Figure 1-1. *The Shift from Before AI to the Age of AI (Anno Artificialis Intelligenciae)*

Turing and the Origins of the Question

In 1950, Alan Turing published his landmark paper "Computing Machinery and Intelligence" [1]. Rather than defining intelligence outright, Turing introduced the "imitation game," later known as the Turing Test. His question, ***"Can machines think?"***, invited a new way of evaluating behavior. If a machine could imitate human conversation convincingly enough to be indistinguishable from a person, might that be considered intelligence?

For enterprises today, Turing's provocation still resonates. Boards and executives now frame the question differently: ***Can AI imitate reasoning in ways that enhance efficiency, reduce risk, and create value?*** Turing's insight, that intelligence can be judged by performance, continues to shape how businesses approach AI adoption.

The Three Booms of AI: A Chronicle of Its Evolution

Boom 1: Symbolic AI and Foundational Theories (1950s–1990s)

This perceived divide is not about when AI was invented. Contrary to popular belief, the technology did not appear suddenly in 2022 when it entered everyday vocabulary. Its roots stretch back to visionaries such as Alan Turing, who introduced the idea of machines simulating human reasoning through the Turing Test, and Claude Shannon, whose Information Theory [4] laid the groundwork for how machines process and quantify data. Shannon's early experiments with mechanical games can be seen as prototypes of early machine learning systems.

The first decades of AI research were defined by symbolic reasoning, handcrafted logic, and expert systems. These approaches were significant, but they were limited in adaptability, learning capacity, integration, and scalability, particularly in enterprise environments.

Boom 2: Neural Networks and Deep Learning (2000s–Mid-2010s)

Decades later, AI research advanced beyond strictly logic-driven methods. Geoffrey Hinton, often called the "godfather of deep learning," proposed the Analogy Machine Theory [5], arguing that human cognition is not purely logical but deeply analogical. We connect ideas, infer relationships, and leap across gaps that rigid rules cannot bridge. When machines begin to operate in this associative, pattern-based mode, their potential extends from task automation to the augmentation of creativity and judgment.

For enterprises, this evolution marked a turning point. Traditional automation depended on deterministic systems: rules, workflows, and predefined conditions. Modern AI, by contrast, is grounded in analogy and pattern recognition, enabling systems to manage ambiguity, learn from data, and adapt dynamically to new contexts. This capacity is what allows AI to reshape industries. The contemporary era of enterprise AI accelerated when Hinton revived neural networks, inspired by the structure of the human brain. With the convergence of big data, natural language processing, GPU-enabled cloud infrastructure, and massive computing power, deep learning became both feasible and scalable across organizations. As we explore in Chapters 5 and 6, these advances form the backbone of today's enterprise-scale AI platforms, from on-premise systems to hybrid cloud architectures. In this context, enterprises are not simply adopting AI but building strategies anchored on four guiding parameters: accessibility, explainability, security, and ethics. These pillars remain central throughout this book, ensuring that enterprise AI is both transformative and responsible.

Boom 3: Generative AI and the Rise of LLMs (Post-2022)

The most visible shift came after 2022, when AI became widely accessible through the rise of large language models (LLMs) and generative AI (GAI). Built on transformer architectures introduced in the landmark 2017 paper "Attention Is All You Need" [6], these systems transformed AI from a specialist's tool into a mainstream capability. Generative AI gained momentum around 2019 and introduced a new dimension to our lived reality: beyond length, breadth, and height, there is now an ambient computational presence, appearing in the form of GAI. Unlike older systems that processed existing data, GAI can produce or "generate" new content: text, visuals, audio, and code. This raises not only operational questions but also philosophical ones: ***Is AI capable of creativity? Is it conscious?***

As we will examine in Chapter 5, these capabilities rest on innovations in LLM training, prompt engineering, fine-tuning, and retrieval-augmented generation (RAG). For enterprises, the challenge lies in adapting these techniques responsibly for secure and scalable environments. This third boom marks a decisive departure from symbolic AI and fragile expert systems. Earlier systems, while significant, were rigid, rule-based, and poorly suited to dynamic enterprise contexts. They struggled with scale and required complex maintenance. In contrast, today's neural and data-driven approaches are built to adapt to complexity and nuance rather than collapse under it. The story of AI does not begin with LLMs, chatbots, or Silicon Valley startups. Its foundations trace back to John von Neumann [7], who laid the blueprint for programmable, memory-based machines, an architecture that continues to evolve into intelligent agents. While text-based LLMs dominate public imagination, multimodal AI is fast emerging as the next frontier. These models interpret and generate across text, vision, audio, and video, moving closer to humanlike perception. They already show promise in tasks that blend modalities, such as analyzing medical images alongside patient histories or answering questions about charts, photos, or videos.

For enterprises, multimodal systems point to powerful applications in manufacturing, diagnostics, and compliance. But meaningful adoption requires re-architecting foundational systems with clarity about design constraints, business objectives, data pipelines, and human values. Chapter 4 will address these data foundations in detail, showing why data, not models, is the definitive enabler of enterprise AI. AI cannot be simply bolted onto legacy systems, a common mistake we examine in Chapter 2. As later chapters will emphasize, successful enterprise AI must be designed like any other lifecycle-intensive system: with forethought, governance, scalability, and alignment to enterprise architecture from day one.

Why This Evolution Matters for Enterprises

Tracing AI's evolution from the Turing Test to GPT models highlights three enduring points:

- AI has always been tied to human definitions of intelligence. From imitation to analogy, enterprises must recognize that how we define intelligence shapes how we deploy it.
- Shifts in AI paradigms mirror shifts in enterprise application. From deterministic automation to adaptive systems, each stage has required new strategies.
- Every breakthrough expands both capability and responsibility. The closer AI systems come to approximating human judgment, the greater the burden on enterprises to ensure ethical, transparent, and responsible use.

This is why AI evolution is the right starting point for this book. It bridges philosophy and practice, skepticism and optimism. It situates enterprise leaders and young professionals alike in a lineage that explains not just where AI stands today, but why its governance and adoption must be approached with care. Later chapters will return to these themes, particularly in discussions of guardrails for innovation (Chapter 7) and the cultural transformations of AI adoption (Chapter 8).

1.2 Navigating the Hype Cycle: Looking Under the Hood to Analyze AI's Real Impact

If you are interested in understanding how to infuse AI into the enterprise, or any technology for that matter, into the enterprise, you need to be familiar with the Gartner Hype Cycle [8] and its five phases:

Innovation Trigger ➤ Peak of Inflated Expectations ➤ Trough of Disillusionment ➤ Slope of Enlightenment ➤ Plateau of Productivity

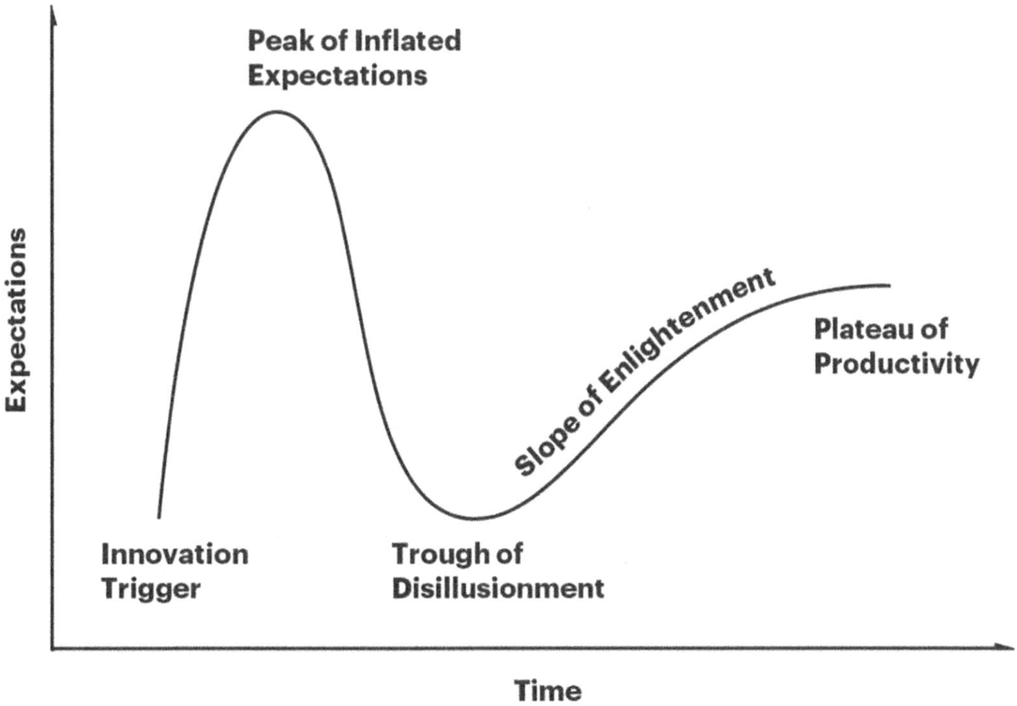

Figure 1-2. *The Gartner Hype Cycle for AI Adoption*

(Yes, subconsciously, you're likely already drawing parallels between these phases and the current trajectory of AI development and adoption. With the widespread use of large language models, we humans have unlocked new ways of thinking and interpreting information. In fact, we've begun to mirror the parallel tokenization approach of LLMs, where context is built layer by layer as tokens are processed simultaneously [9].)

This book is designed to help enterprises move past Phase 3 (the Trough of Disillusionment) and evolve toward Phase 5 (the Plateau of Productivity) and beyond. That framing matters because hype is not only a market dynamic but also an organizational hazard. Leaders who are swept up in inflated expectations often rush into pilots without strategy, only to face disillusionment when results fall short. The challenge is not to avoid the hype cycle but to ride it deliberately. A common narrative persists: AI will eliminate jobs, and autonomous workflows will replace human input altogether. This belief has created urgency across businesses of all sizes to become "AI-ready." But urgency often turns into a hasty sprint without clarity of purpose. In doing so, companies risk undermining their own foundations.

Recent headlines about large IT firms cutting jobs in the name of AI illustrate this point. Many of those same firms quietly rehired for a significant portion of those roles. The optics suggested AI was replacing humans, but the reality was more nuanced. Enterprises discovered that domain expertise, contextual reasoning, and strategic oversight remain indispensable. This episode underscored the risks of rushing from hype to execution without fully grappling with operational complexity. Like the dot-com wave, the generative AI boom is sometimes portrayed as a bubble. On the surface, exaggerated claims and breathless marketing may support that view. In reality, however, generative AI represents a fundamentally new architectural layer within enterprise ecosystems. When implemented thoughtfully, it has the power to enhance core capabilities across industries. Still, AI is no magic wand. It is no guarantee of instant growth. To deliver substantial business value, it must be strategically implemented, aligned with enterprise needs and architecture, and supported by robust systems and capable teams. Without that grounding, organizations risk stalling in disillusionment instead of advancing toward productivity.

Lessons from History

Industrial systems history offers perspective. Japan's lean manufacturing model, refined by Toyota and inspired by Ford's assembly lines, wove autonomous machines into factory workflows as early as the 20th century. These machines could execute tasks with remarkable precision, but the process was never surrendered entirely to them. Human oversight gave the system its rhythm. Quality checks ensured reliability, judgment guided adaptation when conditions shifted, and accountability remained firmly with people.

The balance between machine capability and human judgment gave Toyota its resilience. The system worked at scale because oversight was built in from the start, catching problems early and feeding corrections back into the process. The same principle goes into Anno Artificialis Intelligenciae. Automation delivers substantial value only when it is steered by governance and shaped by human context, allowing enterprises to build systems that perform reliably, adapt to change, earn trust, and remain sustainable over time.

Why Balance Matters

The current excitement around autonomous systems must not be mistaken for a call to remove human input. AI's true strength emerges when integrated into a broader framework that prioritizes human oversight and collaboration. Crucial decision-making points continue to demand human involvement. Ethical governance must remain a human responsibility, not delegated to algorithms. Furthermore, the nuanced understanding of context is a uniquely human capability that no system can fully replicate.

Businesses operate to benefit people, customers, employees, and communities. If a system marginalizes the human element, it risks deviating from the fundamental values and trust that underpin its legitimacy. The essential challenge, then, is to integrate autonomous and human-directed systems as complementary layers, each reinforcing the other. Automation offers speed and scalability, while human oversight ensures judgment and accountability. When designed for coexistence from the start, these layers create a balance, allowing organizations to harness the benefits of automation while maintaining alignment with human requirements and expectations.

1.3 Global Trends in AI Investment and Adoption: From Startups to Enterprises

Global investment trends are dynamic and constantly evolving. Specific funding figures and adoption percentages are subject to rapid change, often shifting even as this book is being read. Therefore, our focus will be on the enduring directions of investment and the consistent structural patterns of adoption observed across various organizational types, rather than on ephemeral statistics.

Investment Patterns That Endure

Over the past decade, AI investment has moved through three predictable waves:

- **Startups As Experimentation Engines:** Startups remain the first movers, testing novel AI applications from generative models for creative industries to agent-based systems for logistics. Their role is less about scale and more about pushing conceptual boundaries.

- **Enterprise Adoption via Partnerships and Acquisitions:** Enterprises often hesitate to build entirely new AI capabilities in-house. Instead, they acquire promising startups or form partnerships with AI vendors, integrating these capabilities into existing systems.
- **Government and Global Policy Catalysts:** State-led initiatives, whether in the EU, US, or Asia, continue to steer AI investment. Policy frameworks, national AI strategies, and regulatory initiatives do more than direct financial flows. They grant legitimacy to certain kinds of research and steer the trajectory of deployment.

Startups bring experimentation to the frontier. Enterprises embed intelligence into their core operations, while governments set the conditions of the field through incentives and oversight. Each of these forces sustains momentum in its own way, and their interaction ensures that AI continues to evolve as both an economic and societal project.

Startups vs. Enterprises: The Volatility Gap

Venture capitalists are accustomed to volatility, making multiple investments with the expectation that only a few will succeed. However, this high-risk approach isn't suitable for enterprises. For enterprises, AI has become a company-wide imperative. It is reshaping the way organizations recruit and support their people, transforming the experience of customers, and redefining the patterns of decision-making that guide daily operations. Implementing it successfully demands alignment that reaches from leadership vision to everyday practice.

Adoption Across Organization Types

- **Startups treat AI as a differentiator.** Their agility allows rapid experimentation, though they face resource and scalability constraints.
- **Small and Medium Businesses (SMBs) are pragmatic adopters.** They look for packaged AI solutions that can be slotted into operations without heavy infrastructure investments. For them, the biggest hurdle is cost-benefit clarity.

- **Large enterprises see AI as both an opportunity and a governance challenge.** Scale amplifies the rewards of successful adoption but also the risks of ethical lapses, compliance failures, or reputational harm.

This segmentation will hold true even as technology shifts. Whether it is today's generative AI or tomorrow's agentic intelligence, the size and structure of an organization will continue to shape how it invests and adopts.

Why Geography Matters

Where an enterprise is based does more than set its regulatory perimeter; it shapes how deeply it can participate in the global AI economy. Forecasts suggest that AI could add over $13 trillion to global value by 2030, but that momentum gathers differently across regions. In the United States, abundant capital and hyperscaler dominance create unmatched research and deployment velocity. China mobilizes industrial scale, weaving AI into logistics, manufacturing, and state priorities. India advances along another path, relying on its vast digital public infrastructure and deep reservoirs of technical talent to drive adoption at pace. The European Union channels its influence through regulatory sovereignty, investing in sovereign cloud and embedding compliance frameworks that transform trust into a competitive advantage. Meanwhile, the United Arab Emirates positions itself as a laboratory of ambition, launching state-backed institutions and bold national projects to claim a place in the future of intelligence.

These trajectories show that geography is never neutral. Capital, scale, governance, and ambition each shape the field in distinctive ways, and enterprises must account for these forces when designing their own AI strategies. Across regions and industries, generative AI is already being deployed at varying scales and for diverse use cases. As we will explore in Chapter 6, these initiatives shape access to data, energy, compute, and talent, the new currencies of the AI era. Just as traditional economies are built on financial capital, the AI economy depends on these four resources, determining who can build, scale, and lead in this new landscape.

Geography also influences regulation and ecosystem support. Enterprises in AI-forward, highly regulated regions often enjoy better access to government funding, vendor partnerships, and market-tested infrastructure. Meanwhile, companies operating in markets with weaker regulatory clarity may face barriers to trust and adoption. Simply bolting AI onto legacy systems without aligning to these ecosystems leaves businesses at a disadvantage. In such cases, enterprises may end up on equal footing with competitors who have not adopted AI at all, just with higher costs and higher risks.

Lessons in Readiness and Transformation

Executives increasingly recognize AI's importance and are seeking ways to implement it sustainably. The distance between awareness and readiness is part of a natural organizational evolution, one that highlights where investment and discipline are most needed. Progress comes when enterprises create the right conditions for success: linking AI initiatives to business outcomes, embedding governance into daily practice, and cultivating trust so that employees and customers move with confidence. This is the essence of readiness. It defines whether adoption remains fragile or matures into a capability that compounds over time. Preparedness, approached this way, becomes an opportunity rather than a hurdle. It allows enterprises to strengthen resilience, to bring strategy and operations into closer alignment, and to ensure that technology deepens rather than destabilizes their core purpose. Organizations that treat AI as a transformation, integrated into the structure of the enterprise rather than bolted on as a tool, discover that the impact endures.

The Convergence Trend

A defining global movement is the convergence of AI with adjacent technologies such as cloud computing, edge systems, and the Internet of Things. In the years ahead, speaking of "AI adoption" as a stand-alone activity will give way to discussions of platforms, where intelligence is integrated across every layer of the technology stack. This convergence channels investment toward solutions that are not isolated tools but connected ecosystems, capable of extending across the enterprise. Governance frameworks are evolving in parallel, shifting from oversight of individual models to stewardship of the broader systems in which those models operate. For enterprises, this trajectory unlocks more resilient operations, stronger compliance, and innovation that draws strength from integration rather than fragmentation.

Enterprise Takeaway

For executives, the key is to watch patterns more than numbers. Quarterly funding totals will fluctuate, but the enduring questions remain: ***Where are the persistent pressures***

in my sector? Where are startups experimenting, and how can my enterprise partner acquire them? What governance frameworks are regulators signaling, and how can we prepare ahead of mandates?

For the next generation of practitioners, the people preparing to shape careers in AI, the message is equally encouraging. The AI economy is durable, and the need for individuals who can connect technical potential with business value will only grow stronger. Careers will be built through integration: the ability to translate between disciplines, align systems with organizational purpose, and sustain innovation over time.

1.4 Consumer-Grade AI vs. Enterprise-Grade AI: Why the Enterprise Playbook Must Be Different

Most people encounter AI in its consumer-grade form, such as GPT chatbots, text-to-image generators, and other applications that showcase the entertainment and creative appeal of artificial intelligence. One of the most prominent examples surfaced in early 2025 with the viral "Ghibli Trend" [10]. Using the artistic style made famous by ***Hayao Miyazaki***, creator of the Ghibli brand, millions of people, from executives to students, turned their photos into Ghibli-style illustrations through publicly available text-to-image models. The trend dominated social platforms, showing how consumer AI thrives on human psychology, ease of use, and social influence. These tools are built for accessibility, producing visually pleasing or conversational outputs at the push of a prompt.

At the same time, the trend sparked ethical debate. If a Ghibli-style image, once requiring painstaking human effort, can now be generated in seconds, ***what does that mean for human creativity and labor?*** Such concerns highlight how consumer AI raises issues beyond entertainment. For artists and audiences, this raised questions of authenticity and value.

Enterprise-grade AI works beneath the surface. Its purpose is deep integration into existing systems, optimization of performance at scale, monetization within complex ecosystems, and stewardship of ethical responsibility. Though it rarely grabs attention, it forms the foundation for many significant digital transformations happening now. By contrast, consumer-facing AI shapes public imagination directly. It influences how people interpret the possibilities of intelligence and how they expect it to reshape human work. For executives, cultural signals deserve careful attention because they shape the environment in which enterprise AI takes root. Public imagination can influence whether new systems are welcomed with trust, questioned with caution, or pushed into the spotlight before organizations are fully ready. The so-called "Ghibli trend" makes it evident that what begins as a moment of fascination in popular culture can ripple outward, strengthening confidence in AI's potential in some quarters while, in others, stirring unease or prompting premature regulatory debate.

Features of Enterprise-Grade AI

Consumer-facing AI is designed to capture attention, rewarding speed and engagement. Enterprise-grade AI serves a different purpose: it must align with the most demanding requirements of business and society. These include transparent data lineage, rigorous regulatory compliance, strong security frameworks, and architectures that integrate seamlessly into complex enterprise environments. The focus of this book is on enterprise-grade AI, because the distinctions matter. Enterprise systems operate under governance regimes that demand accountability, face audit obligations that require explainability, and must withstand scrutiny in ways that consumer systems rarely encounter. A trivial failure in a consumer application may frustrate a user for a moment. An error in enterprise AI, whether in finance, healthcare, aviation, or law, can generate profound financial loss and reputational damage.

Enterprise-grade AI extends far beyond prompting interfaces. It must connect reliably with legacy systems, sustain high availability under strict latency expectations, and demonstrate fairness, interpretability, and secure handling of sensitive information. In this setting, generative AI is expected to produce outputs that are dependable and defensible, not improvisational. Each error carries consequences, and so maturity frameworks, discussed further in Chapters 2 and 5, become essential. These frameworks guide the lifecycle of enterprise models, ensuring they remain effective, compliant, and scalable as organizational needs evolve. These frameworks guide the lifecycle of enterprise models, helping them deliver consistent value, uphold regulatory and ethical responsibilities, and expand reliably as organizational demands increase.

The Hybrid Future

As enterprises progress in AI adoption, one theme emerges with clarity: the future will be hybrid. Agentic AI systems, intelligent software entities capable of perceiving, planning, acting, and learning, are becoming more capable with each cycle of innovation. Their strength lies in autonomy, but their reliability depends on human judgment. This is why Human-In-The-Loop (HITL) design remains indispensable, embedding oversight at key checkpoints so that business intent is never lost. The operational loop behind agentic AI follows a rhythm of perception, planning, action, observation, and reflection. Each stage contributes to continuous learning and adaptation. This cycle is now central to enterprise systems and increasingly visible in smart city initiatives where AI converges with IoT. Early IoT deployments relied on rigid rule-based logic—"if X, then Y." Modern systems evolve through reinforcement learning, sensing and adjusting in real time, and improving as environments change.

Examples of this convergence are already visible at scale. In Hangzhou, the City Brain platform manages the flow of traffic across a vast metropolis, turning congestion into a field where data and intelligence work in tandem. Across Europe, smart grids funded under Horizon programs adjust dynamically to fluctuations in energy demand, demonstrating how infrastructure can learn to balance scarcity and abundance in real time. In Dubai, networks of public safety sensors interpret crowd movement, anticipating risks before they escalate. Meanwhile, cities as varied as Singapore and Houston deploy digital twin platforms to simulate climate resilience, testing scenarios and guiding policy long before crises arrive. Together, these initiatives reveal the outlines of a new architectural imagination. They have moved beyond experimental pilots and are beginning to function as early blueprints of adaptive infrastructure, where agentic AI and IoT converge to make urban systems more responsive, anticipatory, and sustainable.

For enterprises, the lesson is straightforward: infrastructure at scale amplifies both risk and opportunity. Hybrid models succeed when they combine automation with governance, technical power with accountability, and efficiency with trust. This architectural transformation, explored further in Chapter 6, demonstrates how agentic AI is maturing from pilots into enterprise deployments. The most effective designs build HITL checkpoints into the loop, ensuring resilience in regulated environments and responsibility wherever human lives are touched. The trajectory points to coexistence. Humans and AI will not occupy opposing domains; they will operate as partners. Full automation remains an illusion in the complexity of legacy environments. What endures are hybrid models, people augmented by intelligence, systems shaped by oversight, and enterprises strengthened by the balance between autonomy and accountability.

Overcoming Legacy Barriers

Legacy modernization continues to test enterprises in ways that recall the uneven transition from Web 2.0 into Web 3.0. The promise of new models, decentralization, immersive digital environments, and peer-to-peer forms of exchange captured imaginations and attracted investment, but adoption slowed as older infrastructures held their ground. Systems built for an earlier era carried fragile dependencies and were reinforced by ingrained cultural habits. They proved harder to shift than the vision decks suggested. The same tension defines enterprise AI today. Generative systems are accelerating backlog reduction, producing tests, and interpreting legacy code, but the enduring weight of existing architectures continues to restrain the pace of transformation. What emerges is a layered coexistence. Old and new architectures overlap, interact, and at times clash, producing an in-between space where governance and human expertise tip the balance. AI can take over repeatable fragments of work, but continuity depends on people who bring awareness of context and the ability to judge consequences that extend beyond what a system can calculate.

This is more than gradual change; it signals a deeper reset. Service-heavy models are giving way to AI-augmented, IP-driven platforms where humans and machines contribute together to value creation. For enterprise architects, the path forward lies in dual-resource design: human judgment working in concert with AI agents. Human-In-The-Loop systems are not just protective barriers. They boost performance by containing agentic intelligence within secure limits, by ensuring decisions align with ethical obligations, and by guiding outcomes to remain grounded in the enterprise's core purpose.

Human-In-The-Loop (HITL) Mechanism

HITL is more than a safeguard; it is an architectural principle. Its purpose is to ensure that automation evolves in ways that remain aligned with human judgment, reinforcing both trust and governance. Rather than treating oversight as an afterthought, HITL embeds people directly into the operational cycle, at the moments where discretion, context, and ethical reasoning shape the difference between acceptable outcomes and damaging ones. When designed well, hybrid loops elevate performance without diminishing human value. They enable AI to handle repeatable, data-intensive fragments of work, while people contribute what machines cannot: the ability to read situations against history, to recognize consequences that extend beyond immediate metrics, and to weigh tensions between efficiency and fairness. In this design, humans are amplified, freed from rote burdens so their judgment can steer the higher-order direction of the system.

Consider the implications across sectors. In healthcare, HITL enables diagnostic models to highlight anomalies, while physicians interpret those signals in light of patient history and clinical nuance. In finance, anomaly detection can flag suspicious transactions, but compliance officers determine whether those patterns represent fraud, error, or benign irregularities. In aviation, autonomous systems stabilize and optimize flight paths, but pilots retain authority when conditions change in unexpected ways. Each domain demonstrates how the loop functions as a partnership, automation shouldering repetition, and humans guiding intent. For enterprises, the message is evident. HITL mechanisms transform AI from a fragile pilot into an accountable partner. They heighten performance by reducing error, preserve alignment with ethical and regulatory commitments, and give leaders confidence that automation contributes to resilience rather than fragility. Hybrid loops embody the Human Endpoint Principle. They remind us that systems are built to expand what people can accomplish, to safeguard the dignity of those affected by decisions, and to keep enterprise intelligence aligned with its larger purpose.

Enterprise Takeaway

The intention of this book is to move beyond the usual extremes. AI is often framed either as an unstoppable wave to be embraced at any cost or as a disruption to be resisted in the name of caution. For enterprises, both positions are unhelpful. The essential task is to design strategies that balance ambition with responsibility, embedding intelligence into systems in ways that strengthen trust, preserve resilience, and sustain long-term value. Enterprise-grade AI succeeds when architecture carries scalability as a given, when governance is built into the flow of data rather than added later, and when human oversight is treated as integral to performance. These are not abstract ideals; they are practices that shape whether adoption remains fragile or matures into capability. By the time you finish this book, you will have more than concepts. You will have a blueprint for action, one drawn from field-tested lessons and built around the disciplines that enterprises can trust: disciplined architecture, transparent governance, and human alignment that ensures technology continues to serve its purpose.

1.5 Lessons from Early Enterprise AI Adoption: What Worked, What Didn't

The greatest takeaway for enterprises navigating the AI ecosystem in the 21st century is this: hype and urgency must be matched with architectural strategy. Before diving into any AI transformation, enterprises must first ask the foundational question: ***Is the business strategy ready for AI?*** AI is not just another technical layer to be slotted into the enterprise stack; it is a cross-cutting force that permeates every part of the architecture. This can either define an enterprise's growth trajectory or destabilize its foundation, depending on how well integration aligns with key enterprise architecture artifacts. As we'll discuss further in Chapter 3, an enterprise cannot rely solely on being tech-forward. It must also develop organizational maturity models that enable sustainable change. These models ensure that transformation strengthens, rather than undermines, the very architecture it seeks to modernize. In Chapter 7, we'll offer a well-detailed perspective on responsible AI. Enterprises must remain focused on building resilient systems that can withstand ethical scrutiny, unpredictable inputs, and long-term risk. This includes honoring what we define throughout this book as the four pillars of enterprise-grade AI:

1. ***Accessibility***
2. ***Explainability***
3. ***Security***
4. ***Ethics***

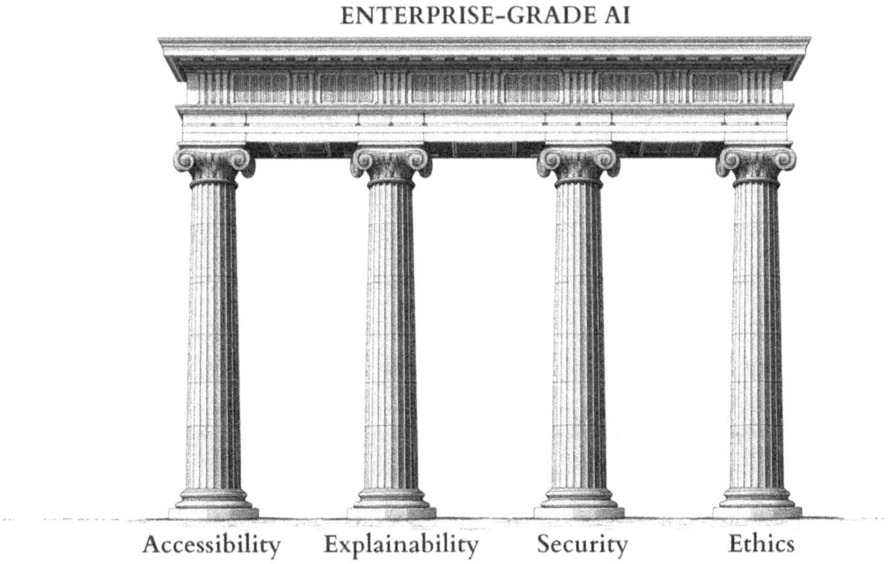

Figure 1-3. *The Four Pillars of Enterprise-Grade AI*

AI has already been adopted across sectors, from finance to healthcare to mobility, sometimes with exceptional results, such as enabling early detection of hard-to-spot health conditions. Other times, results have been less convincing. The differentiating factor, or the **Δ** (delta) as we define it here, is almost always whether the enterprise was strategically ready for AI adoption in the first place. By the end of this book, you will be equipped to assess and identify that readiness.

Agentic AI in Action

Agentic AI systems are already part of enterprise operations today. They run through banking platforms that detect fraud in real time, through urban networks that adapt traffic signals to changing flows, and through hospital systems that coordinate clinicians and resources to keep patients safe. These are not speculative projects; they are working examples of automation that has matured into intelligence able to perceive context, generate plans, act autonomously, and improve through feedback.

A simple analogy makes the difference visible. An ordinary coffee machine, programmed to brew at your preferred time slot, say 7:00 a.m., represents classic automation—reliable, predictable, but indifferent to circumstance. Now imagine a machine that senses when you walk into the room, recalls your preferred strength, notices you slept poorly from biometric cues, and adjusts its brew accordingly. That is a glimpse of agentic intelligence. At home, it feels like a convenience; at enterprise scale, it becomes transformative. Agentic AI enables systems to evolve in ways that static automation cannot. They adapt continuously, responding to new data streams, learning from outcomes, and adjusting to patterns that no engineer could have pre-programmed in advance. This adaptability creates resilience: enterprises can move with uncertainty instead of being derailed by it. Efficiency becomes only one dimension of value. Responsiveness and trustworthiness emerge alongside it. In this sense, agentic AI is already reshaping enterprise architecture, less as a distant possibility and more as a living system that is unfolding in real time.

Oversight As Foundation

Agentic systems only fulfill their promise when guided by deliberate oversight. Human-In-The-Loop (HITL) design is central to this discipline, ensuring that judgment and accountability remain present at the moments when data alone cannot decide. Oversight in this sense is not a restraint. It is the means by which automation becomes more reliable, because computational reasoning is tempered with context and ethical awareness.

When enterprises embed HITL from the outset, they create hybrid systems where machines expand capacity while people shape intent. The result is partnership, not replacement. A clinical model might flag anomalies in a patient record, but the physician determines what action to take. A fraud detection engine may highlight suspicious patterns, but compliance officers decide which investigations to pursue. In each case, oversight secures what raw performance cannot: confidence that systems remain aligned with the institution's obligations and the community's trust. Oversight, therefore, becomes the foundation of sustainable adoption. It is what allows enterprises to transform efficiency into resilience and ambition into measurable Return on AI Investment (ROAI).

Learning from Rollouts

Public deployments of generative and agentic systems have shown how much enterprises can learn in real time. Some rollouts produced surprising or even entertaining outcomes, drawing attention when recommendations strayed beyond expectations. These episodes, widely discussed in the press and boardrooms alike, revealed that adoption is as much about preparation and education as it is about code or models. A telling example comes from airports that introduced AI to identify distressed passengers. On one level, the systems showed genuine promise, allowing staff to intervene more quickly and improve customer care. On another, they highlighted the sensitivity of such applications. Signals drawn from facial expression or movement touch directly on questions of privacy and dignity, reminding architects that safeguards must be embedded from the start, not appended later.

Each rollout, whether celebrated as a success or debated for its flaws, adds to the growing playbook of responsible adoption. There is no doubt that the lesson for businesses is that deployment should be seen as a living process rather than a single event. Enduring systems are characterized by their ability to adapt and evolve. They require constant vigilance, with ongoing adjustments made as conditions change, and a willingness to respond to unexpected outcomes. When systems are built upon thorough preparation, supported by strong governance, and guided by a culture of stewardship, they thrive and remain connected to their communities.

Key Takeaways from Early Enterprise AI Adoption

- **Strategic readiness comes first.** Adoption succeeds when AI initiatives align with business capabilities, not when they chase hype.
- **Architecture must be reimagined, not patched.** Embedding AI requires rethinking workflows, not simply retrofitting tools.
- **Agentic systems are already here.** From fraud detection to clinical support, enterprise-grade autonomy is current and scalable.
- **Governance and trust are foundational.** Data quality, compliance, explainability, and fairness must be built in from day one.
- **Culture is a differentiator.** Enterprises that invest in upskilling, change management, and workforce trust consistently outperform those that rely only on tools.
- **Risks are business risks.** Bias, drift, or hallucinations are not only technical issues; they are business issues with financial and reputational implications.

- **Return on AI-Investment (ROAI) follows maturity.** Organizations that align AI lifecycles with governance and auditability see measurable gains in cost, speed, and resilience.
- **Mind the Δ (delta).** Adoption without readiness multiplies risk. Transformation succeeds when organizations close this readiness gap through intentional design.

Conclusion: Completing the First Blueprint

This first chapter has offered a foundation for how enterprises can approach AI with intention. Early adoption stories reveal that progress does not depend on speed alone; it depends on whether leaders build systems that are stable, accountable, and capable of growth. When AI is embedded into the very fabric of enterprise architecture, supported by oversight, guided by governance, and tied to business purpose, it stops being a fragile experiment and begins to reshape how organizations learn, decide, and act. Beneath architecture, however, lies the deeper ground of data, the focus of Chapter 2. It is data that gives life to every model, and it is through the way data is curated, governed, and secured that enterprises determine whether ambition matures into capability. Poor data foundations widen the readiness gap, Δ. Strong ones close it, creating conditions where ROAI is no longer theoretical but measurable. In that sense, data is not an accessory to strategy; it is the bedrock on which every intelligent system rests.

Artificial intelligence itself is best understood as a continuation of a long human endeavor, where code, infrastructure, and curiosity converge. It is neither a miracle nor a menace. It is a tool that reflects the quality of the systems in which it is housed and the values of the people who guide it. The Human Endpoint Principle reminds us that all these designs exist to serve people, that is, customers, patients, citizens, and employees. Forget this, and architecture becomes elegant but irrelevant. Remember it, and AI becomes the ground for durable transformation. The first blueprint is now complete. The next task is to descend to the substrate of data strategy and ask whether enterprises are prepared to carry the weight of their own ambition. Chapter 2 takes us there to examine the pipelines, governance, and platforms that decide whether AI remains a promise or becomes a capability.

CHAPTER 2

Strategic Foundations: The Role of Enterprise Architecture in AI Adoption

Introduction

Chapter 1 left us with an unsettling thought: the destiny of AI rests less on the brilliance of its algorithms and more significantly on an enterprise's readiness to adopt them. This phenomenon was previously termed the readiness gap delta (**Δ**). It is the reason why some firms transform pilots into enduring advantages, while others are caught in a cycle of forgotten prototypes. MIT's framing of the ***GenAI Divide*** [11] gave voice to what many leaders already suspected. Enterprises are conducting numerous experiments, but only a few successfully transition into production. The models themselves are rarely the cause of failure. Instead, the problems arise from difficulties in integrating systems, teams lacking the knowledge to operationalize ideas, and governance struggling to keep pace with innovation. Uncontained excitement quickly becomes fragile and succumbs to pressure.

This chapter turns to those missing frames. Enterprise architecture (EA), so often dismissed as paperwork or plumbing, takes on a different presence in the Anno Artificialis Intelligenciae. Here it becomes the enterprise's backbone, the connective mesh between ambition and execution, and the set of patterns and decisions that allow intelligence not just to perform at a demo but to seep into the bloodstream of

R. Harjika, *Architecting Enterprise AI Strategies*, https://doi.org/10.1007/979-8-8688-2219-3_2

the business. In the pages ahead, we will trace why AI falters without this foundation. This chapter explores how enterprise architecture (EA) provides the structural support necessary for scaling and how both traditional and modern frameworks can be adapted to the dynamic pace of AI development.

Along the way, we will consider the role of Infrastructure-as-a-Service (IaaS) and sovereign cloud, and we will read maturity models less as checklists and more as mirrors, reflecting back an enterprise's readiness for intelligence at scale. By the end, the claim should feel almost self-evident: architecture is the ground where AI either takes root or dissolves. When the appropriate structures are in place, intelligence transcends its status as a trivial pilot project and becomes an integral aspect of genuine business operations.

2.1 Why AI Without Architecture Fails

The artificial intelligence promise now has a familiar appeal. Executives envision a future of profoundly streamlined, agile businesses, where instantaneous, AI-driven decisions are made. This transforms customer relationships from reactive to proactive, anticipating needs through sophisticated data analysis and nurturing hyper-personalized experiences. The vision, while brilliant in presentations and strategic documents, often meets a quiet reality: an initial surge of optimism and successful pilot programs, followed by eventual fatigue. Researchers at MIT captured this cycle in the idea of the ***GenAI Divide*** [11]. On one side, a crowded world of experiments; on the other, a much smaller circle of enterprises that turn those experiments into lasting transformation. The difference rarely lies in clever models. It lies in the architecture around them.

The Illusion of Early Success

AI integration often begins quietly, with a modest pilot or proof-of-concept championed by a business unit eager to show what is possible. Initially, the excitement is palpable: new patterns emerge from dashboards, efficiency gains are forecast, and leaders envision large-scale potential. However, as the experiment expands beyond its initial scope, the initial promise wanes. Hidden infrastructure weaknesses become apparent, data pipelines struggle under actual demand, governance lags behind deployment speed, and eventually, maintenance costs begin to eclipse the perceived value.

The Core Issue: Architecture As the Missing Multiplier

While algorithms are often blamed, the true vulnerability lies elsewhere. Models are inherently probabilistic, learning, evolving, and sometimes forgetting. For them to succeed, a healthy framework is essential, including regular retraining, consistent feedback, secure data pathways, and explicitly defined ownership. Data provides the fuel, but it is the architecture that provides direction. Without this, organizations remain in the "readiness gap" (Δ, as discussed in Chapter 1), where aspirations are high but tangible results remain elusive.

The neglect extends beyond technical issues, representing a failure to learn from past deployments. Many AI implementations lack proper context and memory, leading to employee frustration and the adoption of unofficial consumer platforms. This informal "shadow economy" of AI, while often useful in the short term, exacerbates fragmentation. The lesson comes into focus: models may ignite interest, yet only architecture turns that spark into a sustained capability. Where architecture is absent, adoption fragments into recurring patterns of fragile data, uneven culture, shallow governance, and runaway cost—patterns we will now explore in detail.

Pattern 1: Compromised Data Quality and Privacy

Data is the ground beneath AI, and in many enterprises, that ground is infertile, unable to yield the harvest of outcomes the organization so urgently seeks. In many enterprises, the data essential for AI to achieve desired outcomes is often insufficient due to silos, legacy systems, and inconsistent formats that undermine reliability. Flawed inputs inevitably lead to flawed outputs, resulting in poor decisions and potential regulatory breaches. This risk is amplified in sectors like healthcare and finance. Generative AI tools further intensify these pressures, frequently relying on sensitive data that introduces new risks of misuse, including the potential for "hallucinations" to reveal confidential information, rapidly eroding trust. To counteract these challenges, architectural solutions are crucial. This involves embedding governance within data pipelines, ensuring visible lineage, controlling access, and designing in privacy from the outset. In the Anno Artificialis Intelligenciae, Security and Explainability, two of the four pillars introduced in Chapter 1, stand as the very foundations on which everything else must rest.

Pattern 2: Organizational and Human Capital Failures

Even with advanced technology readily available, human factors often hinder its effective adoption. The proliferation of "Shadow AI" occurs when individual departments procure tools without proper oversight, leading to duplicated efforts, heightened risks, a deficiency in organizational alignment, and wasted resources. Cultural aspects further complicate this issue. Some employees resist change, preferring familiar routines, while others embrace new technologies too quickly, placing undue faith in their outputs. This results in fragile and inconsistent adoption across the organization. Mature enterprises, however, approach this differently. They begin by reskilling their workforce and then create self-service platforms with safeguards so employees can experiment safely. Over time, they fold technological literacy into daily practice, so adoption is paired with critical judgment rather than blind trust. This empowers employees to both adopt and critically evaluate new tools. In this context, "architecture" extends beyond technical systems; it encompasses the adaptive relationship between people and technology, truly embodying the concept of accessibility.

Pattern 3: Legal and Ethical Compliance Gaps

Bias and ethical considerations are not peripheral concerns; they are fundamental risks that continually challenge an enterprise. When governance is neglected, models begin to drift. They absorb biases that warp decisions, trespass into intellectual property without awareness, produce results so opaque that trust collapses, and in time they erode the very accountability leaders need to defend their systems. Prevention isn't a matter of chance; it stems from deliberate design. Traceability enables the review of past decisions. Comprehensive documentation preserves the evolution of data and models. Proactive oversight integrates accountability throughout the system, preventing problems from escalating. This underscores why ethics, introduced as the fourth pillar in Chapter 1, must be incorporated from the inception. It should be an integral part of the system's framework, just as essential as the data pipelines feeding the models or the APIs exposing them. When treated in this manner, ethics transforms from an abstract concept into a practical discipline, becoming the very foundation upon which AI earns, rather than erodes, trust.

Pattern 4: Operational Limitations and Cost Overruns

Scaling operations often reveals weaknesses within an organization. Legacy ERP and CRM systems are difficult to integrate, leading to slow performance and a poor user experience. Additionally, computationally intensive workloads, particularly those reliant on GPUs, significantly increase cloud computing costs. These issues result in enterprises expending considerable resources with minimal returns. The growing concern for sustainability adds another layer of complexity. Large models consume vast amounts of energy, attracting scrutiny from regulators and investors. Practices like GreenOps, which focus on optimizing compute resources for both carbon emissions and cost, are no longer optional but essential. Furthermore, budgets are frequently misdirected. Resources are often poured into high-profile front-office initiatives that offer visible, but potentially limited, impact, while high-return back-office processes are neglected. In essence, spectacle is prioritized and funded, while genuine substance is starved of necessary investment.

AI-Adaptive Infrastructure and Sustainable Design

Architecture provides adaptability as much as stability. AI-adaptive infrastructure aligns compute choices with workload needs. Lightweight inference flows through CPUs or specialized memory modules, while GPU power is preserved for training cycles that demand it. This balance reduces cost, sustains efficiency, lowers energy use, and strengthens trust with regulators and communities. GreenOps practices extend this principle: scheduling training with carbon awareness, routing inference to efficient processors, embedding sustainability checks into design, and integrating energy metrics into governance. Enterprises that cultivate this mindset discover that scalability, stewardship, compliance, and efficiency reinforce each other, transforming infrastructure into a living discipline.

Case Study: The Fragile Pilot

A manufacturer's attempt at predictive maintenance, successful in a limited trial, faltered once it was scaled across multiple plants. The pilot, designed to predict machine failures and reduce downtime, had delivered strong results in its early stage. But the move to scale revealed how fragile the foundations were. Each factory carried its own peculiarities. One site recorded timestamps in a format no other plant recognized.

Another relied on sensors calibrated in ways that had never been documented. Older facilities used control systems so idiosyncratic that their logs resisted interpretation altogether. A signal of failure in one plant could mean something entirely different in another, leaving the model adrift and its alerts unreliable. As confidence slipped, maintenance teams returned to instinct and manual practice, ownership blurred, and without structured retraining, the system weakened with every cycle. Engineers spent their hours reconciling mismatched data rather than refining the model, until the costs of integration outweighed the savings that predictive maintenance had once promised.

The model itself remained sound; what was missing was the architectural frame that could carry it across environments. Adaptive infrastructure—built through modular pipelines, flexible data standards, compute matched to workload, and governance routines that sustain retraining—would have allowed variation to be absorbed rather than magnified. GreenOps practices, such as energy-aware scheduling and routing inference to efficient processors, would have extended that adaptability into sustainability, turning cost savings and carbon responsibility into twin outcomes of the same design. The failure revealed how prediction alone cannot endure without the architecture that carries it. Across industries, from finance to healthcare to retail, this pattern repeats: pilots succeed in isolation yet falter in scale when the surrounding systems lack coherence. Enduring intelligence depends on an architectural foundation that is adaptive, accountable, sustainable, and built for continuity.

Architecture As the Multiplier

Architecture is the fundamental truth that multiplies value in the realm of AI. While models can spark initial ideas, it is architecture that provides the necessary foundation for sustained growth and realization of those ideas. Without it, organizations risk remaining stuck in a cycle of endless pilot projects. With a standardized architecture in place, enterprises can plant AI in reliable data, integrate intelligence into the routines of daily work, scale their initiatives without losing stability, and govern them with the care needed to sustain trust.

The lesson that settles for architects is this: align AI endeavors with core business capabilities, establish effective feedback loops to transform trials into valuable assets, embed strong governance and ethical considerations into the design process, and measure sustainability not only in terms of cost but also the power footprint. Architecture is the bridge that transforms novel concepts into essential infrastructure.

AI will undoubtedly continue to evolve, but the ultimate success of organizations in achieving real Return on AI Investments (ROAI) hinges on their ability to construct the necessary structures to support its implementation. Those who prioritize this will be well-prepared for the Anno Artificialis Intelligenciae, while those who do not will remain entangled in experiments, perpetually awaiting true transformation.

2.2 Enterprise Architecture As the Strategic AI Backbone

Artificial intelligence (AI) has moved beyond the experimental stage; it now shapes how organizations define their purpose, how they run their operations, how they connect with the people they serve, and how they imagine the futures they want to build. However, as previously discussed, trifling enthusiasm and investment are insufficient to solidify AI's impact. Without the stabilizing influence of enterprise architecture (EA), most AI initiatives remain fragile, little more than isolated experiments or dazzling demonstrations that fail as soon as they meet the weight of reality. EA acts as the unifying force, transforming scattered AI efforts into enterprise-wide capabilities. It serves as the framework that aligns technological ambition with business objectives.

For years, EA lived under an unglamorous reputation. It was seen as a bureaucratic function that catalogued systems, imposed rigid controls, slowed initiatives that demanded speed, consumed attention without obvious return, and left itself cast as an obstacle rather than an enabler. At *Anno Artificialis Intelligenciae* (AAI), this perception has changed. EA's role is no longer to impede but to determine when to accelerate and when to maintain stability. Its primary task is to create a dynamic blueprint that integrates business goals, data flows, applications, infrastructure, and governance into a cohesive whole.

With such a framework in place, AI transitions from a novel concept to an essential tool, evolving from a series of pilots into a systematic discipline of transformation. EA's importance is evident across six dimensions, each demonstrating its shift from a supportive role to a central position in driving enterprise change, as discussed below.

Dimension 1: From Technology Planner to AI Strategist

The role of an architect has evolved significantly. Previously focused on portfolio organization and system standardization, the architect's craft now demands adaptability in an environment where models are frequently updated. This necessitates a shift in governance from strict controls to flexible guidelines. The core inquiry has transitioned from ***what technology to acquire*** to ***what capability to enhance***. Areas like fraud detection, supply chain resilience, and personalized marketing each require a unique transformation from business objectives to data pipelines. This evolution has led to the emergence of new roles, including AI platform owners, data product architects, and lifecycle managers. Enterprise architecture (EA) acts as a collaborative hub, enabling data scientists, engineers, and business leaders to communicate effectively through a common understanding and shared language.

Dimension 2: Anchoring AI in Enterprise Goals

AI's potential remains untapped when it's not synchronized with enterprise objectives; it then serves only as a diversion. Enterprise architecture (EA) ensures this alignment by connecting AI initiatives directly to value streams through capability-based planning, thereby impacting outcomes. This approach integrates AI into EA's four domains—business, data, application, and technology—rather than treating it as an add-on. Architects collaborate with business teams in journey mapping and scenario planning to understand how AI transforms customer experience and operational resilience. This strategic integration is key to converting Return on AI Investment (ROAI) from a hopeful projection into a quantifiable result.

Dimension 3: Data As the Lifeblood

AI depends on data that can be trusted. For many organizations, that trust is undermined by silos, by systems that have grown old, by records that refuse to connect, and by processes that lack oversight. EA offers a way through. APIs and microservices release value from legacy systems without the pain of wholesale replacement. Distributed designs and federated learning prepare for the streams of signals arriving from IoT and the edge. Governance becomes tangible through lineage tracking, stewardship practices, access controls, and audit routines that make data handling visible. Architects also look ahead, planning for synthetic data, building tools for bias detection, designing transparency logs, and preparing for whatever new demands the next generation of AI will bring.

Dimension 4: Architectural Patterns for AI Enablement

To effectively scale AI, repeatable patterns are crucial. Fragile batch pipelines are being replaced by event-driven designs. Models are now packaged as services, managed in containers, and orchestrated on platforms such as Kubernetes or serverless environments. MLOps is becoming standard, offering support for monitoring, retraining, and versioning. Hybrid and multi-cloud strategies provide flexibility, allowing sensitive workloads to remain on-premise, scalable inference to shift to the cloud, and edge deployments to bring AI closer to sensors. Enterprise architecture (EA) teams maintain libraries of these patterns, fostering consistency while enabling customization. Pilot projects are transitioning from one-off efforts into reusable assets.

Dimension 5: Operating Models for AI–EA Integration

Architecture is never only technical; it is also organizational. Without strong structures to hold it, AI cannot scale beyond experiments. A Center of Enablement (CoE) plays a crucial role by curating essential resources such as reference architectures, model libraries, and governance frameworks. Portfolio oversight is vital for tracking initiatives and evaluating them based on maturity, Return on AI Investment (ROAI), and potential for reuse. Capability heatmaps are valuable tools for identifying existing intelligence within an organization and pinpointing areas where it can be further developed. Architects integrate themselves into agile teams, operating as collaborative partners rather than strict gatekeepers. This shift allows for the continuous application of standards throughout the development process, rather than as an afterthought. Consequently, enterprise architecture (EA) evolves from a passive documentation function to an active and engaged participant in delivery.

Dimension 6: Facing the Future

Enterprise architecture (EA) is uniquely positioned to navigate the challenges presented by AI adoption. The rise of "Shadow AI" necessitates structured registries and federated management. Emerging regulations across the globe surrounding AI demand built-in explainability and comprehensive audit trails. Addressing talent shortages requires the development of definitive competency frameworks and learning paths. Furthermore, short-term AI pilots often create architectural debt that EA must resolve. In critical sectors such as aviation and healthcare, the deployment of agentic AI calls for rigorous oversight, dependable fail-safes, layers of redundancy, and upfront lines of accountability. Guardrails are indispensable in these contexts. Ensure output remains structured and boundaries are respected. As the landscape continues to shift, EA must stay adaptive, recalibrating its frameworks to keep pace with both technological change and regulatory demands.

Predictive over Reactive Workflows

Enterprise architecture transforms analytics from reactive to proactive. In industrial automation, vision systems predict faults, while in manufacturing, digital standards disseminate best practices across various locations. These predictive cycles provide resilience, enhance coordination, broaden knowledge, and build trust, all while proactively preventing errors. This partnership between human intuition and advanced systems boosts foresight, leading to continuous learning and greater operational confidence.

Where Intelligence Learns to Live

In the Anno Artificialis Intelligenciae, the worth of enterprise architecture is both effortless to state and demanding in practice: it gives intelligence a place to live. With EA, AI settles into the very infrastructure of the enterprise, stitched into its systems in ways that are ethical, sustainable, resilient, and trusted. Without it, intelligence risks slipping into spectacle, impressive for a moment but gone just as quickly. Treated as a discipline rather than a side function, EA equips enterprises to cross **Δ**, realize a genuine Return on AI Investment, and establish enduring intelligence within their operations.

2.3 Mapping AI to Business Capabilities and Value Streams

AI is often cast as a kind of magic spell, assumed to deliver instant gains in efficiency, faster decision-making, deeper customer insight, sharper risk detection, and seamless personalization. AI is often seen as a magical solution, capable of instantly improving an organization's speed, sharpness, and personalization. However, those with experience in pilot programs know this isn't true. Without being integrated into a business's core structure, AI rarely provides lasting value. All too often, AI initiatives are launched in isolation, disconnected from the actual capabilities and value streams of an enterprise. This results in a series of expensive, uncoordinated experiments. A more challenging but ultimately more rewarding approach is to treat AI as a strategic initiative, deeply embedded in how value is created and delivered within the business.

The starting point cannot be overlooked, for this single question shapes everything that follows. Why ***do companies want to implement AI?*** The answer to this fundamental question will determine everything that follows. An organization focused on efficiency will prioritize different AI capabilities than one aiming for new products or deeper customer relationships. Once the intent is understood, architects can identify the most crucial functions. Take customer experience as an example. If that is the priority, the assessment will point toward service management, personalization, and analytics as the capabilities that matter most. If resilience is the aim, the compass shifts: risk modeling, supply chain monitoring, and workforce planning become the solid foundations. In this way, the choice of capabilities becomes a method of diagnosis, helping architects decide where AI can create the greatest impact.

Capabilities describe ***what*** an enterprise does. Value streams describe ***how*** it gets done, that is, the sequences of activity that create outcomes. ***The distinction matters.*** Mapping AI to value streams reveals where intelligence makes the most difference.

The Transformative Power of AI in Business Operations

AI is revolutionizing business operations, moving beyond elementary automation to integrate intelligence directly into core value streams that drive tangible results. Consider customer onboarding: AI can now verify documents swiftly, proactively identify potential churn risks, contextualize and prioritize support requests, guide real-time fraud detection during identity checks, and maintain accurate compliance records, all without hindering the process. This transforms what was once a disjointed experience into a faster, more consistent, and ultimately more human-centered customer journey.

AI As a Strategic Capability

Seen this way, AI is itself a capability. It has inputs—signals and data. It has processes—models and algorithms. It has outputs—decisions, actions, and recommendations. Around this sits the architectural shell: data pipelines, governance frameworks, guardrails, and monitoring. This reframing turns AI from a fragile pilot into a reusable, governable asset within an enterprise.

Modes of AI Deployment Within Value Streams

AI manifests in three primary modes within value streams:

- **Decision Support:** AI augments human judgment by surfacing patterns and predictions.
- **Automation Loops:** It drives end-to-end bounded processes autonomously.
- **Insight Generation:** AI uncovers anomalies and opportunities that are not immediately visible.

For each mode, a specific architecture is required, encompassing APIs, orchestration layers, and monitoring systems. Feedback, however, is a vital and shared component across all modes. Without feedback, AI remains a static system; with it, AI continuously learns and evolves alongside the business, adapting to new insights and conditions.

The Crucial Role of Infrastructure

Often underestimated, infrastructure is crucial for successful AI integration. The increasing use of Infrastructure-as-a-Service (IaaS) and sovereign cloud investments highlights the strategic significance of data residency, compliance, and readily available compute power. SAP's multi-billion-euro investment in the European sovereign cloud [12], for instance, demonstrated that a strong architectural and infrastructural foundation is essential for securely embedding AI into value streams. IaaS enables departments, from finance to supply chain, to access flexible compute resources while maintaining governance and security.

The Essential Role of Integration in AI Implementation: A Healthcare Case Study

The deployment of a chatbot in a crowded hospital was intended as a remedy for overflowing waiting rooms and relentless call volumes. Leadership believed that by automating symptom triage and appointment booking, staff would be freed from repetitive tasks and patients would gain quicker access to care. Initial signs looked promising as patient complaints were logged more efficiently, the pressure on phone lines eased, dashboards showed favorable trends, and staff felt a brief sense of relief that the load might finally be lifting.

However, a less stable situation existed beneath the surface. Doctors found only fragmented information when opening records, and nurses repeatedly requested details from patients that had already been provided. Patients felt overlooked and disconnected from their caregivers due to this process. The issue stemmed from the chatbot's isolation from the hospital's infrastructure, rather than its functionality or capabilities. It operated independently of the hospital's central systems, was not linked to health records, was devoid of audit trails for accountability, lacked feedback mechanisms for error correction, and was without the system reliability necessary for digital trust. This inherent fragility reflects a larger reality: discontinuous care results from fragmented records. Poor interoperability creates isolated systems that dishearten both staff and patients. A lack of oversight compromises accountability, and without operational governance, initial innovation inevitably leads to disappointment.

Enterprise architects have transformed patient onboarding by meticulously mapping the entire journey, end-to-end. They implemented core digital trust principles: integrating disparate systems, establishing governance for processes and policies, ensuring compliance with comprehensive audit trails, and aligning data flows with care delivery. The introduction of APIs facilitated seamless information transfer into medical records. Regulators and clinicians were appeased by new safeguards. Dashboards were reconfigured to offer a unified, comprehensive view of patient data throughout the system. While the chatbot's external appearance remained unchanged, its underlying integration into the hospital's architecture transformed it from a peripheral experiment into an integral part of the care continuum.

This case demonstrates how architecture concretely establishes trust, with compliance ensured by auditable systems and oversight maintained through active records that uphold accountability. Data flows are synchronized with clinical processes instead of clashing with them, and governance is implemented to guarantee resilience. What started as a fragile pilot program eventually transformed into a strong, enduring capability.

The Four Pillars of trustworthy AI (as we discussed in Chapter 1) are evident here as tangible outcomes. ***Accessibility*** improved as patients no longer had to repeat their information. ***Explainability*** materialized through dashboards that made information readily available to clinicians. ***Security*** was strengthened by audit-ready data pipelines and safeguards. ***Ethics*** was realized through design choices that allowed patients to feel acknowledged rather than dismissed. In healthcare and across all sectors, AI is effective when integrated within existing architecture. When integrated thoughtfully within value-creating frameworks, it thrives as a lasting capability that builds trust and empowers professionals, rather than failing due to disorganized implementation.

The Enterprise AI Architecture Model

Mapping AI to business capabilities and value streams should not be reduced to a checklist. It is better seen as a deliberate act of enterprise design, a practice that turns broad ambitions into sustained performance. This model for AI integration goes beyond a conventional arrangement of technical steps; it strategically links business objectives to organizational structure and then to tangible value, integrating AI as a core institutional practice rather than just an experimental concept. This model can be achieved in six phases, as listed below.

Phase 1: Defining Strategic Intent

The journey begins with business strategy. Enterprises set formal goals, but a closer look at leadership ambitions often reveals aspirations that carry greater urgency and sharper definition. When this intent is articulated with precision, it creates a compass that directs how AI solutions are conceived and applied. The clarity achieved at this stage sets the course for everything that follows.

Phase 2: Critical Capabilities Identification

Next, focus shifts to identifying critical capabilities, the core functions indispensable for achieving the defined strategy. This involves looking beyond industry buzzwords to pinpoint the processes and skills that genuinely drive the organization. Identifying these critical capabilities plants AI initiatives in fertile ground, where they can grow into sustained capabilities rather than scatter as side projects.

Phase 3: Data and Readiness Assessment

This is one of the most crucial stages. A frank evaluation of data and readiness determines how far the enterprise can go. Just as a building's height depends on the strength of its foundation, the success of any AI system rests on its underlying infrastructure. When leaders confront fragmented data, weak infrastructure, absent governance, or shallow skills, the exercise is less about cataloging shortcomings and more about building a shared honesty around where the enterprise truly stands. This is where the ***readiness gap delta (Δ)***, which we introduced in Chapter 1, becomes visible: the gap between aspiration and actual capability. Unless this delta is confronted directly, it grows wider, amplifying risk and eroding trust. Leaders can move forward with conviction only when they recognize the gap, commit to closing it, and align intent with capacity.

Phase 4: Value Stream Mapping

With foundations clarified, mapping extends to value streams, illustrating the actual flow of work across the enterprise. This is the stage where AI's leverage comes into sharper focus, such as follows:

- In financial services, advanced models are running complex risk scenarios and detecting fraud as transactions unfold, narrowing the window between threat and response.
- Healthcare systems are piloting diagnostic tools that analyze imaging, lab results, and patient histories together, offering clinicians a second lens that improves the speed and accuracy of decisions.
- Smart city programs are experimenting with AI to redesign traffic flows, anticipate energy demand, and even simulate civic policies before they are enacted.
- Retailers are deploying personalization engines that adapt digital storefronts in real time, shaping offers and recommendations to each shopper's behavior rather than serving static catalogues.
- And on the factory floor, predictive maintenance algorithms are extending the life of industrial equipment, while intelligent automation is coordinating production lines with a precision no human scheduler could match.

These examples represent more than incremental gains; they signal how AI, when embedded within value streams, reshapes the pace and coordination of enterprise activity. Individual interventions can deliver efficiency, but genuine transformation emerges when they are interconnected across the full chain of value creation, turning isolated improvements into systemic change.

Phase 5: AI As a Core Capability

AI moves beyond being a set of projects only when it is recognized as a capability in its own right. AI becomes a core capability when it is supported by deliberate structures rather than scattered projects. Enterprises need governance that establishes accountability, integration pathways that connect systems across departments, feedback mechanisms that capture learning from everyday use, and resource models that sustain talent and infrastructure. With these four elements in place, AI evolves from isolated pilots into a managed capability that continuously strengthens decision-making, service delivery, and innovation.

Phase 6: Continuous Measurement

The cycle culminates in measurement, though, in reality, it is the point where continuity begins. Enterprises that succeed with AI do not wait for annual reviews; they build steady routines that keep the system alive. Progress is tracked with precise metrics so leaders can see movement against intent. Outcomes are brought into forums where they are openly debated, turning results into shared accountability. Lessons are documented and passed on, allowing knowledge to accumulate rather than dissipate. Each refinement is then carried into the next round of deployment, ensuring that every cycle strengthens the one that follows. Through this discipline, measurement becomes less a closing act and more the engine that keeps AI adaptive and aligned with enterprise priorities.

Generative AI's Impact

Generative AI should never be mistaken for gospel. Its responses often sound natural enough to blur the line between machine and human conversation, close to, and in some cases surpassing, the threshold once described by the Turing test, but that does not make it a source of absolute truth. Technology is predictive at its core. It works by estimating what is most likely to come next—whether that be a word, a sentence, a line of code, or an image—based on vast amounts of training data. Enterprises that forget this distinction risk treating probability as certainty, and that misstep can be costly.

To really see what is happening under the hood, it helps to pause on the mechanics. Generative AI is powered by something called vector embeddings. Imagine every word or token you type being translated into a long string of numbers. These numbers live in a high-dimensional space where words that share meaning are drawn closer together, while those that diverge drift apart. The effect is magnetic in nature: similar concepts cluster, while the distant ones repel. This semantic geometry creates the illusion of understanding. The model does not reason as a human mind would; it moves through a mathematical landscape, bouncing from one coordinate to the next until it arrives at the continuation that is statistically most coherent. It is this almost surreal magic of mathematics, patterns captured in geometry, that lends machines a contextual sensitivity that, when designed responsibly, extends human capability rather than attempting to replace it.

We make this explanation plain, not to diminish the wonder of the technology, but to ground it. Generative AI is remarkable, but it is not divine. It is an instrument of mathematics and probability, and its power comes from how enterprises choose to apply it. Leaders who approach generative AI with clarity can use it to strengthen judgment, expand capacity, improve coordination across teams, and open new avenues of innovation. In doing so, they ground the technology in enterprise reality rather than being carried away by hype.

This is why generative AI intensifies the need for structure. A single application may dazzle, but brilliance in isolation rarely delivers strategic change. The enterprises that endure are those that integrate these capabilities into the very foundation of their value streams, where AI informs decisions with evidence, strengthens the way customers are engaged, accelerates the pace of innovation, and builds an advantage that compounds over time.

Green AI and the Environmental Ledger

Every value stream carries an environmental ledger. Models consume energy as surely as they produce predictions. Architecture transforms this challenge into stewardship by embedding sustainability directly into design. Routing inference to efficient processors, scheduling workloads in alignment with renewable supply, balancing latency with ecological impact, and tracking energy metrics as diligently as financial cost make sustainability a core criterion of enterprise design. An AI-adaptive enterprise harmonizes ambition with ecological stewardship. It constructs systems that perform with efficiency, earn trust through transparency, endure through resilience, and carry legitimacy in the eyes of society.

The Underlying Lesson

AI cannot remain a peripheral accessory for any enterprise; it needs to be constructed into the very core of an organization's operations. When deeply integrated, AI becomes a manageable and scalable capability that can be strategically guided to achieve desired outcomes. Without this foundational integration, AI initiatives remain fleeting experiments, generating temporary excitement but leaving no lasting impact once the novelty wears off.

2.4 From TOGAF to LeanIX: Matching Architecture to AI Ambition

Enterprise architecture (EA) historically operated behind the scenes, mapping system dependencies and creating blueprints, while transformation programs took center stage. However, in the Anno Artificialis Intelligenciae, this understated role is no longer sustainable. EA has now moved into a prominent position, becoming an indispensable framework for AI implementation. This shift emphasizes the critical importance of selecting appropriate frameworks and tools. Outdated static reference models are no longer adequate; businesses now require approaches that offer both structure and flexibility. The evolution from TOGAF to LeanIX perfectly illustrates this transformation.

The Limits of Traditional Frameworks Like TOGAF

For decades, TOGAF provided a strong foundation for IT transformation. Its Architecture Development Method (ADM) offered a structured approach to defining requirements, planning the future, managing transitions, and governing execution. This discipline proved essential for projects like ERP rollouts and data center consolidations. Its layered model—encompassing business, data, applications, and technology—empowered large organizations to confidently navigate complex environments.

However, AI presents a challenge to these linear methodologies. Machine learning thrives on continuous iteration and feedback; models are dynamic, constantly learning, drifting, and retraining. A single predictive model inherently impacts every layer simultaneously: influencing business strategy, integrating with CRM or ERP systems, flowing through real-time data pipelines, and heavily relying on GPUs and cloud infrastructure. TOGAF's sequential assumptions are strained by this inherent dynamism. Furthermore, AI often emerges opportunistically, for example, chatbots in marketing or predictive analytics in operations, making it difficult for centralized frameworks to keep pace. The fundamental difference is noticeable: TOGAF assumes a mature and controlled environment, while AI often arrives in a fragmented manner.

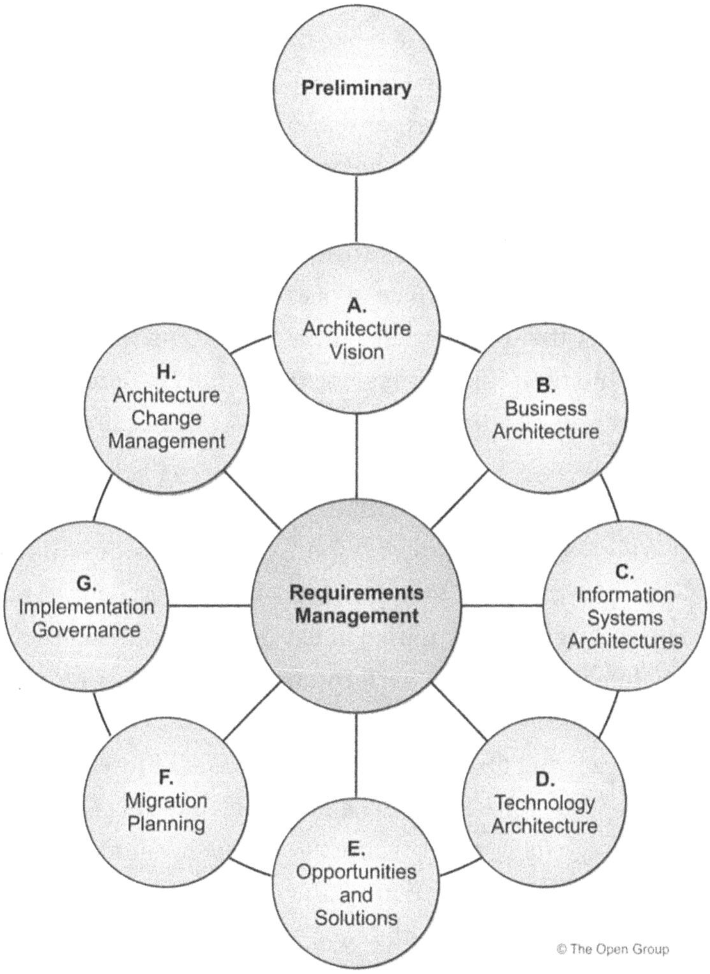

Figure 2-1. *The TOGAF Architecture Development Method (ADM) Cycle Source: The Open Group*

The Shift: From Static Frameworks to Dynamic Platforms

LeanIX was developed to address the challenge of outdated, static architecture diagrams. It transforms quarterly slide decks into dynamic, real-time maps, accessible across teams. This allows architects to visualize application interdependencies, data flow, potential bottlenecks, and failure points.

LeanIX proves most valuable in rapidly evolving environments. It directly supports the modular and composable architectures prevalent in AI-driven organizations. The platform integrates with MLOps workflows, enabling comprehensive tracing, production monitoring, drift-based retraining, and alignment of models with the broader infrastructure. In regulated sectors like finance and healthcare, its lineage dashboards and governance views provide essential operational and auditable visibility. Furthermore, as enterprises expand into hybrid and multi-cloud landscapes, LeanIX ensures continuity by illustrating the practical interactions between legacy and cloud-native components. This shift from static to dynamic architecture transforms documentation from a passive record into an active instrument, governing how systems evolve, strengthening resilience in the face of disruption, opening space for innovation, and creating transparency that builds trust across the enterprise.

As enterprises expand their intelligence portfolios, the challenge evolves from producing ideas to sustaining coherence across them. That's because when pilots emerge in separate departments and tools multiply in silos, the result is often a shadow economy of adoption that grows outside strategy and leaves leaders uncertain about where intelligence truly lives. Architecture responds to this risk by embedding visibility into the fabric of the enterprise, and modern platforms such as LeanIX make that visibility tangible by cataloging every model in use, tracing its lineage across data flows, revealing the dependencies that shape performance, and linking outcomes back to business purpose so that adoption no longer scatters but begins to cohere.

When cultivated as a living discipline, architectural visibility extends far beyond dashboards or static reports; it becomes the enterprise's ongoing awareness of how intelligence moves through its systems, where models reside, how they interact, and what consequences they generate. For compliance officers, this visibility forms an auditable trail that builds regulatory confidence and demonstrates accountability in action. For architects, it creates a working map that exposes duplication, clarifies dependencies, and guides integration so that innovation reinforces rather than fragments. For executives, it delivers a panoramic view of investment, revealing whether intelligence is compounding into durable capability or dispersing into disconnected efforts. Practiced in this way, visibility evolves into a discipline that channels creativity into purposeful alignment, turns governance into a source of momentum, and guides innovation toward outcomes that deepen trust, strengthen resilience, reinforce coherence, and extend the enterprise's advantage across time.

Integration Patterns: TOGAF and LeanIX in Action

Consider a bank deploying an AI-driven risk analytics engine. At the outset, TOGAF's Architecture Development Method (ADM) provides the initial blueprint. It defines the business objective of strengthening fraud detection; establishes governance structures to ensure regulatory compliance in areas such as KYC and anti-money laundering; maps the system's integration with ERP and CRM platforms as well as with data warehouses, customer portals, and transaction monitoring systems; and aligns the architecture with risk appetite and strategic growth priorities set by leadership. This early discipline reflects a truth about the relationship between strategy and structure: strategy provides direction, preventing aimless wandering, while structure gives form, preventing stagnation into bureaucracy. ***Without strategy, structure lacks purpose; without structure, strategy remains an abstract concept.***

Once execution begins, the challenge shifts from design to adaptation. Here, LeanIX becomes the living map. When a regulatory update alters how customer data must be captured, the platform immediately reveals which pipelines, models, and applications are affected. IT can adjust data flows in real time, compliance officers can review audit trails and test safeguards, business units can recalibrate their processes, and executives can respond with informed decisions rather than waiting for static reports. Architecture ceases to be a static blueprint and becomes a responsive instrument that operates at the speed of change.

In this partnership, TOGAF supplies the strategic vision and governance discipline, while LeanIX delivers continuous visibility, operational agility, and regulatory assurance. Together, they embody the principle that effective enterprise AI rests on both deliberate frameworks and adaptive platforms. This balance prevents AI from fading into one-off experiments and enables it to mature into a capability that upholds governance, builds confidence among stakeholders, extends operational resilience, and delivers value that endures over time.

Modeling AI As a Flow, Not a Stack

Unlike traditional architecture's preference for layered stacks (business over data, data over applications, applications over technology), AI architecture embraces a circular, flow-based lifecycle. This involves data arriving, being trained into models, being deployed, being tested, being corrected, and then being retrained with feedback. LeanIX effectively models this flow. AI applications like natural language processing, image recognition, and recommendation engines directly contribute to business outcomes. Architects can track the influence of predictions on decisions and how these decisions, in turn, generate new data for retraining. This shift from a static stack to a dynamic flow fundamentally defines AI-native architecture.

Stakeholder Perspectives and Cross-Silo Collaboration

In this dynamic organizational structure, enterprise architecture acts as the central nervous system that keeps the enterprise connected. For a data scientist, it becomes the map that shows how data travels, where it originates, and how it changes along the way—the lineage that underpins trustworthy models. For a compliance officer, it offers the trail of evidence needed to demonstrate that regulatory obligations are being met. For business leaders, it becomes the lens through which AI initiatives are tied directly to revenue and strategic priorities. And in cross-departmental workshops, it provides the common ground where perspectives converge, gaps are revealed, and fresh opportunities take shape. In this role, EA is not a passive supervisor but the coordinating command center that drives coherence across the enterprise.

Expanding EA Capability: Combining Rigor and Agility

TOGAF's strength lies in discipline; LeanIX's in agility. Together they create a two-speed architecture: one pace for long-term planning, another for real-time adjustment. Both are necessary for AI, where models evolve faster than governance cycles.

Change management reinforces this balance by turning architectural intent into lived practice. Success often begins with the appointment of AI champions within business units—leaders who can translate enterprise strategy into practical adoption. Momentum is built through iterative pilots, small projects that deliver visible wins and create confidence before scaling further. Oversight is strengthened when governance councils bring executives, legal teams, and operations together around the same table, ensuring accountability across functions. Additionally, leadership's unambiguous communication keeps the culture alive throughout the process, bringing people up to speed with technological advancements. In this way, change management becomes the bridge between structured design and tangible organizational impact.

The loop closes with measurement. Key metrics provide the feedback that grounds ambition in reality: the number of processes already augmented by AI, the speed at which models can be retrained, the frequency of data quality incidents, the completeness of audit trails, and the growth of employee literacy. By establishing these measures, a common understanding is developed between leadership and delivery teams. This practice allows progress to be seen as it unfolds, keeps momentum alive across cycles of work, and sustains alignment between leadership intent and the delivery of outcomes.

Living Architecture for Living Intelligence

AI systems are never "set-and-forget." Models drift over time, regulations shift, and business requirements continue to evolve. Without strong observability, organizations accumulate technical debt, unmonitored models that quietly degrade, retraining efforts that go undocumented, hidden integrations that escape oversight, and security gaps that expand unnoticed. LeanIX provides the control plane to counter this drift, showing where models are in use, how APIs interconnect, where dependencies are forming, and which risks are emerging. In this way, architecture shifts from a static plan into an active safeguard for the enterprise.

In the Anno Artificialis Intelligenciae, architecture itself must be alive. Like a living organism, it cannot survive without carrying out essential processes. It must ***"breathe"*** by exchanging information across systems, ***"digest"*** by integrating and processing data, ***"circulate"*** by distributing resources where they are needed, and ***"renew"*** by eliminating outdated components and regenerating new ones. Only by performing these continuous functions does enterprise architecture remain fit to support intelligence that is itself evolving. A static blueprint may record what once was, but a living architecture sustains what is and prepares for what comes next.

Sector-Specific Nuances

The contours of enterprise architecture shift depending on the sector it serves. In manufacturing, resilience at the edge is critical: predictive maintenance depends on AI models that can run directly on factory floors, processing sensor data in real time without waiting for cloud latency. In healthcare, the stakes revolve around privacy and consent. Federated learning allows hospitals to train diagnostic models across multiple sites while keeping patient data local. Fine-grained consent frameworks ensure that ethical boundaries are respected. Retail, by contrast, operates at the junction of speed and legacy. Recommendation engines may personalize online experiences, but they must still connect with decades-old point-of-sale systems that record the final transaction. Smart city initiatives carry their own distinct needs, requiring AI systems that can simulate traffic flows, optimize energy use, and test civic policies before they are deployed to millions of residents.

These variations highlight a deeper truth: no single framework can serve all enterprises alike. Adaptive architectures allow each sector to meet its regulatory obligations but also to pursue competitiveness on its own terms. What matters most is the ***balance***, governance without rigidity, innovation without fragility, and an architecture that grows alongside the intelligence it supports.

TOGAF plus LeanIX: Coexistence and Coevolution

The lesson is not one of replacement but of partnership. TOGAF provides the structure that gives enterprise architecture its discipline over time. It clarifies strategy, defines governance, establishes accountability, and embeds continuity into enterprise design. LeanIX, by contrast, brings those designs to life in real time. It reveals how systems interact, how models change with use, where processes are shifting, and when risks begin to surface. Together, they move enterprise architecture beyond static documentation and into dynamic orchestration.

What emerges is both coexistence and co-evolution. Enterprises cannot afford a blueprint that remains frozen, nor can they depend on platforms without guiding principles. TOGAF offers the compass that sets direction, while LeanIX provides the map that updates as the terrain shifts. One preserves intent, the other enables adaptation. Their co-evolution ensures that enterprise AI matures as a capability that is responsible, resilient, innovative, and strategically aligned with the enterprise.

2.5 Building EA Maturity for AI Readiness

From Cloud-Native to AI-Native

The leap from cloud-native to AI-native is more than a technical progression. Cloud-native enterprises learned to harness elastic infrastructure and scale applications with agility, but AI-native enterprises face a deeper challenge. They must embed intelligence into the very foundation of the organization—into people who make decisions, into processes that shape outcomes, into systems that evolve continuously, and into governance that holds everything accountable.

In this shift, intelligence becomes a core attribute of people, processes, systems, and governance, rather than simply being an add-on. It becomes a capability in its own right, sustained through architecture that is living rather than static, disciplined by frameworks like TOGAF, animated by platforms like LeanIX, and made urgent by the possibilities and risks of generative AI. Sector after sector, whether healthcare, manufacturing, finance, retail, or smart cities, will find its own path, but all must navigate the same imperative: to move from managing technology to cultivating intelligence. To truly embrace an AI-native approach, we must prioritize learning, renewal, adaptation, and trust in our designs. This foundational orientation is what elevates AI from just a collection of "tools" into a lasting and powerful "capability" in its own right.

Traits of a Mature AI-Native Enterprise

Maturity is not a milestone reached overnight; it emerges gradually through recognizable patterns. Decision-making becomes distributed across teams while still grounded in explicit lines of accountability. Data moves more freely across the enterprise, but every access point is reinforced with strong governance. Models are not left to drift; they are monitored in production, retrained when performance falls, adapted as business needs evolve, and retired responsibly when their usefulness ends. Culture itself shifts as openness to automation is tempered with ethical safeguards that protect both people and reputation.

For leaders, these traits become visible through tools that make readiness tangible. Capability heatmaps reveal where strengths lie and where gaps remain. AI road maps translate ambition into sequences of actionable steps. Maturity is transformed from an abstract concept into a practical framework for enterprise decision-making through the use of maturity radars. These tools provide measurable progress over time, without doubt linking effort to value.

AI Credit and Debit As a Readiness Lens

Financial language provides a powerful lens for understanding AI maturity, because just as balance sheets reveal the health of a business, so too can a ledger of credit and debit reveal the health of enterprise intelligence.

Credit represents the value created, from efficiency gains that free thousands of hours to predictive insights that reduce downtime, from customer experiences that deepen loyalty to new revenue streams unlocked through data-driven products, and each successful deployment adds to this account, compounding over time into measurable Return on AI Investment (ROAI). Debt accumulates just as reliably, through rising energy consumption as models scale, through security exposures that expand when monitoring is weak, through workforce disruption when reskilling lags behind automation, and through reputational strain when outputs fail to meet expectations of fairness or transparency. The account therefore shows how every gain carries its counterpart in cost and how the balance between them decides whether intelligence compounds into resilience or drifts toward fragility.

Architecture enables leaders to hold both sides of this ledger in view. Energy metrics embedded into design ensure that sustainability advances alongside speed, governance aligned with data pipelines prevents risks from multiplying, and reskilling programs tied to adoption convert disruption into renewed capability. Culture is measured with the same discipline as technology so that literacy grows, human oversight remains present, and trust is cultivated as an enterprise asset. For the ledger to serve its purpose, it must be maintained with rigor. Enterprises review it as routinely as financial performance, asking where credit is expanding and where debit is building up. They pursue it as a continuous practice, adjusting architectural choices, retraining cycles, governance routines, and cultural investments in response to what the ledger reveals. In this way, credit is nurtured deliberately, and debit is contained before it undermines legitimacy.

Figure 2-2. *The AI Value Ledger: Credits and Debits*

Seen in this light, the ledger functions as a discipline of stewardship. Every architectural decision moves the account upward or downward, shaping not only technical outcomes but also financial durability, ecological responsibility, employee confidence, and customer trust. Enterprises that pursue the ledger continuously, treating credit and debit with equal seriousness, cross the readiness gap delta (**Δ**) with greater certainty. They graduate from scattered wins into a maturity where AI compounds value, strengthens legitimacy, extends human judgment, and sustains advantage across repeated cycles of adoption.

Making Maturity Operational

Maturity is achieved when it transitions from theoretical analysis to practical, daily application. LeanIX facilitates this transition by transforming static diagrams into dynamic, living maps. These maps visually represent where AI is integrated, where it is absent, and where potential risks are emerging. Key issues such as model drift, compliance gaps, fragile dependencies, and new vulnerabilities become apparent. This provides leaders with immediate and actionable oversight. Consequently, architects can offer leadership advice based on concrete evidence rather than abstract assessments.

The Demands of Generative AI

Generative AI pushes enterprise architecture to new levels of discipline. It depends on modular infrastructures that extend across clouds, on-premises, edge, and hybrid environments. It functions effectively only when privacy-preserving techniques such as federated learning protect sensitive data. It remains safe and reliable when continuous monitoring detects drift, bias, anomalies, and security risks in time to act. Above all, generative AI flourishes when architectures are transparent, resilient, adaptive, and open to audit, making unpredictability a managed factor rather than a hidden threat.

Culture and Governance

Technology may enable adoption, but culture and governance determine whether maturity endures. Enterprises that advance deliberately invest in reskilling programs that expand literacy, appoint AI champions inside business units to drive adoption, establish cross-functional councils that connect executives with compliance and delivery teams, and form ethical committees that weave fairness, accountability, privacy, and transparency into everyday practice. As regulatory landscapes expand, these cultural fundamentals turn maturity from a project milestone into a lasting capability.

Real-Time Visibility

LeanIX cultivates trust by integrating architecture with real-time visibility. Its connection with service management and monitoring platforms creates a unified understanding of system readiness. When combined with privacy controls, it strengthens lineage, access, security, and governance throughout the system. In this capacity, enterprise architecture's role shifts from simply planning systems to actively ensuring their legality, reliability, continuity, and overall trustworthiness.

Managing Resistance and Ethical Gaps

Even technically excellent enterprises can falter when their culture presents resistance. This often manifests as blurred ownership, misaligned incentives, growing silos, and decelerated progress. To mitigate these risks, mature organizations implement literacy initiatives that demystify AI, host open forums to encourage dialogue, establish governance structures that clarify accountability, and integrate ethics-by-design principles from the outset. Ultimately, effective change management serves as the crucial link, ensuring technical advancements are seamlessly integrated with cultural acceptance.

Navigating Regulation

Regulation is a dynamic landscape, necessitating continuous adaptation. Enterprise architecture serves as the crucial nexus where legal, ethical, policy, and technological considerations intersect. By integrating fairness checks into operational processes, promoting consistent communication between legal and technical teams, and directly translating policy updates into system safeguards, organizations can maintain agility. This approach allows enterprises to keep pace with evolving regulations while simultaneously driving innovation.

From Systems to Intelligence

An AI-native enterprise is characterized by continuous learning, not just the deployment of models. Strong feedback loops, frequent retraining to preserve accuracy, distinct ownership structures for accountability, and operational procedures that guarantee continuity are the sources of this long-term adaptability. Architects hold a pivotal role in making intelligence sustainable. They map where impacts will land, clarify who carries responsibility, shape systems that can renew themselves over time, and ensure continuity even as technologies evolve. The absence of these practices leads to failed initiatives, while their integration empowers AI to become a lasting organizational asset.

AI Across Sectors

AI adoption varies significantly across sectors, yet consistently drives mature outcomes. Legal firms using AI for contract review prioritize compliance, traceability, auditability, and speed to reduce turnaround times. Manufacturers leverage edge AI to predict machine failures and maintain production stability. Healthcare institutions utilize federated learning to advance diagnostics while upholding patient privacy and consent. Retailers improve personalization by integrating recommendation engines with existing point-of-sale systems, modernizing without discarding valuable infrastructure. Across these diverse sectors, one lesson stands out: architectural maturity consistently delivers outcomes that endure. Systems become resilient under stress, progress can be measured with confidence, scale is achieved without fragility, and strategies remain solidified as the enterprise evolves.

Architects As Advisors

In this ever-changing environment, architects serve as trusted advisors. They leverage platforms like LeanIX to show executives the tangible value of AI, pinpoint accumulating risks, highlight misaligned resources, and identify promising opportunities. Their role expands beyond drafting architectural maps; they become guides who shape enterprise journeys, navigating through complexity with foresight. While technology is constantly evolving, the architectural vision of these advisors provides a vital North Star for the enterprise, offering the consistent guidance needed to stay on course.

Future Frontiers

New demands like edge AI, digital twins, spatial computing, and immersive interfaces are challenging existing enterprise structures, which older frameworks weren't built to handle. Traditional methods alone cannot manage this growing complexity. LeanIX, when integrated with observability practices and continuous integration pipelines, acts as a control center for adaptive design. It empowers architects to monitor evolving dependencies, adapt systems to changing conditions, strengthen governance in high-pressure areas, and guide enterprises in real time.

The AI Compatibility Score

Assessing an enterprise's readiness for AI adoption is intricate due to its unique history, limitations, and aspirations. We propose the AI Compatibility Score as a structured framework to visualize this readiness, examining the adaptability of systems to change, the trustworthiness of data, the depth of governance, and the cultural preparedness to integrate intelligence as a core competency. This approach transforms disparate indicators into a comprehensive understanding of both strengths and deficiencies.

The score rests on eight dimensions, each capturing a critical layer of preparedness:

1. **Legacy System Modernity**: How modular, decoupled, and adaptable core systems are when new demands arise
2. **Data Lineage and Quality**: Whether data pipelines can be traced end to end, metadata is reliable, datasets remain trustworthy, and validation routines are in place
3. **Cloud and Integration Readiness**: The maturity of APIs, the flexibility of hybrid deployments, the elasticity of cloud infrastructure, and the interoperability of tools across environments
4. **Privacy and Governance**: The ability to follow frameworks such as GDPR, the EU AI Act, and HIPAA while also adhering to internal codes of conduct
5. **MLOps and Observability**: Monitoring mechanisms that track performance, retraining cycles that address drift, explainability features that create accountability, and audit logs that capture model history
6. **Alignment with Strategy**: Whether AI initiatives are correlated to business outcomes, linked to capability maps, supported with investment, and aligned with leadership intent

7. **Cultural Readiness**: The literacy levels of employees, openness to experimentation, willingness to adapt roles, and retention of human judgment alongside automation

8. **Sector Benchmarks**: How the enterprise compares with peers in its sector, whether gaps are narrowing or widening, and where differentiation is possible

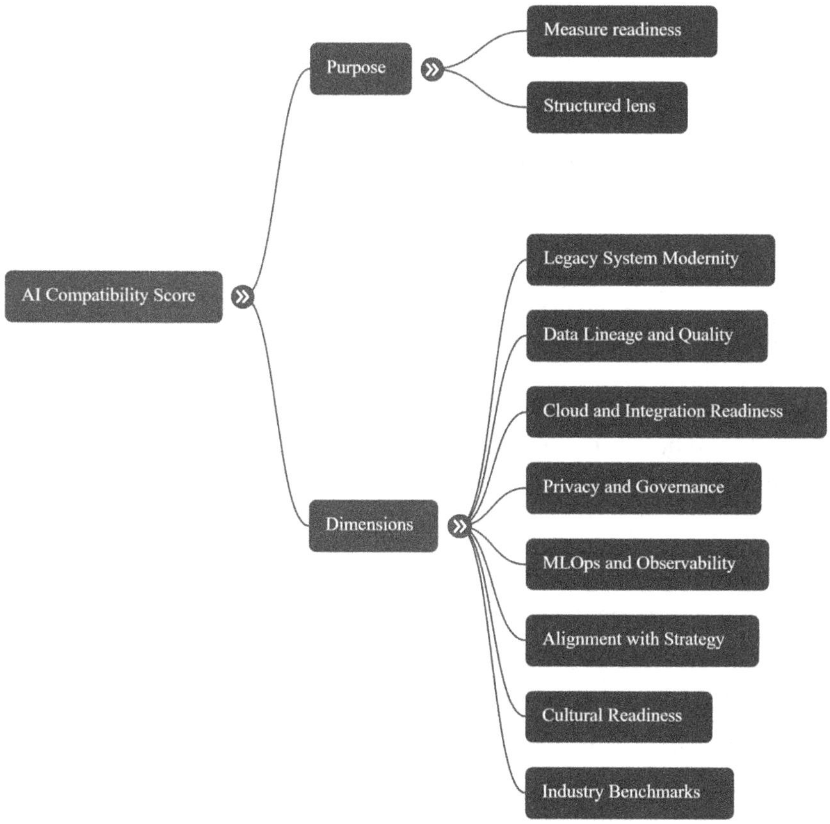

Figure 2-3. *The AI Compatibility Score Framework*

How to Score the AI Compatibility Score

The AI Compatibility Score is applied consistently across all eight dimensions. Each dimension is scored on a 1–5 scale, where the numbers reflect maturity rather than raw performance. The goal is comparability—so leaders can see how their enterprise stacks up within itself, across dimensions, and over time.

- **1 (Initial)**: The enterprise has little or no structured capability in this dimension. Practices are ad hoc, and risks are high.
- **2 (Emerging)**: Early initiatives exist, but they are fragmented, inconsistent, or heavily dependent on individuals rather than processes.
- **3 (Developing)**: Formal structures and processes are in place, though gaps remain. Capabilities are repeatable but not yet standardized across the enterprise.
- **4 (Established)**: The enterprise demonstrates consistent, enterprise-wide practices. Systems, data, governance, and culture are integrated into daily operations.
- **5 (Leading)**: The enterprise is proactive, adaptive, and benchmarks above its peers. Practices are not only consistent but continuously improved and innovated.

With eight dimensions scored on a scale of 1-5, the maximum score is 40. As a result, the Compatibility Score becomes a consistent baseline for comparison across time and context, giving leaders a crown line against which the ascent of enterprise intelligence can be traced and judged. Each enterprise rates itself across all eight dimensions we mentioned above. A score in the range of 8–16 signals ***Fragile Readiness***, where AI adoption risks outpacing capacity and foundations remain weak. A score between 17 and 28 reflects ***Developing Maturity***, where progress is visible but uneven, and bottlenecks limit impact. Scores from 29 to 36 indicate ***Established Foundations***, where systems, data, and governance support AI adoption, though continued investment is needed to scale. Scores of 37–40 define an ***AI-Compatible Enterprise***, where ambition is matched by structure, culture is reinforced by governance, adaptation is continuous, and outcomes remain strategically aligned.

This scoring mechanism offers a one-size-fits-all baseline. The Compatibility Score is designed to provide visibility, offering a direct view of readiness rather than a judgment. With regular reassessment, the AI Compatibility Score becomes a living health check. It reveals where an enterprise is strong, highlights the areas that remain fragile, points to the investments needed for improvement, and shows how close the organization is to closing the readiness gap delta (**Δ**).

The Compatibility Score serves as a reflective tool for leadership, guiding decisions rather than catering to shareholders. Different sectors will emphasize different aspects: financial institutions may weigh compliance most heavily, healthcare providers may give precedence to privacy and ethics, manufacturers may elevate resilience at the operational edge, and smart cities may stress transparency for civic trust. The key lies in discipline—turning early assessments of readiness into evidence that can be monitored, debated, improved, and shared.

So, where do you start with a Compatibility Score? With the Compatibility Score, the first step is always at the foundation: modernizing core systems so they can support change, strengthening data quality so insights can be trusted, expanding integration capacity so information flows without friction, and embedding governance so accountability is built in from the start. These foundations create the conditions for every other dimension to function. Still, the eight dimensions are not a sequential checklist; they are interdependent and can be advanced in different orders depending on context. A bank may focus on compliance first, a manufacturer may begin with edge resilience, and a healthcare provider may prioritize data privacy. What matters is completeness. Only when all dimensions are addressed together does an enterprise achieve AI compatibility, positioning itself to capture sustained value and avoid the barriers that so often stall initiatives.

Enterprise architecture is well placed to steward this process. Just as financial audits provide an account of organizational health, the Compatibility Score should be refreshed routinely in partnership with compliance, governance, digital strategy, and operational teams. In this way, it evolves from a scorecard into a shared language for progress. Above all, the Compatibility Score connects to the central question carried through this chapter: ***Is the enterprise ready for AI?*** Applied consistently, it highlights where AI should be implemented, to what degree, and how the readiness gap delta (**Δ**) we introduced earlier can be closed. It stands as both a measure of the present and a guide for the future.

AI Compatibility Score in Action: A Banking Example

Consider a mid-sized bank preparing to launch an AI-driven fraud detection platform. Leadership decides to apply the AI Compatibility Score as a readiness check before scaling the initiative. Each of the eight dimensions is rated on the 1–5 maturity scale.

- **Legacy System Modernity**: Core systems remain monolithic, difficult to decouple, and only partly modular. **Score = 2**
- **Data Lineage and Quality**: Transaction data is traceable, but metadata is inconsistent, and audit trails are incomplete. **Score = 3**
- **Cloud and Integration Readiness**: APIs are available but not standardized; hybrid deployments exist but lack elasticity. **Score = 3**
- **Privacy and Governance**: Compliance with GDPR and KYC is strong, with dedicated audit teams and policies. **Score = 5**
- **MLOps and Observability**: Basic monitoring exists, but retraining cycles are ad hoc, and explainability tools are minimal. **Score = 2**
- **Alignment with Strategy**: AI initiatives are tied directly to fraud reduction targets and operational efficiency goals. **Score = 4**
- **Cultural Readiness**: Employees understand compliance but lack broader AI literacy; there is hesitancy about automation. **Score = 2**
- **Sector Benchmarks**: Compared to peer banks, resilience is solid in compliance but weak in system agility. **Score = 3**

The total score is 24, placing the bank in the ***Developing Maturity*** range. The profile reveals identifiable patterns. Governance is exemplary, and strategy is well aligned, but weaknesses remain. Legacy systems are still rigid, cultural readiness is fragile, MLOps practices are immature, and integration capacity is uneven. These gaps represent the areas where risk accumulates.

Leadership chooses not to press ahead blindly but to act with discipline. They sequence investments rather than scatter them, modernizing core systems to reduce rigidity, establishing structured retraining cycles to strengthen model reliability, launching an internal AI literacy program to prepare employees, and improving integration pipelines so applications can connect more fluidly.

Within a year, the bank reassesses its Compatibility Score. Scores for systems, MLOps, culture, and integration rise to 4, lifting the overall profile into the ***Established Foundations*** range. The benefits are immediate and visible. Fraud detection models begin to retrain automatically as new threats emerge. Compliance teams gain confidence because explainability and audit trails are now embedded. Employees feel equipped rather than threatened, supported by literacy programs and enhanced guidance.

Integration improvements reduce friction across business units, creating faster response times. The Compatibility Score, once an abstract measure, now gives the leadership team a common language to track readiness, align resources, reassure regulators, and steer AI adoption as a structured, transparent process.

What began as a vague question, as an enterprise, ***"Are we ready for AI?"***, turns into a measurable, repeatable process that bridges ambition with capacity. This is the power of viewing compatibility as a strategic lens that brings clarity to complex choices.

Case Study: From Pilots to Portfolio in Financial Services

Picture a mid-sized European bank, proud of its heritage but quietly anxious about falling behind the fintech wave. Its early experiments were cautious and limited in scope. While individual initiatives such as a customer service chatbot, a fraud-detection pilot, credit-scoring models, and personalization tools for digital portals showed promise in isolation, they lacked integration into a cohesive strategy.

In boardrooms, while impressive on presentation slides, the true value of the bank's AI initiatives became questionable when regulators demanded audit trails and executives sought measurable returns. A pivotal moment occurred after a tense meeting when an executive posed a critical question: ***"Do we actually know how many AI models are live across this organization? And do we trust them?"*** The subsequent silence highlighted a significant lack of clarity and marked the beginning of the bank's AI maturity journey.

To respond, the architects applied the ***AI Compatibility Score*** we proposed above. It became the lens through which every model was assessed. Instead of vague impressions, leaders now had a structured view of how reliable the data was, how frequently retraining occurred, whether governance safeguards were in place, and how closely each system aligned with business priorities. The score made the invisible visible. Models with promise but weak compliance showed up as risks. Others that delivered value but lacked monitoring and demanded urgent attention. A handful that met the highest standards stood out as strengths worth scaling.

LeanIX served as the bank's dynamic blueprint, revealing the locations of embedded intelligence and existing deficiencies. Over subsequent months, this depiction evolved. Certain models were decommissioned, while others were reconstructed with pipelines that adhered to GDPR and preempted the EU AI Act. New models were introduced, consistently incorporating lineage, observability, governance, and integration into their fundamental design.

The cultural shift proved as significant as the technical one. Leaders stopped asking, ***"What's the next impressive pilot we can show the board?"***, and started asking, ***"Where does AI genuinely extend our capability map?"*** Compliance officers participated in design sessions, which were followed by training programs. This allowed business leaders to directly link AI deployments with strategic outcomes. The Compatibility Score gave everyone a common reference point—executives, compliance teams, delivery units, and data and risk teams could finally speak the same language about the enterprise's AI readiness.

As we discussed earlier, thinking of AI in terms of credit and debit provides leaders a practical way to balance enthusiasm with stewardship. The bank adopted this lens alongside the Compatibility Score, and it quickly shifted boardroom conversations from impressions to accountability. Credit could now be named and measured in reduced fraud losses, stronger customer loyalty, and efficiencies in risk modeling. Debit was made visible in rising compute costs, regulatory compliance overhead, and the cultural investment required to reskill staff. By treating AI adoption through this ledger, executives created a discipline in which benefits were nurtured deliberately, costs were managed before they eroded trust, and every new deployment was judged for both its technical promise and its financial and cultural resilience.

Two years later, the change was visible across the enterprise. Fraud models retrained automatically as new threats appeared, customer-facing systems produced explanations regulators could follow, employees had developed the literacy to use AI with confidence rather than suspicion, and data and risk teams relied on dashboards that revealed how models were performing and when intervention was required. The leadership team could finally point to something more durable than hype: measurable Return on AI Investment (ROAI), models that stood up to compliance scrutiny, systems that stayed resilient under stress, and a workforce that trusted the technology it helped to shape.

AI maturity was achieved by progressively strengthening and aligning systems, governance, culture, and strategy. The AI Compatibility Score was crucial to this process, offering leaders concrete direction, facilitating the transition from isolated trials to intentional advancements, and establishing a universal framework for evaluating the enterprise's AI preparedness. This framework allowed for ongoing discussion, action, and refinement. Consequently, AI progressed from a series of pilot projects to a dependable and sustainable enterprise capability.

Design for the Human Endpoint

As we opined in Chapter 1, the endpoint is always ***human***. That is our guiding fact and our moral constraint. When an enterprise treats AI as a route to raw efficiency or a contest for the biggest model, it risks losing sight of why products and services exist in the first place: to serve people. For the architect, design begins the journey and also completes it. It is both the blueprint that sets direction and the conscience that ensures alignment at the end. When design acts as the conscience of a system, intelligence becomes sustainable, trusted, and genuinely useful. When design is absent, intelligence grows brittle, misaligned, and ultimately unworthy of trust.

Across sectors, the logic is the same. Finance moves because humans earn and spend. Healthcare exists because humans fall ill and need care. Manufacturing thrives because products are created for human use. Even in B2B systems, what looks like business-to-business on the surface ultimately ends in choices and experiences that shape individual lives. This is not nostalgia or an argument to slow technical progress. It is simple economics and simple ethics. If systems stop serving human needs, they lose the only source of durable value they have, which is trust.

Design that centers the human endpoint looks different from a checklist. It threads a path for human judgment through every interaction, allowing people to intervene and redirect when systems drift away from purpose. It ensures that decisions are not only explained but explained in terms people can actually understand. It measures outcomes that matter to both users and employees. And it treats governance, culture, engineering, and leadership as parts of a single living practice. These are practical commitments, not abstractions. They require measurable artifacts and routines, metrics that capture trust and usability, governance gates that safeguard dignity, and training programs that let people work with systems rather than be displaced by them.

Two complementary practices help turn human-facing design into reality:

I. **Collective Intelligence** keeps people in the loop as active contributors. It draws on user feedback and the insights of employees, but it also extends to the lived perspectives that surface when diverse voices are invited into the process. In our premise, this means building systems that learn from frontline experience as much as from community review and that take shape through collaborative decision-making. In this way, AI remains grounded in the realities it is meant to serve.

II. **Design Thinking** offers a second safeguard by asking three questions in sequence: Does the solution hold meaning for people, can it be integrated smoothly into enterprise workflows, and will it create value that endures? In practice, this approach shifts attention toward outcomes that people recognize as relevant while still keeping the enterprise aligned with purpose and societal trust. It helps architects design with the human endpoint always in sight, steering them away from technical feats pursued for their own sake.

Taken together, Collective Intelligence and Design Thinking form a discipline of balance. The first ensures human voices remain present in how systems evolve. The second ensures those systems mature into designs that reflect trust, usability, longevity, and enterprise purpose. Implemented together, they reinforce architecture in service of humanity while also sustaining advantage for the enterprise. Together, they allow the architect to translate ambition into services people can accept, trust, and ultimately value. In the Anno Artificialis Intelligenciae, architecture is less a diagram and more an operating system that links vision to action and ensures value endures.

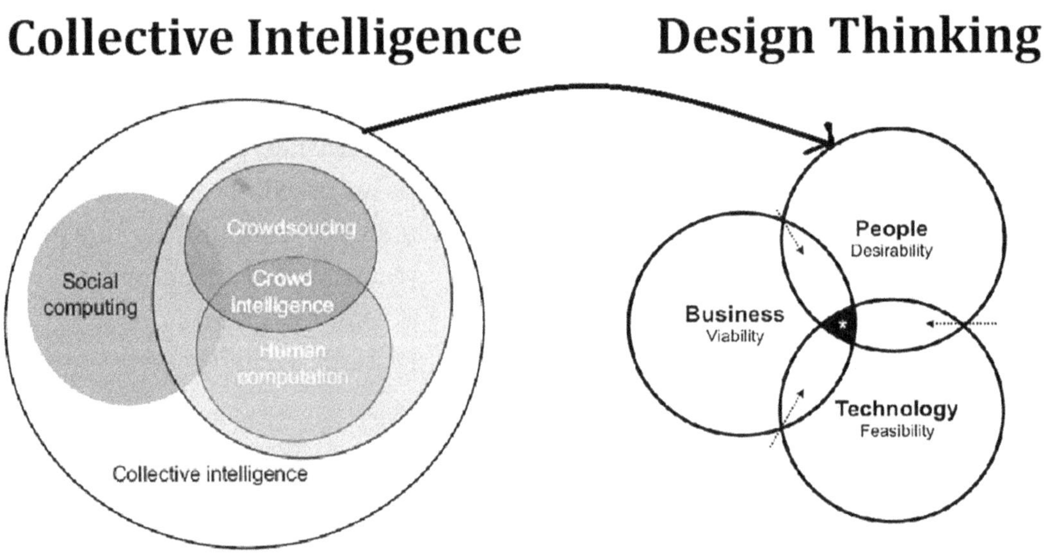

***Figure 2-4.** Collective Intelligence and Design Thinking as Human-Centered Safeguards*

We should be explicit about the hazard and the remedy in affirmative terms. When enterprises pursue blanket automation as a first-order strategy, they risk hollowing out the very foundations of demand: empathy, judgment, cultural fit, and human trust. Instead, adopt AI selectively and strategically in places where it augments human capabilities and where automation genuinely improves outcomes for real people. The AI Compatibility Score we discussed above will give leaders a concrete way to replace guesswork with governance and to base decisions on evidence rather than instinct. Pilots then become disciplined spaces for learning, showing where systems earn acceptance and where they truly deliver value before being scaled. Alongside this, literacy cannot remain a side initiative; it must be a core investment so that employees and customers alike gain the confidence to understand, question, and shape the systems that affect their work and their lives.

This is not an argument to hesitate or deter innovation. It is a call for stewardship. ***Progress that is blind to human consequence is progress that will be resisted. Resistance will reduce value rather than increase it. The enterprise that embeds human-facing design gains a competitive edge. Trust becomes an asset that compounds, explainability becomes a differentiator in crowded markets, and a workforce reskilled and partnered with machines becomes a source of innovation rather than a cost to cut.***

As we now near the end of this chapter, let this be the charge we carry forward: to shape systems that remain answerable to people, to judge progress by the weight of outcomes that touch real lives, and to guard the human endpoint as the compass at the heart of every implementation.

Conclusion

Enterprise architecture transforms ambition into tangible capability. This chapter has outlined a journey of progress: modernizing legacy systems for flexibility, fortifying data pipelines for reliability, cultivating a culture where skepticism yields to understanding, and integrating governance into daily routines so accountability becomes inherent rather than superficial. These advancements transform intelligence from mere innovation into an indispensable element of the enterprise.

Architecture breathes life into fragile models, transforming them into living intelligence. As seen in the evolution from TOGAF to LeanIX and the shift from static frameworks to dynamic maps, effective design is what allows AI to move beyond isolated demonstrations and become a lasting capability. However, tools alone are insufficient, which is why we put forward the AI Compatibility Score above as a reflective discipline. It creates a unified picture of readiness by bringing together the state of systems, the discipline of governance, the cultural capacity for change, and the strength of leadership intent. Its role is to guide leaders toward clarity, showing how intelligence can be embedded in the enterprise, how far it can extend without strain, and how to recognize the moment when scaling becomes sustainable.

As highlighted in Chapter 1, the ultimate goal remains human-centric, a fundamental premise that should not be overlooked even when developing frameworks. Every sector, including finance, healthcare, manufacturing, and B2B platforms, derives its legitimacy from the individuals at the furthest reach of its value streams. An enterprise loses its essence if it sacrifices the human element for the sake of efficiency or revenue. Therefore, sustained advantage is achieved through stewardship, rather than the fleeting promise of speed, the lure of scale for its own sake, or the pursuit of efficiency without regard for trust. The lesson settles with weight: systems must answer to people, outcomes must carry meaning in real lives, safeguards must protect the trust on which every enterprise ultimately depends, and leadership must ensure that these commitments are renewed over time. With such architecture in place, AI can evolve from a series of scattered pilots into a capability that endures.

The path forward now turns toward governance. If architecture provides the frame, governance provides the discipline that keeps it intact under stress. Chapter 3 will step into this terrain, exploring the hurdles faced by startups, SMBs, and global enterprises, and the universal challenges of talent, technical debt, and regulation. The focus has shifted from the feasibility of building AI to the imperative of implementing it responsibly across diverse applications. Designing intelligence is one challenge; coexisting with it presents another entirely.

CHAPTER 3

Challenges Across the AI Journey: From Startups to Global Enterprises

Introduction

Achieving AI maturity is never a uniform path. Its shape shifts depending on the size of the organization, the pace at which it moves, and the weight of its existing structures. Startups approach the journey with restless energy, eager to prove themselves through experiments that feel like wagers on the future. Small and mid-sized businesses lean toward pragmatism, sensing the pull of innovation but living each day under the constraints of budgets, limited expertise, and time. Large enterprises face a different kind of challenge: their hierarchies, processes, and legacy systems provide stability but often resist rapid adaptation. Fragmentation across departments can slow progress even further. In all these contexts, one question persists: ***How does an organization move from fragile pilots to capabilities that endure?***

As we established in Chapter 2, enterprise architecture acts as an intelligence multiplier. It provides the root system that allows AI implementations to withstand pressure and grow with stability. Although architecture alone does not guarantee success. Between ambition and capability lies **Δ**, the readiness gap. Every organization, regardless of size, must navigate this space. For startups, the gap appears as a tension between agility and scalability. For SMBs, it appears as the trade-offs between ambition and limited resources. For enterprises, it manifests in silos, cultural inertia, and

R. Harjika, *Architecting Enterprise AI Strategies*, https://doi.org/10.1007/979-8-8688-2219-3_3

accumulated technical debt. Beyond these distinct hurdles lie constraints that cut across the spectrum: scarce talent, governance demands, fragile trust, and the rising cost of computation and energy. Together, they set the outer boundaries of what AI adoption can realistically achieve.

Game theory, first formalized by ***John von Neumann*** and ***Oskar Morgenstern*** in 1944 [13], set out to study how individuals and groups make strategic choices when outcomes depend on the decisions of others. At its heart, game theory is a way of framing interdependence. Some games are ***zero-sum***: a win for one side equals a loss for the other, as in chess or war. Others are ***non-zero-sum***: through cooperation, all sides can create value that grows the total outcome, as in trade or alliances. Within this framework lie concepts that will shape the discussions in this chapter. The ***Prisoner's Dilemma*** illustrates how players, acting in their immediate self-interest, can converge on an outcome that leaves everyone worse off. ***Nash equilibrium*** describes the point where no player can improve their position by changing strategy alone, because stability emerges from mutual adjustment. ***Repeated games*** reveal how credibility and trust accumulate over time, making today's move inseparable from tomorrow's reputation. Although conceived as mathematics, these ideas travel well into the world of enterprises.

Organizations play by different rules, that is, startups with speed, SMBs with efficiency, and enterprises with resilience, but they all operate in shared arenas where choices intersect. The language of payoff functions, strategies, and equilibria becomes a way to make sense of adoption patterns that might otherwise appear chaotic. This chapter approaches those challenges through the lens of ***game theory***. Each type of organization is a player in the same arena, but each plays by a different set of priorities.

Startups act as high-risk players, optimizing for speed in hopes of disruption before their resources are exhausted. SMBs play the efficiency game, seeking ways to stretch limited budgets into meaningful outcomes. Enterprises focus on resilience, aware that scale magnifies both opportunities and risks. These dynamics are not locked into a zero-sum contest. The adoption of AI is a non-zero-sum game: trust, legitimacy, capability, and societal acceptance can all rise together or collapse together if recklessness prevails. If startups pursue unchecked shortcuts and enterprises rush into adoption without governance, the result resembles a prisoner's dilemma: every player makes moves that appear rational for immediate gain, but the collective outcome is fragile pilots, wasted resources, and public resistance. A more stable outcome, akin to Nash equilibrium, only emerges when organizations align their strategies with the Four Pillars of Enterprise AI—Accessibility, Explainability, Security, and Ethics—and measure readiness through reflective disciplines such as the AI Compatibility Score.

Patterns of investment reinforce these dynamics. Startups continue to act as experimentation engines, pushing conceptual boundaries. Enterprises tend to integrate through acquisitions and partnerships, absorbing external innovations into existing frameworks. Governments and policy bodies act as catalysts, channeling both capital and legitimacy toward approaches society is willing to accept. These patterns, visible across the last decade, show little sign of disappearing. They will shape the contours of the Anno Artificialis Intelligenciae as surely as they shaped the years leading up to it. In the chapter ahead, we will explore these dynamics through concrete cases. We will meet startups grappling with volatility, SMBs applying off-the-shelf solutions to reduce friction, and enterprises confronting shadow AI and architectural debt. Each narrative illustrates a unique struggle, but together they define a common landscape.

Operationalizing AI requires more than a string of pilots; it demands capabilities designed to scale with discipline and legitimacy. When organizations treat adoption as a repeated game rather than a series of disconnected wagers, credibility compounds across every move. Agility, pragmatism, resilience, and stewardship may take different shapes in startups, SMBs, and enterprises, but they converge on a shared destination: intelligence that endures, legitimacy that strengthens, and trust that carries forward. The endpoint, always, is human. The challenge is deciding how each player chooses to achieve it.

3.1 Unique Hurdles for Startups: Agility vs. Scalability

Startups stand at the entry point of the AI journey. They are restless players in a larger strategic game, defined by bold bets, short runways, and a constant struggle between speed and structure. When artificial intelligence is introduced, the stakes intensify. Speed has evolved into a larger commitment, the assurance that systems will continue learning and adjusting, responding in ways that sustain trust over time. Game theory helps illuminate this challenge, because each decision becomes a move with uncertain payoffs whose effects travel outward, shaping not only investors' confidence but also the experiences of customers and the judgments of regulators.

Agility As Promise and Risk

Agility is the hallmark of startups. They move quickly, disrupt incumbents, and seize opportunities others hesitate to touch. In game theory, this can be expressed through a payoff function:

We can think of their payoff function in simple terms:

$$U = p \times B - C$$

Here, ***U*** is the expected payoff, ***p*** the probability of success, ***B*** the benefit when success is achieved, and ***C*** the cost of failure. The multiplication between ***p*** and ***B*** shows how probability scales potential reward: a small chance applied to a large prize still produces only a modest expectation, reminding us that bold visions alone cannot carry outcomes. The subtraction of ***C*** highlights the weight of costs, which are unavoidable and immediate—burn rates, wasted time, legal exposure, and the erosion of trust count against the payoff regardless of whether success materializes.

For startups, ***p (probability of success)*** is usually modest, ***B (benefit of success)*** can be immense, and ***C (cost of failure)*** can be devastating when failures lock out customers, draw regulatory scrutiny, or exhaust scarce capital. In this light, agility pursued without structure becomes fragile. It resembles gambling, where each move risks credibility as much as capital. But when agility is paired with practices that raise probabilities, constrain costs, and preserve trust across repeated rounds of play, the function tilts upward. What looks like volatility becomes resilience, and speed becomes a lever for endurance rather than a countdown to collapse.

The difference between a promising experiment and a damaging failure lies in whether agility is guided by a structure that sustains credibility over time. This tension creates what we call the volatility gap. Venture capital aims to absorb volatility through diversified investments. Startups can afford to fail in the eyes of investors; they cannot afford to fail in the hands of customers. Businesses adopting their solutions expect stability from day one. In game-theory terms, if every startup pursues unchecked speed, the system converges on a prisoner's dilemma. Each player optimizes for short-term payoff, but the collective outcome is fragile, as users and markets lose trust. The path toward a higher equilibrium, akin to a **Nash equilibrium**, requires startups to balance speed with governance, shifting from one-shot gambles to repeated games where reputation compounds.

Rethinking Agility As Structured Experimentation

Escaping the volatility trap requires agility to be practiced as experimentation with intent. Well-designed experiments surface weaknesses while there is still time to respond, contain risks before they accumulate into crises, build resilience that strengthens as growth unfolds, and generate learning that compounds into future advantage. Each move becomes a considered play in the larger game, made in full awareness of those whose confidence sustains the enterprise: investors who measure reliability, regulators who test accountability, customers whose trust determines longevity, and employees whose daily adoption ultimately decides whether systems take root. Safeguards deepen this discipline. A kill switch halts damage before it spreads, protecting both continuity and reputation. Documented assumptions bring fragile premises into view early enough for course correction. Data treated as a product, held with ownership, guided through oversight, cultivated with care, and monitored for fairness, evolves into a foundation that strengthens resilience over time.

Resilient startups carry this mindset into their technical foundations. They match computing resources to the task at hand, reserving heavy capacity for training, routing inference through leaner options, relying on orchestration layers to knit these choices together, and monitoring performance to prevent drift. The result is leaner spending that extends the runway, a flow of progress that compounds steadily, credibility with partners who see responsibility as maturity, and legitimacy with regulators who equate architectural discipline with trustworthiness. In this light, scale is measured less by raw size than by coherence, that is, the degree to which ambition, architecture, stewardship, and accountability move in alignment.

Case Study: A Fintech Divergence

Consider two fintech startups developing fraud detection systems.

The first rushed ahead, training on curated historical data that produced impressive demonstrations and won early applause from investors. But when the system was deployed in live environments, it began producing false positives, struggling with metadata inconsistencies that confused the model, quirks in legacy systems that had never been documented, and edge cases that the training data failed to anticipate. The impact was immediate: legitimate customers were locked out of their accounts, frustration spilled over into formal complaints, regulators stepped in with scrutiny, and costs mounted until the payoff equation turned decisively negative.

The second fintech startup followed another path. From the very beginning, they tested with noisy, multi-source data, invested in observability tools that provided continuous monitoring, embedded rollback mechanisms to restore stability when failures appeared, and established feedback loops so that insights from errors directly informed retraining. Failures continued to surface, but they were diagnosed early enough to prevent escalation, managed with openness that preserved stakeholder confidence, corrected in ways that restored stability, and folded back into the training process so that each weakness became a lesson. As a result, clients maintained trust in the system, contractual relationships remained stable, reputation grew steadily in the market, and credibility accumulated round by round. Both firms began with agility, although only one managed to transform that agility into structured experimentation, converting volatility into resilience.

The Role of Enterprise Architecture

At this point, a fair question arises: ***Isn't enterprise architecture something reserved for large corporations with sprawling systems and not a concern for small startups?*** The distinction lies between EA as a ***formal function*** and EA as a ***way of thinking***. The function may belong to big enterprises, but the thinking belongs everywhere. Even at the startup stage, lightweight practices such as documenting data conventions in ways that reduce ambiguity, embedding monitoring that reveals problems as they emerge, aligning AI features with the daily processes that sustain the business, and setting early norms for governance create disproportionate advantages. They shift adoption from ad hoc tinkering to deliberate design, raising the probability of success while containing costs before they spiral.

Many founders encounter this lesson under immense pressure. The startup arena is filled with investor expectations to display AI features, sometimes more for appearance than for substance. The demand to pivot toward what is fashionable can be overwhelming, pulling leaders toward choices that consume capital but fragment strategy. The cultural parodies circulating online exaggerate these struggles for humor, but they resonate because they reflect a real vulnerability: the strain of building under relentless hype. Enterprise architecture cannot remove those pressures, but it disciplines how they are met. Even in lightweight form, EA practices give startups a framework to filter noise, to decline features that undermine integrity, and to chart a path where speed is matched by coherence.

The AI Compatibility Score, first introduced in Chapter 2 and developed within this book, extends this reflection by offering leaders a lens through which to examine their readiness with discipline and honesty. By encouraging founders to look beyond models into systems, governance, culture, and leadership, it acts as a mirror that reveals whether the organization can genuinely carry scale. When readiness grows in this balanced way, the payoff function bends upward, guiding the startup toward an equilibrium where credibility compounds into resilience.

Case Study: The Healthtech Dilemma

A healthtech startup set out to build a chatbot, fine-tuned on medical language models, to triage patient symptoms. Early tests on curated datasets looked promising, and investors responded with enthusiasm. But when the system entered clinical settings, the everyday messiness of healthcare quickly surfaced, such as shorthand notes that defied interpretation, coding practices that varied from one department to another, and the unpredictable complexity of patients whose conditions rarely followed textbook patterns. The model faltered, generating diagnoses that could not be trusted, and liability concerns soon followed. What had seemed a breakthrough was in fact a prototype, placed into practice without the architecture of governance to sustain it.

A peer startup chose another path. It began with checkpoints that kept clinicians in the loop, designed logs that captured the full flow of interactions, and built auditing routines that allowed outcomes to be traced back with clarity. When mistakes appeared, they became moments of learning: flagged by physicians, corrected through retraining, and folded back into the system so that confidence grew instead of eroding. In this approach, speed was treated as an early advantage but not the endpoint; the real aim was to let trust compound across each round of use.

Beneath these technical contrasts lies an ethical seam that runs through all health technology. When AI systems direct patients to the wrong pathway, misinterpret symptoms, or mishandle access to treatment, the consequences are lived immediately: delays that erode health, financial pressures that deepen stress, and in some cases outcomes that change the course of a life. In such moments, the system is no longer offering a neutral calculation; it is shaping who receives attention, who waits, and who is quietly excluded. Enterprise architecture provides the means to meet these stakes responsibly. It creates environments where design choices are visible rather than hidden, where decisions leave a trace that can be examined, and where human oversight is built into the flow of care. With these foundations in place, prototypes mature into governed systems, and accountability is treated as a property of the design itself instead of being an afterthought. Far from being abstract, these disciplines are what keep technology in service to people, ensuring that innovation extends care rather than diminishes it.

Here, the Human Endpoint Principle comes into view with full force. Systems exist to extend care, not to diminish it. The discipline of architecture ensures that ***patients are regarded as people first and never reduced to probabilities on a screen.***

Culture and the Temptation of Noise

The cultural challenge within startups is often less visible than the technical one, although it shapes outcomes just as profoundly. Founders carry the constant expectation to demonstrate progress through visible AI features, while investors search for signs of momentum, and teams hope their effort will translate into lasting impact. In such an atmosphere, the temptation is strong to chase what looks impressive in the moment, even when it drains focus from the deeper work of building systems that endure. The weight of these expectations is real, and it presses on every participant in the journey.

Parodies of startup life exaggerate this reality, such as cryptocurrency schemes promoted to extend runway, high-profile hires made under impossible conditions, or cultures branded as "founder mode" while fatigue spreads through teams. But exaggeration only resonates because it echoes genuine anxieties. Everyone inside this world feels the tension: the founder balancing vision with survival, the employee working late nights in the hope their effort matters, and the investor wondering if discipline will hold when hype surges. Enterprise architecture steadies culture in these moments. In startups, it may not appear as formal frameworks or departments, but as a way of bringing structure and foresight into decisions. It turns choices into visible commitments rather than invisible gambles, encourages leaders to articulate trade-offs so their weight is understood, and frames values in terms of continuity and resilience. Practiced in this way, EA gives founders a compass to navigate difficult calls, offers teams a sense of coherence that makes their work meaningful, and provides investors with a structured way to assess progress that reaches deeper than surface signals.

Agility, shaped through this discipline, becomes less about racing for attention and more about renewal. It is expressed in the capacity to rework quickly without losing direction, to learn from the feedback of real deployments, and to align every choice with the Four Pillars of Accessibility, Explainability, Security, and Ethics. Cultures that grow in this way find that trust is not won in a single dramatic moment but accumulates slowly, interaction by interaction, until credibility itself becomes the strongest form of capital they hold.

Startups in the Repeated Game

Startups move through what game theory describes as a repeated game, where each move influences the next and, over time, defines how the venture is remembered. A client call might resurface months later when a contract is negotiated. A product launch is compared against earlier promises. An investor briefing becomes part of the story circling the market. Nothing is isolated; reputation accumulates from these strands. When choices are made with care, trust builds quietly. Investors feel secure extending capital, customers grow comfortable relying on the service, and employees begin to see their work as part of something durable. But when decisions are hurried, the consequences ripple outward in another way. Doubt creeps in among customers, pressure weighs heavier on teams, and investors begin to hesitate, sensing the strain beneath the surface. The equilibrium worth pursuing in such a game is one where governance is seen as a foundation that holds everyone, not a burden to be endured. In such an environment, steady conduct earns reward, while shortcuts quickly expose their cost. The caricatures of abrupt pivots or founder crises that fill online forums strike a chord precisely because they capture what unfolds when that balance collapses. Enterprise architecture steadies the course in those moments. It provides the orientation that keeps momentum coherent, so each step taken adds to legitimacy and pushes the venture toward endurance rather than fragility.

From Fragile Pilots to Enduring Systems

The startups that endure in the Anno Artificialis Intelligenciae treat agility, scalability, governance, and culture as moves within a single game, each reshaping the payoff landscape of the others. Founders who succeed think like architects even when their teams are lean. They embed responsibility directly into design, hold trust as a defining element of leadership, and keep the human endpoint visible as the compass that guides every decision. Agility brings the first momentum, but it is scalability that allows momentum to grow rather than fade. Governance steadies that growth, channeling energy toward coherence, while culture gives it texture, such as deciding whether the experience builds commitment or wears it down. Survival in the repeated game grows through layering, where fragile pilots mature into enduring systems and volatility gradually transforms into resilience across round after round of play.

3.2 SMBs: Balancing Innovation with Budget Constraints

If startups play the speed game, small and mid-sized businesses enter a different contest. Theirs is the efficiency game, where every choice must stretch resources to their fullest, and each outcome leaves an imprint larger than the enterprise itself. The same payoff equation introduced earlier continues to hold:

$$U = p \times B - C$$

But its variables take on a distinct contour in the SMB setting. ***Probability of success (p)*** needs to remain high because resilience depends on outcomes that arrive with reliability. ***Benefits of success (B)*** are usually modest rather than spectacular, and still, their steady presence supports growth and keeps a business moving forward. ***Costs of failure (C)*** press heavily: an overspent budget, a service outage, or reputational damage can quickly weaken both financial and human reserves.

For SMBs, efficiency is the core principle of survival. The task is to keep probability strong enough that success becomes the norm, to treat benefits as building blocks of continuity, and to hold costs firmly in check. Efficiency in this sense works as resilience itself, enabling smaller firms to turn limited resources into a platform that can sustain the future.

Playing the Efficiency Game

Small and mid-sized businesses seldom chase moonshots. Their attention stays closer to ground level, on tactical choices where success feels attainable, costs stay visible, and returns can be traced. This is why packaged AI features embedded within familiar systems such as CRMs, finance platforms, and logistics suites carry particular weight. By selecting solutions already proven in the market, SMBs raise their probability of success while holding costs in check. The outcomes may not capture headlines, but they shift the balance sheet in ways that matter. A predictive scoring module inside a CRM, guiding sales teams toward higher-probability leads, can be the margin that turns a quarter into profit. The logic resembles a repeated game played within shorter cycles. Startups may absorb volatility, and enterprises may sustain long experiments, but SMBs live with quicker judgments. Each adoption is assessed in the near term, and credibility with staff, customers, suppliers, and investors builds or weakens with every round. In this setting, discipline becomes the decisive trait. Incremental gains accumulate into resilience, while a single unchecked failure can drain both trust and capital, leaving little space for recovery.

Choosing the Right Problems

Efficiency extends beyond budgets; it rests on judgment. The resilience of an SMB depends on whether its leaders select problems where AI can truly matter. Many failures arise when pilots are launched outside value streams, producing demonstrations that appear novel but do little to advance enterprise goals. In game-theory terms, this is a coordination failure: moves that make sense in isolation but fail to align with collective progress.

The payoff equation introduced earlier remains the same, although its terms shift with the quality of the problem. Poorly framed initiatives lower the ***probability of success (p)*** because signals prove noisy or incomplete. ***Benefits of success (B)***, even when delivered reliably, weaken if they do not connect to core business value. ***Costs of failure (C)*** grow heavier when compliance risks emerge, when customers feel unsettled, or when fragile operations are pushed beyond their limits. By contrast, problems chosen with care, whether improving the clarity of decisions, relieving teams from repetitive effort, extending visibility into customer needs, or uncovering new opportunities, tip the equilibrium firmly in favor of resilience. Furthermore, suitability should be weighed across four fronts: whether the data offers stable signals, whether the benefit advances business priorities, whether the risks fall within tolerance, and whether the outcome can be sustained without draining energy or legitimacy. A model that demands more resources than the value it creates cannot be considered viable. Suitability, in this sense, is architectural as much as technical and ethical as operational.

Case Study: Retail Chatbots as Targeted Operational Leverage

A regional retail chain struggled with mounting service backlogs. Customer queries clustered around the same concerns, such as store hours, return rules, and delivery schedules, and frontline staff spent much of their day repeating answers. Leadership chose an off-the-shelf chatbot, introduced in a matter of weeks at a modest cost. The system absorbed the routine questions, lowering resolution times by nearly half. Employees gained the space to address complex issues where judgment mattered, while customers experienced shorter waits and improved responses.

The payoff equation reveals why this modest step worked. The probability of success (p) was high because the problem was readily defined and the data was straightforward. The benefits of success (B), while limited in scale, were steady: efficiency gains, better morale, and improved customer experience. The costs of failure (C) remained low because the chatbot ran in parallel with human agents, creating little risk to reputation or compliance. In this balance, a small investment delivered a durable return. The lesson is that SMB efficiency rests less on grand innovation and more on well-framed problems, modest deployments, and results that can be measured quickly. Each step taken in this way builds credibility for the next, reinforcing trust with employees, customers, and partners while preserving the capacity to adapt.

Decision Support As Leverage

For SMBs, some of the most valuable applications of AI involve strengthening human judgment rather than seeking to replace it. Predictive analytics in finance, demand forecasting in supply chains, trend analysis in retail, and staffing models in services all show how intelligence augments decision-making across domains. These are cooperative games: people and machines working together, each improving the other's effectiveness, and together raising the overall payoff.

A mid-sized logistics firm demonstrates this in practice. Demand shifted constantly, and managers often leaned on intuition, choosing to overstock to avoid shortages. This habit protected service levels but tied up working capital and eroded margins. By embedding predictive analytics into their planning, the firm altered the terms of the payoff equation. The probability of success (p) rose because forecasts were consistently more accurate. The benefits of success (B) expanded as inventory costs declined and customer satisfaction held steady. The costs of failure (C), once magnified by excess stock or sudden shortages, were reduced to manageable levels. Managers remained the final arbiters of decisions, but their intuition was now supported by evidence.

The results went beyond numbers on a balance sheet. Customers noticed greater reliability, and service commitments held even during volatile periods. Employees trusted the system because it clarified their judgment instead of constraining it. Investors recognized that the firm was managing uncertainty with discipline rather than luck. In this way, decision-support AI became more than a tool: it acted as a structural reinforcement that preserved authority, improved efficiency, deepened trust among employees and customers, and strengthened credibility with every cycle of play.

Driving Automation Loops

Another category of suitable problems lies in repetitive, bounded tasks that consume energy without advancing strategic goals. Automating these loops allows human effort to shift toward higher-value work. Consider a small business weighed down by invoice processing. By introducing AI-based categorization through its accounting software, the firm raised the probability of success (p) because errors diminished. The benefits of success (B) grew as more time was freed for customer-facing work and financial records gained accuracy. The costs of failure (C) eased as compliance risks receded. Just as important, employees experienced a boost in morale when repetitive duties gave way to work that required judgment and interaction.

A retailer piloting AI-driven inventory management illustrates the same dynamic. The system adjusted stock automatically, drawing on sales data and supplier schedules. Out-of-stock incidents fell by a fifth, margins recovered as overstocks were contained, and customers faced fewer disappointments at the shelf. Staff no longer spent their days in reactive firefighting; instead, they planned ahead with confidence. The organization as a whole gained credibility with investors who could see that adoption was holding steady. Over time, these gains accumulated across four dimensions, that is, financial stability, customer experience, employee engagement, and market trust, each reinforcing the others in the repeated game.

Generating Insights Beyond Human Reach

AI creates distinctive value when it surfaces anomalies and patterns that human review cannot reliably detect. In finance, this may take the form of fraud detection; in manufacturing, the spotting of irregularities in production flows; in marketing, the mapping of complex customer journeys; and in healthcare, the early identification of clinical risks. Each of these applications carries risk if handled poorly; even when governance is present and outputs are integrated into daily workflows, the payoff equation shifts. The probability of success (p) rises as false alarms are reduced, the benefits of success (B) expand through faster and more accurate interventions, and the costs of failure (C) shrink because oversight and transparency limit reputational harm. The Four Pillars—Accessibility, Explainability, Security, and Ethics—act as safeguards that sustain this balance.

A banking example illustrates the stakes. One firm rushed anomaly detection into production without securing data lineage or establishing confidence thresholds. Legitimate transactions were repeatedly blocked, customers voiced their frustration, and regulators began to question whether oversight was in place. A competitor approached the same problem differently. From the start, it invested in explainability, attaching confidence scores to every flagged transaction and building audit trails that supervisors could review. Customers accepted occasional false positives because transparency preserved their trust, and regulators recognized that governance was present. The divergence lay not in the algorithms themselves but in the maturity of the architecture that carried them.

Resistance and Cultural Friction

Cultural readiness often determines whether adoption succeeds. Employees whose expertise was built on manual processes may feel anxious when automation appears. Others hesitate to trust systems whose reasoning they cannot follow. These concerns operate as hidden costs within the payoff equation. They lower the probability of success (p) by creating resistance, diminish the benefits of success (B) when adoption is partial, and raise the costs of failure (C) when morale weakens or turnover increases.

Game theory frames this tension as a coordination game. Progress depends on alignment between leadership intent and employee confidence. When that alignment is absent, equilibrium falters. The most effective remedy is structured participation. Involving employees in choosing tools, shaping pilots, and sharing feedback turns them from reluctant observers into active contributors. A service agent who sees routine tasks lifted from their workload begins to view AI as a collaborator that extends their capacity. When participation is genuine, hesitation gives way to trust, and the readiness gap **(Δ)** narrows in practice rather than in theory.

Governance at the Right Scale

Governance does not belong only to large enterprises with compliance departments. For SMBs, it remains central, even if it must be lightweight. The Four Pillars—Accessibility, Explainability, Security, and Ethics—still form the ground on which trust is built. Accessibility matters when systems are designed so employees without technical training can use them effectively. Explainability allows managers to understand how outputs are generated, building confidence in decisions. Security protects customer data, a non-negotiable even when infrastructures are modest. Ethics ensures adoption carries genuine value so that efficiency gains also preserve legitimacy.

Additionally, many SMBs adopt consumerized AI stacks, often embedded in platforms for sales, logistics, or finance. These tools achieve scale quickly, but they require careful framing. Lightweight governance such as usage tracking that shows where tools are active, registries that catalog which models are in use, and simple "AI manners" that guide responsible behavior creates early habits of accountability. Such measures avoid unnecessary overhead while still signaling that oversight is present. They give employees confidence that systems are monitored, reassure customers that data is protected, and show investors that ambition is paired with discipline. In this way, even small enterprises can establish the cultural and architectural foundations for trust.

The Role of Policy and Shared Ecosystems

Small and mid-sized businesses rarely have the deep reserves of enterprises or the venture backing that fuels startups. Their capacity to adopt AI often depends on the environment around them, and it is here that policy and shared ecosystems alter the balance. Subsidies and tax incentives reduce financial strain, while shared data platforms create access that individual firms could never afford alone. Industry associations pooling resources, consultants offering fractional expertise, cloud providers lowering barriers with entry-level packages, and universities opening applied research centers all widen the field of participation. Each intervention reshapes the payoff equation by lifting the probability of success (p), expanding the benefits of success (B), and containing the costs of failure (C). Without these supports, adoption narrows to the privileged few, and the divide between those who can engage and those who cannot grows wider.

Pragmatism As a Winning Strategy

The strength of SMBs lies in pragmatism. Their maturity grows through a sequence of deliberate moves that steadily build resilience. Automating invoices, improving service response times, stabilizing inventory flows, and nurturing customer loyalty may appear incremental in isolation; however, together they form the foundation of endurance. Each improvement strengthens credibility with employees, reinforces trust with customers, reassures investors, and creates a platform for the next initiative. Occasional failures, when bounded, become sources of learning rather than threats to survival, and in this way, fragility is gradually converted into discipline. This is the essence of Return on AI Investment (ROAI) for SMBs: value expressed not through abstract accuracy metrics but through time reclaimed for productive work, customers retained, revenue secured, and reputations protected.

As Chapter 2 established, enterprise architecture multiplies intelligence when AI is mapped carefully to workflows. Pilots mature into enduring assets, reinforced by the AI Compatibility Score, which offers leaders a structured way to test whether systems, governance, culture, and leadership are aligned for scale. In the Anno Artificialis Intelligenciae, SMBs illustrate pragmatic adoption in practice. Their maturity is expressed through carefully chosen moves that fit their boundaries while still building durability. When the efficiency game is played with intention—guided by the Four Pillars, measured through ROAI, and assessed with the AI Compatibility Score—outcomes hold their ground. Endurance emerges from alignment and stewardship, and at the close of every equation, the endpoint remains human.

3.3 Enterprises: Complexity, Silos, and Organizational Drag

Enterprises enter the AI arena with resources that smaller firms cannot match, such as budgets that span continents, pipelines of talent from leading universities, and global networks capable of deploying at scale. These advantages open extraordinary possibilities, but they also introduce structural risks. In game-theory terms, the payoff equation carries a distinctive profile at this scale. The benefits of success (B) are immense. The probability of success (p) should, at least in principle, be elevated by the depth of available resources. Even so, the costs of failure (C) expand dramatically because of visibility and reach. A single misstep can trigger regulatory penalties across jurisdictions, reputational damage that cascades worldwide, operational breakdowns that ripple through supply chains, and erosion of customer trust that spreads quickly across markets.

Where startups experiment in relative obscurity and SMBs pivot within shorter cycles, enterprises operate under constant scrutiny and within systems that touch millions of lives. Their task is to adopt AI in ways that transform complexity into resilience, ensuring that the scale of their reach strengthens rather than destabilizes them.

The Resilience Game

Enterprises play what may be called the resilience game. Their payoff is shaped less by speed or raw efficiency and more by the ability to sustain operations under pressure while layering intelligence into inherited structures. Agility must evolve into repeatable processes, governance must grow in step with innovation, and new intelligence must reinforce rather than strain legacy systems. In game-theory terms, enterprises are engaged in a repeated coordination game with themselves—departments, functions, and geographies must align so that local decisions accumulate into collective progress rather than pulling the organization apart.

At this scale, the variables of the payoff equation take on sharper dimensions. Resources should raise the probability of success (p); however, silos and fragmented data often drag it downward. Benefits of success (B) can be extraordinary when projects align with enterprise priorities, but they shrink when investment favors high-visibility experiments over essential but less glamorous processes. Costs of failure (C) rise steeply when governance lapses, whether in the form of a compliance breach in finance, the mishandling of patient records in healthcare, the compromise of customer data in retail, or the bias of an algorithm in legal contexts. Stability emerges only when coordination, architecture, governance, and culture are treated as foundations, that is, the pillars on which enterprise survival rests.

Organizational Drag and Cultural Inertia

Culture often determines how far and how steadily enterprises move with AI. Employees shifting from established routines to AI-enabled workflows frequently experience unease. Their concern is rarely with the system itself but with what its arrival suggests about the future of their roles and the continuity of their expertise. These reactions deserve attention. They remind leaders that trust and identity are part of the adoption architecture. When intent at the top races ahead of confidence on the ground, organizations lose balance. Game theory helps explain this as a coordination challenge. Each department acts with its own priorities, watching how others move, but the absence of shared alignment prevents their actions from compounding into collective progress. The effect is felt in slowed productivity, hesitation from customers, strain within teams, and unease among regulators and investors.

Drag also emerges through what has been called shadow AI. In the absence of a unifying architecture, departments procure tools independently to signal progress. What begins as an initiative soon fragments into parallel systems, disconnected data streams, and accountability that drifts without clear ownership. The probability of success (p) falls because outcomes cannot be compared or trusted. The benefits of success (B) are narrow, since isolated pilots rarely scale. The costs of failure (C) expand as unmanaged systems open vulnerabilities in security, compliance, customer trust, and operational continuity.

The way forward is to channel experimentation through a centralized architectural framework that sustains accountability, coherence, and visibility. Enterprise registries clarify which systems are active, who carries responsibility for them, and how they connect to strategic priorities. From there, codes of practice, what we describe as ***"AI manners,"*** extend architecture into culture by shaping the way people and intelligent systems interact. Manners are what sustain shared spaces: they guide how meals are taken together, how traffic moves without collision, and how conversations unfold with respect. Enterprise AI requires the same kind of discipline, a grammar of interaction that allows intelligence to serve within patterns of trust.

These manners shape practice in concrete ways. They indicate when judgment returns to humans, how decisions are documented, what disclosures are required, and how fairness is protected. In this sense, AI manners transform governance into something lived, an etiquette practiced collectively rather than a structure observed from a distance. Within such an environment, employees recognize how their contributions fit into a larger design, leaders embody stewardship by sharing responsibility, and the enterprise preserves the alignment on which resilience rests.

Architectural Debt

Enterprises often carry a quieter burden, one that remains hidden during early experiments but becomes impossible to ignore with scale, that is, the burden of architectural debt. Pilots launched in haste to demonstrate momentum frequently bypass the standards that make systems sustainable over time: data lineage, interoperability, monitoring, and observability. While such omissions may remain invisible at first, they surface with relentless force as adoption widens, workloads expand and pipelines strain, regulations grow more demanding and gaps in explainability stand exposed, errors cascade through interdependent systems, and the costs of correction mount quickly. What once seemed agile reveals itself as fragile, weighed down by decisions deferred and shortcuts taken.

A multinational bank offers a vivid illustration. In an effort to showcase innovation, its regional divisions introduced customer-service chatbots independently, each pursuing its own design, integration, and vendor partnerships. Some initiatives attracted attention and delivered short-term benefits; others faltered quietly, but together they produced a patchwork of disconnected systems. Data lineage was inconsistent across regions, audit logs were incomplete, and accountability drifted across multiple reporting lines. When regulators eventually demanded explainability, leadership faced escalating compliance costs and reputational strain. By contrast, competitors that had invested in governance and observability from the beginning appeared slower in their rollouts. But once scrutiny arrived, they advanced steadily, scaling with confidence rather than scrambling under pressure. The contrast revealed the deeper cost of debt: speed purchased at the expense of architecture erodes resilience, while early discipline converts governance into strength that endures.

Misaligned Investment and the Illusion of Progress

Another source of fragility for enterprises lies in misaligned investment. Large budgets often flow toward projects that sit in the spotlight, especially customer-facing initiatives that promise visible gains, while the quieter but essential foundations of resilience remain underfunded. A retailer may lavish resources on personalized recommendation engines, showcasing an experience that feels modern, while its supply chain forecasting remains brittle and vulnerable to disruption. In the short term, the payoff equation appears favorable because benefits of success (B) seem high and highly visible; however, the probability of success (p) erodes as neglected systems drag performance down, and the costs of failure (C) begin to accumulate beneath the surface. Game theory helps reveal the flaw. This is a strategy that optimizes for a single round, where attention is rewarded, at the expense of repeated play, where durability is tested. Sustainable equilibrium is achieved when investment balances front-end innovation with back-end discipline, customer experiences with robust supply chains, and attention-grabbing pilots with enduring infrastructure.

Governance Failures and Trust at Scale

For enterprises in high-stakes arenas such as finance, healthcare, and law, governance stands as the foundation of legitimacy. The consequences of lapses reach far beyond financial penalties; they extend into the erosion of confidence, the disruption of lives, and the weakening of institutions. A single misaligned output can trigger lawsuits, invite regulatory sanctions, fracture reputation, and cause customers and partners to withdraw their trust. At this scale, governance must rest firmly on the Four Pillars of enterprise AI: Accessibility, Explainability, Security, and Ethics. Dashboards that display reasoning in terms managers can follow, audits that verify the integrity of data, ethical reviews that bring risks to light before they spread, and interfaces designed for use beyond technical teams together form the beams of credibility that support enterprise systems. The AI Compatibility Score introduces another layer of discipline. It provides leaders with a reflective lens to examine whether their architecture, governance frameworks, culture, and leadership can sustain adoption at scale. A score that signals fragility points to areas where intervention can reinforce trust before weaknesses multiply. Seen in this light, governance becomes a force for enablement. It shifts adoption from guesswork to guided play, closes the readiness gap (Δ), and ensures that enterprise intelligence advances with resilience and legitimacy intact.

Case Study: Manufacturing at Scale

A global manufacturer set out to apply predictive maintenance through edge AI, aiming to reduce costly downtime and extend the life of its equipment. Initial pilots in individual plants were promising, delivering substantial savings and demonstrating measurable Return on AI Investment (ROAI). Encouraged by these results, leadership chose to accelerate adoption by deploying the system simultaneously across dozens of factories. At scale, however, the hidden weaknesses of the architecture came into view. Legacy systems differed from site to site, sensor data lacked consistency, and local teams resisted processes that felt imposed rather than integrated. The probability of success (p), high in the controlled conditions of the pilot, fell sharply in the fragmented reality of global rollout. Benefits of success (B) shrank as uneven adoption undercut results, while costs of failure (C) rose through mounting delays, escalating expenses, and declining trust among staff.

A competitor approached the same challenge differently. Instead of a single dramatic rollout, it progressed step by step, scaling plant by plant. Data collection was standardized at each stage, and governance checkpoints were introduced to ensure that results were observable and explainable. Human-In-The-Loop practices gave local engineers confidence that their expertise remained essential, transforming potential resistance into participation. The pace looked slower from the outside, yet credibility grew with each successful cycle. By embedding governance, stabilizing architecture, and pacing adoption deliberately, the second firm avoided architectural debt and reached an equilibrium where predictive maintenance could expand without eroding trust. Its resilience was not the product of speed but of sustained design, where scale was achieved through coherence rather than momentum alone.

Toward Resilient Equilibrium

Enterprises reveal that readiness is never secured by resources alone. What matters is how those resources are structured within architecture, how culture absorbs change without fracturing, and how legacy systems adapt to carry new layers of intelligence. When silos deepen, when incentives diverge, and when organizational drag slows momentum, the probability of success (p) begins to fall, the benefits of success (B) narrow against expectations, and the costs of failure (C) grow heavier as hidden weaknesses surface.

Resilience appears when adoption is treated as a long game rather than a sprint. Innovation is introduced in ways that extend the strength of legacy systems rather than colliding with them. Cultural adaptation is cultivated through genuine participation, so employees understand how new intelligence complements rather than displaces their expertise. Governance is embedded as a daily discipline that guides decisions at every level, instead of an afterthought introduced once systems are already in motion. In game-theory terms, equilibrium emerges when departments, geographies, and leadership tiers coordinate their moves so that local progress reinforces collective resilience.

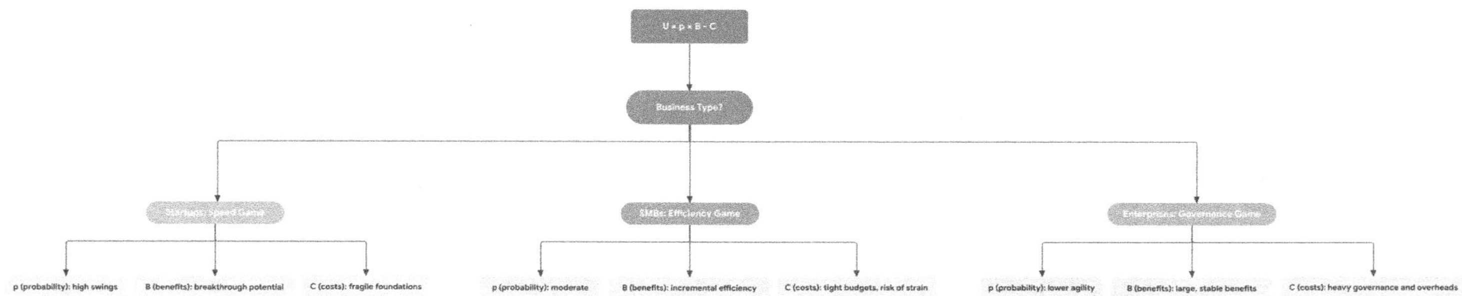

Figure 3-1. *Payoff Dynamics Across Startups, SMBs, and Enterprises*

In the Anno Artificialis Intelligenciae, enterprises that endure will be those that treat adoption as a repeated endeavor, where each round, whether a pilot within a division, a rollout across regions, or an audit under regulatory scrutiny, adds another layer of credibility. The critical outcome is the compounding of trust across cycles and the steady layering of capability that transforms isolated projects into durable systems, standing in contrast to a single successful initiative. Leaders who think architecturally, who steward trust with the same diligence as financial capital, who invest with patience in both visible innovations and the quieter infrastructures beneath them, and who cultivate cultures capable of adaptation, decisively improve the payoff in their favor. For these enterprises, AI no longer disperses as a collection of experiments; it becomes a capability integrated with governance, strengthened by architecture, sustained through culture, and directed always toward the human endpoint. Intelligence carried in this way persists beyond transient excitement, embedding itself into the foundational structure of enterprise operations and enabling organizations to maintain their position across cycles of change, scrutiny, and renewal.

3.4 Universal Challenges: Talent Gaps, Governance, and Technical Debt

Across startups, SMBs, and enterprises, certain challenges stretch beyond size, sector, or strategy. They are structural in design, human in impact, and systemic in consequence. These universal hurdles determine whether organizations close the readiness gap (Δ) or remain locked in fragile pilots. In game-theory terms, they are the shared constraints of the adoption game: the rules of play that apply to every participant, however different their strategies may appear.

Talent Gaps and Workforce Dynamics

The first of these shared constraints is talent. AI adoption requires more than technical specialists. What enterprises of every scale require is hybrid fluency, that is, the ability to link business priorities to technical design, to interpret algorithmic patterns in ways managers can act upon, and to carry insights from models into the markets where value is realized. Across industries, this capacity remains scarce. Startups stretch limited funds to recruit selectively. SMBs lack the financial means to compete for premium hires.

Enterprises employ large technical teams, but expertise often remains siloed, detached from the decisions it was meant to guide. When this gap persists, the probability of success (p) declines while the costs of failure (C) increase. Bottlenecks form around a few specialists, decisions slow, and untrained staff misapply tools they do not fully understand. Cultural dynamics intensify the strain: employees long accustomed to manual routines may hesitate to reskill, while others lean too heavily on AI outputs, allowing automation bias to weaken judgment. Over time, the benefits of success (B) are diminished, as creativity and critical thinking erode and adoption risks slide into complacency.

Resilient equilibrium emerges when talent is cultivated as a shared capability rather than concentrated as a scarce resource. Startups can integrate learning directly into projects so that each initiative strengthens people and products. SMBs can appoint "AI Scouts," encouraging staff to explore features embedded within consumerized platforms and circulate practical knowledge. Enterprises can design reskilling programs that connect explainability and oversight to daily managerial practice, ensuring decisions remain accountable. In each case, the Four Pillars of Accessibility, Explainability, Security, and Ethics provide the orientation for cultural alignment. Skills shift across domains, moving toward areas where judgment, empathy, and leadership matter most. Through this process, adoption remains grounded in the Human Endpoint Principle: that every system exists to serve people.

Governance and Trust

The second shared constraint is governance. Where discipline is absent, adoption fragments. Organizations move quickly on their own terms, chasing speed, but the collective field begins to corrode. Customers hesitate, regulators respond with heavier scrutiny, partners question reliability, and the broader legitimacy of AI things. Stability comes when governance is built into practice as deliberately as any technical design, shaping choices day by day rather than appearing as decoration after the fact. The fault lines are familiar. Weak data quality or poor privacy protection undermines confidence. Generative models that invent outputs create risks that stretch across industries, destabilizing clinical decisions in healthcare, exposing portfolios in finance, and clouding judgment in legal and regulatory contexts. As rules shift across jurisdictions, those who cannot keep pace invite costs that outweigh any temporary advantage claimed through speed.

The Four Pillars offer a frame for discipline. Accessibility ensures that governance is experienced in the daily work of employees, not confined to compliance teams alone. Explainability allows reasoning to be traced and understood by managers, regulators, customers, and staff who depend on outputs. Security safeguards against adversarial threats and prevents fragile infrastructures from collapsing under pressure. Ethics directs adoption so that intelligence elevates human dignity and institutional trust. Taken together, these principles increase the probability of success (p), extend the benefits of success (B), and keep the costs of failure (C) within tolerable bounds. Governance then shifts in character: from something perceived as a brake on momentum into the stabilizer of credibility. The AI Compatibility Score extends this logic. It works as an internal mirror, enabling leaders to reflect on readiness across architecture, culture, governance routines, and leadership intent. Where weaknesses surface, there is room for early intervention before fragility multiplies. So governance becomes more than a control mechanism. It becomes a long-term investment in resilience, an assurance of trust across stakeholders, and the infrastructure through which legitimacy endures.

Technical Debt and the Hidden Costs of Scale

The third shared constraint is technical debt. In the urgency to showcase momentum, organizations often accept compromises such as skipping architectural standards, postponing integration, or overlooking monitoring and observability. These choices remain invisible during early pilots, although scale makes them impossible to ignore. As adoption widens, pipelines buckle under heavier workloads, regulatory scrutiny exposes the absence of explainability, and errors spread across interdependent systems until correction becomes both costly and disruptive. What seemed to preserve agility in the beginning slowly undermines credibility, leaving enterprises to rebuild at a price far higher than the savings once claimed.

A multinational consumer enterprise illustrates this pattern. Determined to deploy personalization rapidly, it extended AI across multiple regions without standardizing its data models or aligning governance routines. The first results looked promising, but inconsistencies soon weakened recommendations, customers began to complain in large numbers, and remediation costs escalated. Competitors that invested early in common standards advanced at a slower pace, but when scrutiny arrived, they moved with stability, securing durable returns without reputational strain. The lesson is straightforward: speed bought through shortcuts produces fragility, while discipline in architecture builds resilience that compounds over time. Technical debt also carries consequences beyond engineering. Fragile architectures create fragile experiences. Customers encounter delays when integrations fail, employees repeat tasks when workflows collapse, and communities may suffer flawed decisions that engineers never witness. Every technical compromise eventually arrives at a human endpoint, for the integrity of systems is measured not only in efficiency but also in the trust they preserve.

With equal weight, debt gathers in the environment as surely as it does in technical systems. Large-scale AI demands immense computation, and that demand carries a trail of emissions, energy consumption, and resource depletion. When this dimension is overlooked, adoption risks losing its legitimacy at the very moment it claims progress. GreenOps practices offer a path forward: treating energy use as a first-class design variable, aligning workloads with renewable supply, and optimizing compute cycles with the same discipline applied to code. Through these practices, technical stewardship extends outward into societal trust, reminding leaders that the costs of adoption reach far beyond servers and pipelines, touching the environments and communities on which enterprises themselves depend.

Drawing the Threads Together

Talent, governance, and debt cannot be separated into tidy categories; they intertwine. Scarce expertise creates pressure to cut corners, weak governance allows poor practices to spread, and accumulated technical or environmental debt magnifies both, locking organizations into cycles of fragility. Together, they shape the shared conditions of the adoption game. Game theory frames these conditions as boundary rules, constraints that apply to every participant regardless of size or strategy. When talent is underdeveloped, the probability of success (p) decreases. When governance lacks depth, the costs of failure (C) mount. When debt accumulates, the benefits of success (B) erode. Only when all three are addressed in concert does the payoff function sustain its balance across repeated rounds of adoption.

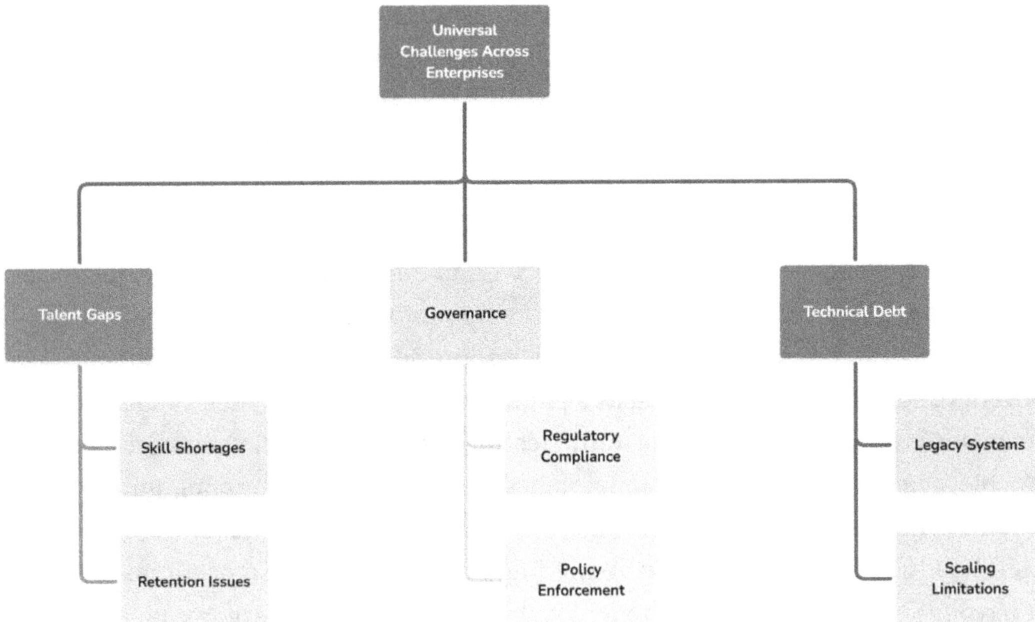

Figure 3-2. *Talent Gaps, Governance, and Technical Debt As Universal Challenges*

In the Anno Artificialis Intelligenciae, the organizations that endure will be those that recognize these constraints as design parameters and act accordingly. Talent will no longer be concentrated in a few roles but cultivated as a distributed capability that strengthens every layer of the enterprise. Governance will be practiced not as a compliance ritual but as a discipline present in daily decision-making, shaping choices as naturally as financial oversight or strategic planning. Technical and environmental debt will be treated as the foundation of resilience, carrying adoption steadily when scrutiny or disruption arrives. And above all, every architectural choice will be understood as one that eventually touches a human life, reminding leaders that the endpoint of intelligence is not efficiency or scale but people themselves. By holding this principle, adoption gains legitimacy, equilibrium is preserved, and the repeated game of AI becomes a path of endurance rather than fragility.

3.5 Operationalizing AI and Agentic Intelligence: From Pilots to Scalable Programs

Having examined the hurdles of startups, the efficiency plays of SMBs, the resilience games of enterprises, and the universal constraints of talent, governance, and debt, we arrive at the culmination of this chapter: operationalization. This is the stage where scattered experiments must be translated into enduring capabilities, when repeated plays converge toward stable equilibrium. Pilots may reveal potential, but operationalization determines whether intelligence matures into a core capability or dissolves into a patchwork of disconnected moves.

From Pilots to Core Capabilities

Pilots often carry the appearance of momentum. A chatbot in customer service, a fraud detection engine in finance, a predictive tool in logistics, or a vision system in manufacturing can all deliver local benefits. Yet without integration into the larger architecture, they remain isolated gambits, strong in promise but fragile in practice. In controlled conditions, pilots raise the probability of success (p) because the scope is narrow, and the benefits of success (B) appear significant. But once they extend into production, the failure costs (C) begin to multiply. Systems fragment across silos, governance lapses surface, and trust erodes as inconsistencies spread.

Operationalization reframes pilots as stepping stones within a longer sequence. It calls for readiness across several dimensions: governance routines that sustain accountability, integration pathways that connect departments, feedback loops that turn use into learning, and resource models that provide for both talent and infrastructure. Each of these dimensions increases the probability of success, extends the benefits realized, and constrains the costs that emerge at scale. Taken together, they allow organizations to cross the readiness gap (Δ) and to reach a condition where positive payoffs repeat across multiple rounds of play.

The Emergence of Agentic AI

Generative AI first captured attention through its ability to produce text, images, and code, but the more transformative change is now emerging in systems that act within operations themselves. Agentic AI extends the scope of adoption into continuous cycles of perception, planning, decision, and execution. These systems observe workflows as they unfold, coordinate across platforms, trigger actions when thresholds are reached, and bring humans into the loop when choices require judgment. Strategically, they function less like static tools and more like semi-autonomous participants in the adoption game, shaping outcomes from within and altering payoffs across repeated rounds of play.

The progression can be understood as a series of layers that expand outward in capability. At the center lie large models that generate content and patterns. Surrounding them are agents that manage memory, break tasks into components, and interact with external functions. Extending further are agentic systems in which multiple agents collaborate, specialize, and coordinate across domains. Encasing all of this is the agentic infrastructure: the orchestration frameworks that connect workflows, the observability mechanisms that track performance, the Human-In-The-Loop processes that safeguard accountability, the governance routines that align adoption with enterprise priorities, and the cost and energy management practices that ensure systems remain sustainable. Each layer enriches the one beneath it, turning isolated predictions into ongoing cycles of action, feedback, and adaptation that hold their reliability over time.

An enterprise case shows how this shift takes form. A retailer confronting rising demand in customer service began with generative systems that produced automated replies but faltered whenever queries spanned multiple functions. As adoption deepened, leadership advanced toward agentic systems that connected logistics, inventory, and customer records. The new design resolved routine issues from start to finish, escalated ambiguous cases with full context, and integrated lessons from each cycle back into operations. Outcomes extended beyond cost savings. Customers experienced greater reliability, frontline staff felt supported by a system that handled repetitive strain, and managers gained confidence in decisions reinforced by evidence. In payoff terms, integration raised the probability of success (p) by improving consistency, learning expanded the benefits of success (B) by uncovering insights across silos, and reliability reduced the costs of failure (C) by containing errors before they spread. Adoption in this form moves beyond scattered pilots and settles into coordinated equilibrium, where intelligence becomes part of the enterprise structure, strengthening resilience and carrying decisions with credibility over time.

Case Study: Scaling Beyond Pilots

A consumer goods company began cautiously, piloting an AI agent that automated the production of marketing summaries. Early results showed potential, but leadership chose not to scatter pilots across departments. Instead, they invested in an orchestration layer that connected the agent to enterprise systems, from the data lake to customer relationships and supply chain operations. With this foundation in place, the scope widened within a year. Agents were reallocating budgets based on campaign performance, identifying risks within supplier networks, alerting managers to operational anomalies, and drawing links across functions that had previously operated in silos.

The payoff equation shifted as the program matured. The probability of success (p) increased because agents operated reliably across diverse workflows. The benefits of success (B) expanded, surfacing insights that informed strategic planning and day-to-day execution. The costs of failure (C) remained contained because governance was present from the outset, with thresholds for confidence, defined escalation protocols, oversight dashboards, and explainability built into the design. What began as a modest pilot grew into an enterprise-wide capability delivering measurable Return on AI Investment (ROAI). Equilibrium stabilized as adoption moved beyond demonstrations and settled into a repeatable discipline, turning intelligence into a structural component of the organization rather than a series of experiments.

Governance and Hybrid Intelligence

Operationalizing agentic AI demands governance that is embedded directly into system design and expressed through collaboration between human and machine. Human-In-The-Loop (HITL) structures ensure that choices carrying ethical, legal, or reputational weight remain under human judgment, while agents assume responsibility for tasks that require scale, speed, or repetition. This distribution of responsibility aligns with the Four Pillars of enterprise AI. Accessibility allows staff without technical training to oversee outputs and exercise control. Explainability provides reasoning in terms that managers, regulators, and customers can understand. Security establishes confidence that workflows are protected against intrusion or misuse. Ethics guides automation so that its outcomes strengthen dignity, legitimacy, and institutional trust.

Game theory frames this balance as a coordination strategy. Attempts to chase complete autonomy often drive costs upward as mistakes spread, scrutiny intensifies, and systems fracture under pressure. Hybrid intelligence, by contrast, enhances the probability of success (p) by pairing human judgment with computational reach, expands the benefits of success (B) by uniting efficiency with credibility, and contains the costs of failure (C) by keeping oversight active where consequences are most severe. The equilibrium that emerges is sustainable cooperation, in which human and machine reinforce one another, each compensating for the limits of the other, and adoption advances with resilience.

Technical Debt and Human Consequences

Scaling agentic AI requires ambition to be matched with architectural discipline. Orchestration prevents fragmentation across functions, monitoring surfaces drift before it expands into cascading errors; standardized pipelines keep data coherent across domains, and governance structures provide accountability as adoption grows. These investments carry their own cost, but they reduce fragility and make scale sustainable rather than fragile. The consequences of neglecting this discipline extend directly into lived experience. A claims-processing agent that misclassifies cases delays settlements and leaves customers uncertain. Fragile integrations force employees back into duplicate work, draining morale and reducing productivity. Weak oversight allows flawed outputs to shape decisions in ways that engineers never intended, eroding confidence among managers and staff alike. Technical debt, seen in this way, is not an engineering detail; it is a set of choices that ripple outward into the lives of customers, the routines of employees, and the trust that society places in its institutions. Every architectural decision ultimately arrives at the human endpoint, where dignity and confidence serve as the true measures of rigor.

As introduced earlier, AI credit and debit provide a readiness lens that makes this balance visible. Credit grows when adoption generates operational efficiency, delivers sharper insight for decision-makers, sustains revenue growth, and builds credibility with stakeholders. Debit builds in parallel, through the energy required for compute-intensive workloads, the compliance risks that emerge when oversight lags, the disruption that unsettles employees when reskilling falls behind, and the reputational strain that follows when expectations of fairness or transparency are missed. Sustainability takes shape only when leaders hold both sides of this ledger deliberately, ensuring that the pursuit of gains is matched by stewardship of the risks that accompany them. In this balance, adoption matures with legitimacy, carries resilience across cycles, and secures the trust that allows intelligence to endure.

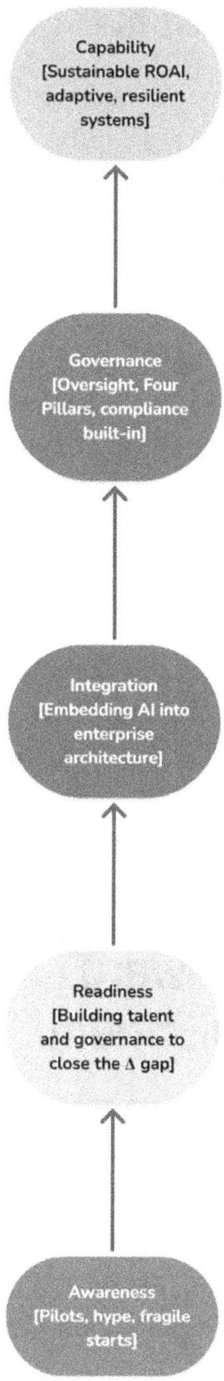

Figure 3-3. *From Fragile Pilots to Enduring Enterprise Capability*

Toward Enduring Equilibrium

Operationalization marks the decisive test of adoption. Startups experiment, SMBs refine efficiency, and enterprises orchestrate at scale, but each must ultimately move beyond pilots and construct systems capable of holding their ground. In game-theory terms, this is the stage where repeated plays converge toward equilibrium: govern and adopt with responsibility. The AI Compatibility Score offers the reflective discipline to assess this progress, showing whether architecture, governance, culture, and leadership intent are aligned to carry intelligence at scale. Crossing Δ, the readiness gap, is achieved not through spectacle but through deliberate design and steady alignment.

At every turn, the endpoint remains human. Employees experience new contours in their work, customers engage with systems that must strengthen their confidence rather than weaken it, investors and regulators look for signals of credibility, and societies at large decide whether adoption deserves their trust. In the Anno Artificialis Intelligenciae, those organizations that thrive will be the ones that treat intelligence as a living capability: investing in governance as carefully as in technology, aligning design with human need, and using agentic AI to reinforce resilience. Through these choices, adoption moves toward an equilibrium that carries stability and legitimacy, where intelligence matures beyond experiments and becomes part of the enterprise design itself, serving as a foundation of trust that endures.

Conclusion: Playing Toward Human-Centered Equilibrium

This chapter has shown that the challenges of AI adoption differ in form but converge in rhythm. Startups combat volatility, where speed without structure can become fragile. SMBs advance through efficiency, stretching limited resources into stable gains. Enterprises pursue resilience, working against silos, inertia, and architectural debt that threaten to pull them apart. Across every scale, three universal hurdles—that is, talent, governance, and debt—set the conditions within which maturity must be forged.

Game theory sharpens this picture. Each organization plays with the same payoff function, but the values of its terms change with context. For startups, the probability of success (p) remains low, the benefits of success (B) can be extraordinary, and the costs of failure (C) strike with existential force. SMBs work with higher probabilities and narrower margins, seeking stability in repeated returns. Enterprises push for resilience, amplifying benefits while managing the heavy costs of large-scale breakdowns. What decides advantage is not a single bold move but the repeated game: credibility earned over cycles, trust compounded through decisions that prove consistent, and resilience built step by step into the architecture of adoption.

Patterns of investment sustain this logic. Startups act as experimentation engines, pressing into new territory. Enterprises integrate innovation into their architectures through acquisitions, partnerships, and orchestration at scale. Governments and regulators intervene as catalysts, steering flows of capital and legitimacy through policy. These patterns have marked previous hype cycles and will continue into the Anno Artificialis Intelligenciae. However, the line between fragility and durability is always drawn by architecture, governance, culture, and readiness moving in alignment.

Agentic AI reinforces both opportunity and responsibility. These systems perceive, plan, act, and adapt in continuous loops. They coordinate across workflows, monitor for anomalies, and bring humans into the loop when judgment is required. They do not stand outside the adoption game; they participate in it, shaping payoffs from within. When structured without discipline, they drive adoption toward collapse, as short-term advantage gives way to eroded trust. When designed as part of hybrid intelligence, they guide adoption toward equilibrium, a condition where cooperation and governance create stability and where trust becomes the highest form of return. The lesson carries beyond strategy into lived experience. Technical debt surfaces in misclassified claims, brittle pipelines, and fractured integrations, but its weight is felt by employees repeating tasks, customers waiting for answers, and citizens confronting disrupted services. Talent shortages register in diminished confidence and unequal access to opportunity, weakening the promise of inclusion. Governance, when expressed as practice rather than paperwork, sustains dignity, accountability, and trust. Even the environmental costs of adoption, such as the energy consumed, the emissions released, and the waste accumulated, settle their bill with communities.

To play the adoption game responsibly is to design intelligence that strengthens accountability, that carries resilience through pressure, and that holds legitimacy over time. True maturity lies in architectures that extend human judgment, in cultures that protect human dignity, and in governance that serves human purpose. This is the essence of sustainable equilibrium: intelligence that endures as trust, evolving through institutions and decisions and finding its meaning in the lives it touches.

CHAPTER 4

Data: The Real AI Enabler

Introduction

In the previous chapter, we traced the hurdles that shape the enterprise AI journey. Startups live in the tension between agility and scale, moving fast enough to prove their promise yet struggling to hold that pace as systems grow. Small and mid-sized businesses stretch ambition against finite means, often advancing further than their infrastructure can bear. Global corporations, despite their power, remain bound by their own weight, such as silos, legacy systems, and the sediment of technical debt. The forms differ, but each returns to a single fault line: the condition of enterprise data. When data is brittle, fragmented, or confined within walls that resist connection, every aspiration meets its limit.

This truth is neither new nor abstract. According to our research, supported by field interviews and enterprise case studies, it affirms what most practitioners know instinctively but rarely confront without hesitation: data quality and privacy are the decisive determinants of success. A promising initiative collapses when records are flawed or incomplete, when the lineage of information fades into obscurity, or when sensitive detail slips unguarded into public space. From such lapses emerge erosion of trust, reputational damage, and the gradual decay of confidence that spreads faster than any breach itself. In the *Anno Artificialis Intelligenciae*, data is no longer a passive resource; rather, it is the current that sustains intelligence, the living element that decides whether an enterprise closes its ***readiness gap (Δ)*** or drifts into it.

R. Harjika, *Architecting Enterprise AI Strategies*, https://doi.org/10.1007/979-8-8688-2219-3_4

Data As a Living Current

For much of computing history, data was treated as residue, that is, an exhaust trail left behind once transactions were complete. Mainframes processed activity but did not learn from it. Records were stored for compliance, never animated for discovery. Even as decades passed, language still betrayed the same logic. Data was called "***the new oil***," a metaphor of extraction and depletion, implying something to be burned, not nurtured. In the *Anno Artificialis Intelligenciae*, that metaphor dissolves. Data is not a fossil to consume; it is air. Without circulation, the organism of intelligence suffocates; with clean and continuous flow, it adapts and evolves. Enterprise architecture therefore inherits a moral and technical duty: to keep this air breathable. It must design circulation that sustains clarity, preserve provenance so confidence remains intact, and make knowledge usable by every actor who depends on it. The task is ecological rather than mechanical, creating balance between abundance and restraint, between access and protection, and between the demands of progress and the ethics of care.

Why AI Strategy Cannot Stand Apart from Data Strategy

To speak of AI strategy without data is to speak of architecture without a foundation. Intelligence cannot be an ornament appended after platforms are chosen or algorithms procured; it must arise from the structure of the data itself. When data flows mirror the logic of value creation, when pipelines endure stress without distortion, and when governance matures as a habit rather than an audit ritual, intelligence finds stable ground. Only then does ambition turn into capability, and capability into measurable ***Return on AI Investment*** (ROAI).

The Movements of This Chapter

This chapter unfolds less as sections than as a sequence of transformations.

- **Movement I:** It begins with a recognition that every AI vision must be born as a data vision, shaped around outcomes that matter to people and institutions alike.
- **Movement II:** It then enters the machinery, the architecture of pipelines that sustain continuity, reliability, and reach.

- **Movement III:** From there, it turns to governance, treating it not as paperwork but as the architecture of trust where explainability, security, and ethical practice become lived habits.
- **Movement IV:** Thereafter, it explores the textures of data itself: unstructured, semi-structured, and synthetic forms that blur the boundary between signal and imagination.
- **Movement V:** The chapter closes by tracing how modern data fabrics and adaptive platforms create the conditions where intelligence can evolve without losing coherence.

Each movement extends the previous one, forming a single argument: that data architecture is the living skeleton of enterprise intelligence.

The Economics of Readiness: Datanomics

Every age creates its own economy of value. The industrial era organized progress around capital and labor; the digital era around networks and scale. The age of intelligence introduces a new equilibrium, ***Datanomics***, the economics of readiness. The term *Datanomics* has appeared in recent years within commercial and journalistic circles, often used to describe the expanding economic significance of data. In this book, the concept acquires its architectural and ethical form. This book advances a distinct interpretation of ***Datanomics: the economics of readiness***, the study of how enterprises create, exchange, and sustain value through the responsible and disciplined governance of data. It fuses the reasoning of economics with the design language of architecture, recognizing that information behaves as both capital and covenant: a productive asset that generates intelligence and a moral contract that sustains trust. By articulating *Datanomics* in this way, this book gives structure to a term that has long floated at the edges of discourse. It formalizes a framework where stewardship, not accumulation, defines economic advantage. Data ceases to be exhausted from operations and becomes the primary currency of legitimacy, a living asset whose worth compounds through governance and erodes through neglect.

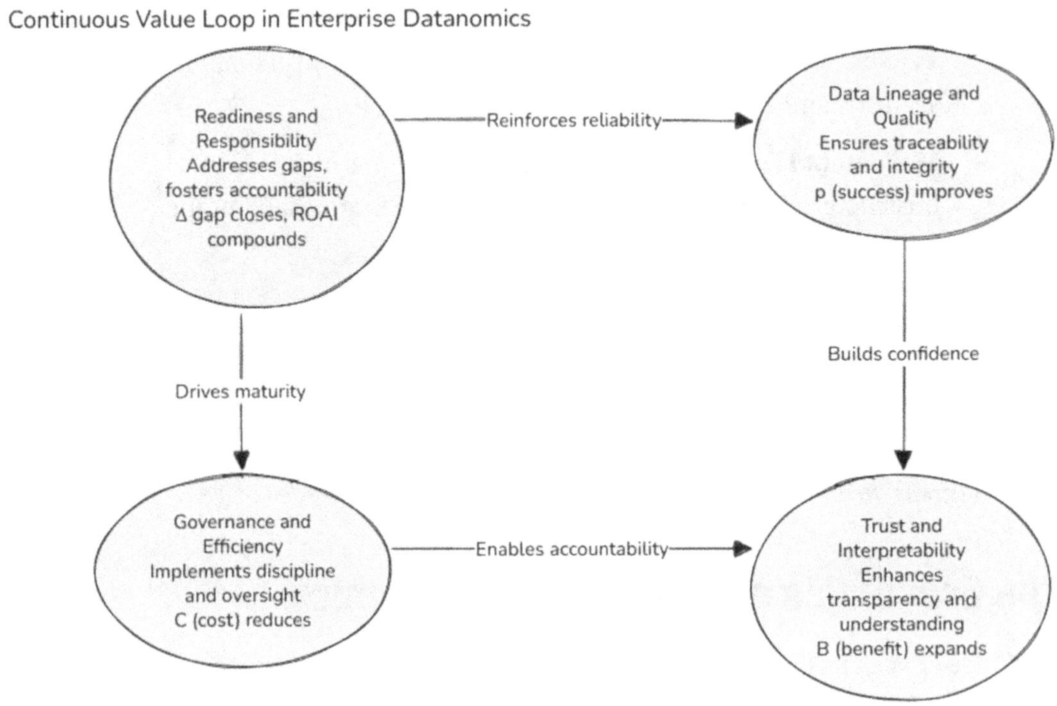

Figure 4-1. *The Architecture of Datanomics*

The logic of game theory brings the terrain into focus, reviving the payoff equation from Chapter 3 as a compass for data maturity. $\boldsymbol{U = p \times B - C}$, where the probability of success (p) strengthens as data gains lineage and reliability; the benefits (B) expand when outcomes inspire trust and interpretability; and the costs (C) decline as pipelines become coherent, efficient, and observable. Each term in the equation carries an ethical dimension. Lineage translates into accountability, precision into credibility, and efficiency into sustainability. The formula thus becomes not merely a calculation of utility but a reflection of institutional maturity. Through this lens, *Datanomics* reveals the enterprise as a living economy of intelligence. Well-governed data behaves like sound capital: it appreciates with use, compounds through trust, and circulates freely without losing coherence. Poorly governed data behaves like debt: it accrues hidden interest in the form of bias, opacity, and inefficiency until correction becomes costly. The readiness gap ($\boldsymbol{\Delta}$) represents this differential, the distance between declared ambition and realized capability, between data's potential and its discipline.

In this architecture of value, the AI Compatibility Score becomes the mirror of enterprise conscience. It functions less as a metric and more as an ethical audit, a portrait of how an organization conducts itself beneath its algorithms. It reveals whether governance breathes as a living culture or settles into routine, whether privacy is upheld as an act of care, and whether stewardship arises from conviction that endures through scrutiny. The Score, in this sense, measures the compound interest of responsibility, the trust that accrues discreetly, accumulates across decisions, and endures as the most tangible return on intelligence. *Datanomics* therefore expands the very notion of return. The Return on AI Investment (ROAI) cannot be reduced to throughput or margin; it must account for legitimacy earned, risk contained, and confidence sustained. In this new economy of intelligence, resilience becomes the highest dividend. The enterprises that endure will be those that treat data as both capital and conscience, an asset that generates efficiency, embodies integrity, and builds its highest dividend in the form of trust.

The Unseen Architecture Beneath

Beneath every dashboard and model lies a more physical truth, that is, the data centers themselves. They hum at the peripheries of cities, consuming water and energy at scales that reconfigure entire grids. Their glow is unseen by the users they serve but felt by communities who share their power and landscape. These are the lungs of the digital age, and like all lungs, they draw from the world around them. The ecological weight of this infrastructure becomes the bridge to the next chapter, where sustainability emerges as the language of survival, a principle of design as vital as intelligence itself. For now, it is enough to remember that data is never abstract. It breathes through material things: metal, heat, water, and human labor.

The Physical Cost of Data: A Hidden Chapter of Intelligence

Every abstraction of cloud and algorithm rests upon a physical foundation. In many parts of the world, vast data centers have begun to alter local landscapes. One such example emerged in Mansfield, Georgia, where families live beside vast data centers that illuminate the horizon day and night, their presence shaping air, water, and community life. Wells draw from aquifers that cool computational engines, while the hum of servers becomes part of the landscape's texture. What appears as instantaneous intelligence, each query, prediction, or generated phrase, depends on networks that consume power, space, and human attention. These infrastructures sustain the world's cognition while reshaping the environments that host them. This material dimension gives data its ethical weight. Every dataset, every model, and every request draws from shared ecological and social reserves. Stewardship, therefore, extends beyond privacy and accuracy into the domains of energy, locality, and human consequence. The governance of data must include the care of the systems that hold it, ensuring that the intelligence we build strengthens the environments it occupies. This awareness defines the bridge to the next chapter, where the architecture of scale becomes an architectural responsibility, designing intelligence that grows in coherence with the world that sustains it.

Toward a Human-Centered Foundation

If enterprise AI is to mature into lasting capability, data must be understood as its moral and structural ground. This is not an exercise in precision alone; it is an ethical commitment to build systems that strengthen human judgment, enhance institutional memory, and preserve dignity. The Human Endpoint Principle reminds us that all this machinery—data, models, and governance—exists to serve people, not to measure them. Chapter 4 therefore begins where every architecture must: with the foundation. What follows traces how data takes form through design, finds integrity through governance, and gains renewal through continuous dialogue with the society that grants it purpose.

4.1 Data Strategy As the Foundation of AI Strategy

Every enterprise proclaims that data is its most valuable asset; however, few treat it with the seriousness of architecture. The adoption of AI exposes this contradiction with unsparing clarity. Leaders chase after models, drawn to their surface intelligence, while overlooking the structural design that gives those models endurance. It is like admiring the light that filters through stained glass while forgetting the stonework that holds the window in place. Intelligence cannot flourish without that foundation. In the *Anno Artificialis Intelligenciae,* data has ceased to be an exhaust trailing behind transactions. It has become the lifeblood of systems that learn, reason, and act. The shift is more than technical; it marks a change in temperament. Where the mainframe era regarded data as an afterthought to be stored and archived, modern architecture treats it as the primary material of decision-making. Neglected, it decays. Cultivated and governed, it turns into living capital. Embracing this change calls for transformation at the level of leadership itself, a recognition that data now defines the movement of enterprise, guiding processes, influencing decisions, and composing the rhythm through which value takes form.

Legacy Workhorses and the Art of Evolution

Across industries, legacy systems remain the dependable workhorses of daily operations. Banks, insurers, telecom providers, and public institutions trust them for their resilience and transactional integrity. Still, these same systems often imprison what they protect: decades of records, institutional memory, and patterns of behavior that could enrich every modern initiative. Their data lies hidden behind proprietary formats, reachable only through brittle connectors or nightly batch transfers. The irony is painful. The infrastructure that preserves continuity also constrains renewal. Modern data strategy does not demand that these workhorses be discarded in the name of novelty. Its wisdom lies in evolution, not rupture. Through replication streams, event-driven connectors, and application interfaces, enterprises can let legacy data breathe, feeding contemporary analytics and AI pipelines while the old cores continue their reliable function. Such incrementalism is not hesitation; it is discipline. It honors the stability that past generations built, even as it prepares the ground for what follows.

Discovery As a Living Dialogue

The first gesture in any credible data strategy is discovery. An organization must learn to see its own data before it can govern or apply it. But discovery is not an audit of tables and files; it is a conversation that crosses boundaries of business, technology, and oversight. It begins with questions that sound simple but unsettle habits: ***What do we truly hold? Who touches it, under what conditions, and toward which ends? What value does it conceal, and what risk does it carry?*** As these questions deepen, hidden realities begin to emerge: documentation once believed complete reveals its gaps, systems praised for automation expose the concealed dependence on human hands, and forgotten repositories resurface carrying data that no one remembers owning; through this unfolding, discovery transforms from a technical exercise into an act of reflection, showing leaders both the wealth they command and the fragility of the culture that holds it together.

Governance As Compass and Shield

Discovery without discipline soon devolves into voyeurism: seeing without responsibility. The credibility of AI rests on the reliability of its inputs, which means that every flow of data must be bound by provenance, quality, and accountability expressed in daily practice. Rules hidden in legacy code must be surfaced and translated into policies that living systems can observe. Governance is therefore not a bureaucratic layer but an ethical framework woven into architecture itself. Stewardship becomes the defining act of maturity. When ownership of data products is explicit, quality and privacy are not repaired after failure; they are sustained as a continuous cycle. Governance, in this sense, functions both as a compass and a shield: orienting data toward purpose while protecting the enterprise from reputational and legal harm. It embodies the Four Pillars of enterprise AI—Accessibility, Explainability, Security, and Ethics—as living habits that shape every transaction, guide every transformation, and leave their trace in each decision the system makes.

Integration and Coherence

Once discovery and governance take root, integration follows naturally. The challenge is to connect what exists without dismantling what works. Enterprises can no longer accept isolation, although few can afford a wholesale rebuild. Modern data strategy therefore pursues coherence rather than centralization. Change-data-capture tools, replication layers, and streaming architectures create channels through which information flows between worlds: on-premise cores, hybrid clouds, and edge environments, without loss of fidelity. Coherence emerges when data reaches the right moment in the right context, remaining traceable, interpretable, and useful across systems. In this design, architecture takes the shape of **a living structure**, which is adaptive, continuous, and capable of renewal through every interaction that sustains it.

From Architecture to Outcome

Even the most elegant architecture means little unless it translates into lived results. A data strategy earns its legitimacy when its flows illuminate the value streams of the enterprise, such as detecting fraud before it spreads, strengthening supply chain resilience, personalizing services with integrity, and safeguarding patients through clearer signals. Here, the AI Compatibility Score becomes an instrument of reflection. By examining lineage, quality, privacy, and cultural readiness, it makes the ***readiness gap (Δ)*** visible, allowing leaders to invest deliberately rather than reactively.

Case Study: A Bank's Journey from Archive to Action

For decades, the bank's heart had pulsed inside a mainframe—a dependable core that balanced accounts with ritual precision but moved at the pace of another age. Its reliability was a legend; its rigidity, an unspoken cost. Then came the twin pressures of rising fraud and a new expectation from customers who wanted recognition, not routine. Urgency gathered quietly across boardrooms and corridors: innovation was essential; nevertheless, the institution's memory, that is, its data, its history, and its proof of trust, lived inside the very system many now wished to replace.

Amid voices arguing for demolition or defense, leadership chose a subtler path: **evolution through design**. The architecture team reimagined connection rather than replacement. Transaction streams began to flow from the mainframe into a modern cloud lakehouse, where analytics and machine learning could interpret behavior as it happened. Slowly, patterns that had once taken days to detect appeared in seconds. Unified customer profiles began to take shape, such as threads of credit, savings, and digital interaction interlacing into a single portrait of belonging. Each data point found its place within a broader story of relationship, turning transactions into traces of trust. Within months, the numbers gradually testified to the change: fraud receded, alerts arrived as events unfolded, and customers felt the presence of a bank that listened before they had spoken. Transparency became its language; even regulators sensed a new steadiness beneath the surface of compliance. But the transformation's essence was never in velocity but in reconciliation, the moment when permanence and agility ceased to compete and began to converse. The mainframe's discipline met the cloud's curiosity, and between them arose a pattern both familiar and renewed. Modernization revealed itself not as erasure but as continuity refined, proving that systems, like institutions, mature when they remember what made them trustworthy in the first place.

Beneath the technical outcome lay a subtler victory. Operational risk dissolved into resilience; efficiency ripened into credibility. Trust, once an intangible promise, became a measurable flow within the enterprise, a subtle currency that gained value through every transparent act. In uniting its past with its potential, the bank discovered that progress endures only when it carries memory forward and that intelligence attains grace when it learns to honor the history that sustains it.

Closing Δ and Compounding ROAI

This example distills the true meaning of data strategy in the *Anno Artificialis Intelligenciae.* It represents not an extension of enterprise ambition but the foundation that allows ambition to endure. When data is shaped as a living product, protected as an ethical resource, and guided toward outcomes of real consequence, intelligence gains coherence. Investments in AI begin to accumulate value organically; readiness matures into capability, and capability matures into trust.

In this maturity, the Return on AI Investment (ROAI) evolves beyond its numeric appearance. It becomes a property of the enterprise itself, a flow through which insight, governance, and responsibility reinforce one another, compounding carefully with time. Readiness deepens as systems learn to explain themselves, as data governance becomes instinct rather than instruction, and as trust grows into the currency that sustains continuity. Enterprises that root their architecture in this discipline experience progress that endures. Their intelligence retains form through change, drawing strength from transparency and grace from accountability. The reward is subtle while enduring: a system that learns without fracturing, advances without forgetting, and serves with a constancy that reflects the people for whom it was built.

4.2 Designing Scalable, Reliable Data Pipelines

If data strategy offers the blueprint, pipelines provide the circulation through which intelligence comes alive. They move insight from the places where it is born to the decisions that depend upon it. When those channels falter, the entire organism weakens. Many enterprises learn this truth the hard way: a proof-of-concept dazzles in a laboratory but collapses under real-world strain. What seemed elegant on a developer's machine buckles when faced with live traffic, schema drift, or the noise of daily operations. With each failure, credibility erodes, and with it the confidence of the people who must trust these systems.

Too often, pipelines are built as disposable code, that is, hastily assembled scripts to answer a one-off report or enable a fleeting experiment. That mentality belongs to a vanished age. In an enterprise preparing for intelligence at scale, a pipeline must be designed as a product, not a project. A product has purpose, stewardship, and a lifecycle. It evolves through design, deployment, refinement, and renewal. It learns to endure stress rather than crumble beneath it. A pipeline unable to survive turbulence is not a pipeline at all; it is a rehearsal mistaken for performance.

Stress As the Normal Condition

Every data system lives within a state of tension. The moment it meets the world, it encounters forces that test its design, volumes that swell without warning, connections that strain under new velocity, and dependencies that reveal fragility long concealed beneath stability. What appears as stress is, in truth, the natural flux of enterprise intelligence, the pulse that separates experimental prototypes from living architecture. Resilience arises when systems are designed with this flow in mind. Modern architectures embody flexibility through event-driven design, modular interfaces, and agile middleware that allow data to move with the ebb and flow of demand. Workloads migrate seamlessly, from sensors that speak at the edge to deep computational engines in the cloud, from instant inference close to the user to longer cycles of retraining in controlled environments. The architecture breathes with the enterprise itself, adjusting, regenerating, and continuing to serve even as conditions evolve. Scalability, then, is not a measure of size but of grace under pressure, the ability to remain composed while expanding, to adapt without rupture, and to distribute weight without losing balance. A truly scalable system behaves like a living circulatory network: elastic, self-repairing, and aware of its own continuity. Through such design, stress ceases to be a threat and becomes a signal, a constant reminder that intelligent systems, like the organizations they serve, stay vital only when they keep moving.

Reliability As Discipline

Reliability begins with humility. In complex ecosystems, failure is ordinary. Records arrive twice or not at all; schemas evolve midstream; a single misconfigured network rule can silence an entire region. Systems designed for a perfect world are destined to disappoint the real one. Mature pipelines are built on the expectation of imperfection. They process repeated events without contradiction, resume work from where they left off, and expose disruption rather than conceal it. Checkpoints, recovery logs, and compensating transactions replace the illusion of flawlessness with the practice of resilience. Reliability, understood in this way, is less a technical specification than a cultural stance: a belief that trust is preserved through transparency in recovery and the grace of swift restoration whenever disruption arises.

Observability As Sightline

No pipeline can be reliable if it remains opaque. Observability gives systems their sightline, the ability to know what is happening while it happens. Every transformation, ingestion, and emission must be traceable. Lineage reveals how data has changed; metrics signal drift or delay; logs capture early tremors before they grow into crises. Without that visibility, operations teams fly blind, unable to defend the decisions their systems produce. With it, they gain coherence. Data flow becomes an open record of movement, a structure of accountability rather than an invisible utility. Observability stands as the condition through which confidence becomes sustainable and trust gains permanence within intelligent systems.

The Medallion Architecture: Structuring Flow into Value

In mature data ecosystems, strength lies in structure. The Medallion Architecture expresses this discipline by organizing the movement of data into three deliberate layers—**Bronze**, **Silver**, and **Gold**—each serving a distinct purpose in preserving integrity while enabling flow. The **Bronze layer** holds data in its native form, complete and unfiltered, maintaining the authenticity of its source. The **Silver layer** introduces refinement through validation, standardization, and harmonization, transforming raw inputs into dependable records that can sustain operational use. The **Gold layer** represents synthesis, where information becomes governed, trusted, and ready for analytical and intelligent application. Together, these layers form an ordered sequence of transformation, ensuring that every transition enhances clarity and confidence rather than complexity.

Figure 4-2. *The Medallion Architecture: Structuring Flow into Value*

The Medallion model reinforces the principles of Datanomics, the economics of readiness, by ensuring that value compounds through structure. Each progression increases usability while protecting provenance, translating technical order into institutional reliability. Within the enterprise payoff equation ($U = p \times B - C$), the model strengthens probability (p) by centering decisions in verified lineage, expands benefit (B) through dependable insight, and contains cost (C) through disciplined reuse and coherence. In this way, architecture becomes the language of assurance. The Medallion design enables organizations to transform raw accumulation into accountable intelligence, aligning data movement with purpose and allowing every layer to sustain the trust upon which intelligent enterprise depends.

Case Study: A Logistics Company Finds Its Form

The transformation began on the move, somewhere between ports and warehouses, as the enterprise tried to keep pace with its own expanding network. For years, nightly batch reports had governed the movement of goods, a cycle once sufficient, even graceful in its predictability. But as new hubs opened and time zones stretched, that cycle fractured. Packages advanced faster than the systems that tracked them; customers waited for answers that no longer arrived in time. Change came when the architecture team decided to rethink continuity rather than capacity. They redesigned the data landscape around continuous flow, building event-driven pipelines that could ingest, transform, and distribute information as it was created. Data began to travel seamlessly into the enterprise cloud, enriched as it moved, and surfaced through dashboards designed for transparency and observability. Every shipment could now be followed from departure to delivery, and discrepancies emerged in minutes rather than days.

The improvement unfolded slowly but with unmistakable consequence. Uncertainty gave way to clarity; decision-making regained confidence; customers sensed reliability returning to every interaction. Transparency became the unseen infrastructure, the connective tissue linking operations, insight, and service. What had once been hidden code evolved into coherence itself, an architecture capable of moving with the enterprise and sustaining the trust that kept its world in motion.

Case Study: A Bank Learns to Outpace Fraud

For years, the bank's mainframe extractions had followed a familiar tempo: overnight reconciliation, morning reports, and day-end assurance. The pattern worked in an earlier era of predictability, but as digital payments accelerated, that structure fractured. The systems built for yesterday's closure could not serve today's continuity. Transactions moved faster than their verification; genuine payments were blocked in caution, while fraudulent ones escaped in the gaps between updates. Confidence wavered at every level, from customers who felt interrupted to analysts who could no longer see the whole picture in time. The architecture team resisted the impulse to rebuild from scratch. Instead, they pursued renewal through precision. By implementing change-data-capture (CDC), they began to stream live transaction data directly into a cloud-based lakehouse, where analytic and machine-learning models could interpret behavior as it unfolded. Monitoring was integrated from inception rather than appended after failure, and models retrained themselves continuously as new patterns emerged. Gradually, the system moved from reaction to anticipation. Over the following months, the signals began to shift, transactions once flagged in error passed smoothly, patterns of fraud that had evaded detection now surfaced with clarity, and the experience on both sides of the counter settled into a steadiness that felt newly trustworthy.

The transformation owed less to algorithmic novelty than to architectural clarity. The bank had learned to think in motion, to treat data not as a periodic report but as a continuous dialogue between system and signal. In the language of payoff, the probability of success grew with visibility, operational cost diminished through automation, and benefit compounded as trust re-entered the equation. Although beyond this calculus lay something more enduring: the recognition that technological speed acquires meaning only when joined with ethical attention. In aligning vigilance with design, the bank rediscovered what true intelligence demands: systems that protect as they perform and architectures that hold faith with the people they serve.

Designing for Sustainability

Sustainability in data architecture reaches beyond elastic compute or flexible contracts. It resides in discipline: metadata catalogs that establish meaning, schema registries that guard compatibility, federated ownership that prevents drift, and cost awareness that keeps ambition within bounds. Poorly governed pipelines can silently consume fortunes through redundant queries or oversized clusters. Efficiency is therefore an ethical choice as much as a financial one. A sustainable pipeline respects both the enterprise budget and the planet's resources, minimizing waste of energy and computation while preserving performance.

Pipelines As Arteries of Decision-Making

To imagine pipelines as mere plumbing is to underestimate their significance. They are arteries of decision-making, carrying signals that determine outcomes in human lives. Their fragility can appear in the smallest moments, such as a customer unable to access funds, a patient misclassified, or a delivery stranded in transit. Their strength appears just as tangibly: a timely fraud alert, a treatment chosen correctly, and a supply chain that stays balanced through uncertainty. Pipelines, in this sense, embody the ***Human Endpoint Principle***. When they falter, consequences are immediate and personal. When they endure, trust deepens subconsciously, often unnoticed until a crisis arrives and systems hold firm. The lesson is enduring: good pipeline design disappears into reliability; great pipeline design endures as an act of care. Enterprises that treat pipelines as products, built with discipline and tended with foresight, discover that their intelligence does more than function. It persists. And in persistence lies the truest mark of maturity: technology that continues to serve when the world around it shifts.

4.3 Data Governance for Trustworthy and Compliant AI

Trust is no longer a soft virtue in the age of intelligent systems; it has become a strategic asset. As enterprises embed intelligence into the architecture of their operations, the integrity of the data that sustains it becomes the measure of their accountability. Without governance, pipelines grow opaque, models drift, and credibility collapses. A single lapse of stewardship can undo years of careful architecture. In the *Anno Artificialis Intelligenciae*, governance demands a different imagination. Data is no longer a passive resource to be stored and catalogued; it is both an asset and a liability, capable of enabling new forms of intelligence while equally capable of exposing the enterprise to risk. Governance, therefore, must transcend the old caricature of bureaucracy. It provides the architecture within which innovation can take shape, granting it form, direction, and the strength to evolve without fracture. Its purpose is to embed accountability directly into the movement of data so that explainability, traceability, and ethical alignment become natural properties of the system rather than afterthoughts appended to it.

Lineage As Accountability Made Visible

Lineage is the simplest concept and the hardest discipline. It asks that enterprises know where their data originates, how it has been altered, and what decisions it ultimately informs. In practice, lineage is not only metadata or logs; it is memory. It holds the choices made during preprocessing, the assumptions recorded during labeling, and the record of who accessed information and why. Lineage converts intelligence from opacity to transparency: a black box turned glass, auditable by regulators, explainable to customers, and defensible before law. Enterprise architecture becomes the medium through which this visibility takes form. Platforms such as SAP LeanIX enable architects to map, in living diagrams, where AI models operate, which datasets they consume, and how those elements shape business logic. Governance thus ceases to be a static report and becomes a living cartography. The architect evolves from custodian of documentation to enabler of trust.

Quality, Bias, and the Lesson of Spam and Ham

Governance serves as the silent conscience of intelligence. It preserves systems from two slow erosions that can undo entire architectures: the decline of quality and the invisible seepage of bias. Each begins as something almost trivial, such as a missing field, a misclassified record, or an unexamined assumption, and subsequently, when magnified through machine learning, these details become structural truths. This understanding is older than the digital age itself. In 1957, a U.S. Army mathematician named William D. Mellin used a phrase that would echo through decades of computing: ***Garbage In, Garbage Out*** [14]. His words reminded early programmers that machines do not create meaning; they follow it. Even Charles Babbage, a century earlier, had framed the same principle with wonder and disbelief, asking how anyone could imagine that wrong figures might yield right answers. From those early reflections arose a lesson that remains unchanged in the *Anno Artificialis Intelligenciae*: intelligence cannot transcend the integrity of its inputs.

The same truth reappeared decades later in a more humble setting: email filtering. Engineers tasked with distinguishing unwanted messages, or *spam*, from legitimate correspondence, affectionately called *ham*, discovered that the problem was not computation but curation. Each example in the training set mattered. A single mislabeled message could tilt the entire balance, letting malicious mail slip through or silencing genuine communication. The challenge became an allegory for all data work: discernment mattered more than scale, judgment more than volume. Today, that early discipline has become the foundation of ethical AI. Modern datasets contain the vast residue of human behavior, records shaped by privilege, omission, and history. When those asymmetries pass unexamined into machine learning, systems learn to replicate them faithfully. Credit models inherit geographic inequalities; recruitment engines echo old prejudices; clinical algorithms misread the bodies of those absent from their data. The same logic that once sorted email now shapes the contours of human experience, deciding who gains access, who feels secure, and whose worth is passively affirmed by the systems that see them.

Governance responds by restoring awareness. It invites enterprises to treat data quality as an act of care and bias management as an act of responsibility. It shifts the focus from accuracy alone to the completeness of understanding, from the perfection of models to the integrity of the reality they mirror. In this light, governance becomes more than a safeguard; it is a philosophy of attention. It reminds those who design intelligent systems that precision without fairness diminishes truth and that every dataset carries an ethical inheritance. When cultivated with sincerity, data turns from raw material into reflection, a record of how deeply a civilization chooses to know itself.

Privacy and the Promise of Decentralization

Privacy stands at the center of responsible architecture. Every intelligent system depends upon data that carries traces of human life—transactions, choices, movements, emotions—and those traces create an enduring obligation of care. In the *Anno Artificialis Intelligenciae*, privacy is not the resistance to innovation; it is the principle that gives innovation its legitimacy. Around the world, nations and regions are shaping this duty through evolving legal frameworks. The General Data Protection Regulation (GDPR) in Europe, India's Digital Personal Data Protection Act (DPDP), China's Personal Information Protection Law (PIPL), and the African Union's Convention on Cyber Security and Personal Data Protection (Malabo Convention) all articulate a shared conviction: that data originates with people and must remain accountable to them. Each law may shift in scope, interpretation, or enforcement, but together they express a single global movement, the recognition that dignity is measurable through design. For enterprises, this recognition translates into architecture. Consent travels with every record as metadata; minimization governs what is collected; erasure operates as an engineered feature rather than an administrative promise. Privacy is expressed in system behavior.

Decentralization gives this principle its living form. Instead of gathering every fragment of personal data into vast repositories, enterprises are designing federated systems in which intelligence learns across distributed nodes. Each node retains its data locally, sharing only learned representations or gradients. This model achieves balance: knowledge circulates, but ownership remains grounded. The enterprise gains insight without possession; individuals gain assurance without withdrawal. Within this federated world, a new generation of privacy-preserving techniques sustains the balance between learning and restraint.

Privacy-Preserving Computation: The Instruments of Ethical Architecture

Secure multiparty computation, differential privacy, and homomorphic encryption extend the philosophy of decentralization into the realm of computation itself. Where decentralization disperses control, these techniques safeguard trust within that dispersion. Each offers a different path toward the same principle: intelligence that learns without intrusion, collaborates without exposure, and reasons without possession.

- **Secure multiparty computation** allows several parties to collaborate on a shared computation while keeping their data private from one another. Hospitals can measure treatment effectiveness collectively without sharing patient records; banks can analyze systemic risk while keeping individual ledgers sealed. Collaboration becomes an act of mutual respect, with knowledge generated through cooperation rather than surrender.

- **Differential privacy** introduces measured uncertainty. By adding controlled randomness to data or outputs, it ensures that no single individual can be traced or identified within the whole. The system learns from patterns, not persons, treating anonymity as an architectural right. Privacy here is active presence, the practice of protecting identity even as insight expands.
- **Homomorphic encryption** extends this principle into the mechanics of computation. It allows algorithms to perform operations on encrypted data, enabling analysis without ever unveiling the raw content. Regulators can audit, researchers can innovate, and enterprises can extract value, all while the data remains veiled within its cryptographic shell. This is transparency without exposure, the capacity to reason through protection.

Together, these methods form the ethical machinery of modern intelligence. They transform privacy from a defensive posture into a creative force. Each reveals that progress flourishes when restraint is built into design, when computation itself becomes an expression of respect. In this light, privacy and innovation are not parallel ambitions; they are the same discipline, viewed through different lenses. In this vision, decentralization becomes more than an engineering pattern; it becomes a moral geometry. Power disperses outward from the center to the edges, where individuals, institutions, and communities retain sovereignty over their digital selves. Knowledge circulates freely, but possession no longer defines control. Privacy, built in this way, transcends compliance. It becomes a form of architectural empathy, a recognition that learning can occur without domination, that intelligence can grow without consuming its subjects. When designed with this balance, AI systems move beyond efficiency into trustworthiness. They embody what every civilization ultimately seeks in its technologies: power guided by conscience, insight governed by respect, and progress aligned with human worth.

Community Sovereignty and Reciprocal Data Stewardship

A rising consideration in responsible enterprise AI is **data colonialism**, that is, the practice of collecting data from communities, customers, and citizens and using it primarily for organizational benefit. As organizations derive insight from behavioral patterns, location histories, health indicators, and preferences, meaningful consent and tangible benefit for all participants become essential values. The movement of data outward to enrich enterprise capability calls for thoughtful stewardship, partnership, and transparency. Progressive enterprises are advancing beyond routine compliance toward shared benefit. They establish data-sharing agreements and recognize source communities as true stakeholders, ensuring that consent is informed and that returns are both clear and genuine. Regular transparency reporting communicates how data is gathered, for what purposes, and by what safeguards. Many organizations then close the loop, such as by returning insights, supporting local initiatives, or involving communities in governance, thereby fostering reciprocity rather than extraction.

Recognizing data colonialism as both an ethical and strategic concern builds trust and resilience. When governance is rooted in dignity, openness, and reciprocal value, the practice of intelligence grows in legitimacy and strength. This stance is directly aligned with the Accessibility and Ethics pillars of responsible AI. Through such practices, organizations ensure intelligence serves all stakeholders, enriches relationships, and builds enduring social license for innovation.

Ethics, Fairness, and the Experiment of Constitutional AI

Governance and ethics emerge from the same foundation. Every dataset carries within it the culture of those who create it, their norms, priorities, and blind spots. Numbers may appear neutral; however, they inherit the shape of human judgment. When patterns formed by human choice flow unexamined into models, they harden into invisible structures of influence, deciding who gains access, who receives care, and who slowly recedes from visibility. Ethical governance therefore begins not in reaction but in creation, in how representation is balanced, how absence is recorded, and how difference is understood as information rather than anomaly. By tracing distribution, documenting skew, and acknowledging silence as a kind of data in itself, governance turns awareness into architecture. Ethics becomes measurable through the precision of design, through the questions asked, the perspectives that define accuracy, and the principles that shape code as constraint rather than ornament.

The idea of Constitutional AI first appeared within research circles as an attempt to guide model behavior through written principles rather than reactive correction. Early experiments, most notably by Anthropic in the early 2020s [15], trained systems to critique and refine their own outputs against a constitution of values drawn from human rights declarations and institutional codes. It was an early effort to give machines a textual conscience. Even so, its implications extend far beyond model training. In this book, the concept evolves into an ethical architecture for enterprise intelligence. Constitutional AI becomes the practice of embedding guiding principles, privacy, fairness, dignity, proportionality, and respect for human agency directly into the logic of systems and the governance that sustains them. These principles act as a living charter within learning itself, defining the boundaries of exploration and orienting intelligence toward outcomes that reflect shared human purpose. The constitution, in this sense, is less a document than a discipline: a continuous dialogue between design and conscience.

By expanding Constitutional AI from a technical mechanism into an architectural ethic, we extend its reach from model alignment to institutional integrity. It becomes the connective framework between governance and innovation, translating moral intuition into computational form. This approach treats intelligence as a participant in civilization rather than an instrument beneath it. To give an AI a constitution is to affirm that power gains meaning only when tethered to purpose. Through this lens, governance ceases to be oversight and becomes companionship, a perpetual negotiation between autonomy and accountability. Constitutional AI, as conceived here, mirrors the deeper history of governance itself. Just as societies have built constitutions to keep power coherent with justice and ambition aligned with restraint, the same architecture now finds expression in code. It marks the moral evolution of systems design: the deliberate act of ensuring that progress moves in step with conscience and that learning, however rapid, remains bound to the responsibility to care.

Case Study: Healthcare and the Governance of Consent

Among all domains, healthcare most vividly reveals how governance matures from regulation into care. A leading provider set out to design a predictive model that could anticipate patient readmissions, but the challenge lay not in algorithms but in the tangled landscape of data itself, with structured clinical records sitting beside narrative physician notes, historical encounters scattered across institutions, and repositories rich in detail but poor in coherence. Each dataset carried both insight and fragility, holding stories that could illuminate patterns of recovery yet expose patients if handled without discipline. The organization approached the problem as an act of architectural reform rather than technical experimentation. Consent metadata was carried directly from electronic health records into analytic pipelines, ensuring that every computation respected the permissions under which data was gathered. Clinical notes, filled with the nuance of human judgment, were translated into structured form under the supervision of medical experts so that context survived even as content became analyzable. Population balances were studied across age, gender, and condition, establishing fairness not as adjustment but as design. Outcome definitions, long inconsistent across facilities, were reconciled through inter-hospital collaboration until the model rested on shared meaning instead of local convention.

As these structures settled into practice, the results became visible first as confidence and then as culture. Predictions grew more precise, but precision was only part of the gain. Clinicians began to treat the system as a partner in discernment; regulators saw in its transparency the promise of accountability; patients, knowing how their consent travelled within the system, began to extend a cautious trust rarely given to data-driven tools. The transformation was as much ethical as technical, a demonstration that governance, when conceived as design, turns intelligence into a form of care.

Governance As Enabler, Not Burden

Governance often suffers from misinterpretation. It is too easily imagined as a brake on creativity or a ritual of compliance, when in reality it forms the skeleton that allows progress to stand upright. Within the evolving ecosystem of intelligent enterprise, governance is the silent architecture of continuity. It aligns curiosity with discipline, ensuring that the momentum of innovation does not outrun the legitimacy that sustains it. When governance is incorporated into daily practice, it ceases to feel external. Embedded within workflows, expressed through policy-as-code, and carried by living metadata, it transforms from oversight into guidance. Automated checks become invisible courtesies that preserve coherence. Approvals arrive not as interruptions but as confirmations that the system remains aligned with its own values. Through this integration, governance becomes a routine rather than a restriction. As adoption deepens, this routine must evolve. The future belongs to intelligent governance, frameworks capable of interpreting policy dynamically, auditing themselves, and distributing responsibility across domains without fracturing unity. In such architectures, rules adapt in real time, learning from context just as models learn from data. Governance thus matures from static enforcement to responsive stewardship, a system that preserves agility even as accountability expands.

Enterprises that invest in this evolution discover an unexpected reward. Their trust compounds. Regulatory reviews proceed with confidence; investors recognize resilience rather than risk; customers sense stability beneath innovation. The benefits emerge gradually, like interest accruing on credibility. In this light, governance fulfills its truest purpose. It becomes the architecture of trust, the invisible framework that carries intelligence forward with dignity. Every safeguard, every audit, and every encoded policy contributes to a deeper assurance: that technology and responsibility can grow together, that ambition can move swiftly without losing its moral center, and that progress, when guided by structure, acquires the grace of permanence.

4.4 Handling Complex Data: Unstructured, Semi-structured, and Synthetic

Enterprises once imagined data as orderly, neatly tabulated, cleanly labeled, and ready for analysis. That era has receded. In the *Anno Artificialis Intelligenciae*, the richest signals and the most decisive risks live in forms far less compliant: physician notes scribbled at midnight, scanned contracts buried in shared drives, audio fragments from customer calls, telemetry from IoT sensors, streams of online transactions, and even synthetic simulations of rare or hazardous events. To design for intelligence in this new epoch is to embrace disorder as material, to treat complexity not as failure but as frontier.

The Rise of Unstructured Data

Unstructured data now defines the enterprise landscape. From diagnostic images and legal documents to client emails and social feeds, it resists the rows and columns of relational logic. However, within that apparent disarray lies immense value: the X-ray that reveals what structured variables miss, the clause in a contract that shifts an entire deal's risk, and the tremor in a customer's voice that signals distress before it becomes a complaint. Architecting for such data demands more than repositories and scale. Object stores such as Amazon S3 or Azure Blob provide capacity, but without metadata, they devolve into digital storage fields, spaces that hold without revealing. Meaning arises through enrichment: tagging, indexing, classification, and contextual embedding. Vector-based representations now allow these unstructured fragments to be mapped into multidimensional spaces where relationships emerge, making discovery intuitive and retrieval purposeful. In such architectures, intelligence is less about volume and more about recoverability, that is, the ability to find, interpret, and act upon what once lay buried.

But governance must mature alongside capability. A scanned PDF may contain a passport number, a medical image, biometric detail, a voice recording, or a private confession. Without content-aware controls, enterprises risk exposing far more than they learn. Privacy-preserving design therefore becomes inseparable from data architecture. Encryption, redaction, and differential privacy must extend across modalities, allowing enrichment and containment to coexist. The architect's responsibility is not merely technical; it is ethical, to protect the dignity implicit in every record while enabling its legitimate use.

The Challenge of Semi-structured Data

Semi-structured data occupies the shifting ground between order and freedom. JSON logs, XML feeds, and IoT payloads all contain fields that can drift, expand, or vanish. This partial structure offers flexibility but also fragility. A schema change introduced by one supplier may cascade downstream, disrupting integrations or corrupting analytic models.

Customer event streams reveal this tension with particular clarity. Each interaction produces hundreds of fields; however, only a few remain constant as systems evolve. The rest shift with product releases, marketing trials, or interface changes, reflecting the living nature of the enterprise itself. Architects therefore design for transformation rather than resistance. Schema registries and event contracts preserve coherence amid drift, while schema-on-read practices allow data to be interpreted as it arrives, without forcing premature structure. Modern query engines extend this flexibility, enabling teams to explore changing data in context, and registries record each version so that evolution becomes visible, deliberate, and ultimately governed by design rather than discovered through failure. Beneath this technical discipline lies a cultural one. An undocumented schema change may appear minor in isolation, but multiplied across teams and systems, it creates opacity that carries real cost. Inconsistent flows can inflate operations, distort reporting, and steadily widen the readiness gap, Δ, the distance between what the enterprise aspires to achieve and what its data can sustain.

Synthetic Data As Enabler and Risk

Synthetic data marks the newest chapter in the story of intelligence. Unlike natural data, it is created rather than captured, designed to occupy the spaces where reality is rare, protected, or perilous to observe. Fraud scenarios too infrequent to model, clinical histories constrained by privacy law, safety tests impossible to conduct in physical environments—all find expression through synthetic generation. The methods range from rule-based synthesis to advanced systems such as generative adversarial networks (GANs), diffusion models, and agent-based simulations. When applied with rigor, these techniques expand the enterprise's field of learning, allowing systems to mature in domains once defined by scarcity or constraint. A manufacturer with limited examples of microfractures extended its dataset using synthetic images rendered under varied conditions of light and pressure, improving recall without bias inflation. In healthcare, federated learning coupled with synthetic augmentation enabled hospitals to train models collectively while preserving the privacy of their patients.

But the same creative power that extends possibility can also introduce fragility. Poorly generated data can produce illusions of accuracy, patterns that imitate truth without embodying it. Synthetic samples may even retain traces of their origins, softly echoing the private details they were meant to obscure. The discipline, therefore, lies not in invention alone but in stewardship. Synthetic data must be held to the same standards as natural data: verified, versioned, and governed by transparent lineage. Its promise is real only when imagination remains accountable to evidence. In that balance between creation and control, synthetic data reveals its highest purpose: to make learning both safer and more just.

Case Study: Legal Firm and the Architecture of Insight

A multinational law firm offers a clear window into how intelligent architecture transforms complexity into capability. The firm's archives contained hundreds of thousands of legal contracts, scanned images, and multilingual correspondence accumulated over decades. For years, its teams catalogued only superficial metadata—author, date, jurisdiction—while the deeper structures of meaning remained sealed inside dense paragraphs and handwritten annotations. The true risk, as well as the hidden advantage, lay within these unexamined details. The firm's architects designed a layered analytic pipeline capable of seeing what storage alone could not. Optical character recognition unlocked text from images; named-entity recognition and clause classification surfaced relationships; and multilingual embeddings linked provisions across languages and jurisdictions. Together, these layers formed an environment where documents once inert became interpretable. Review cycles shortened from weeks to hours; risk assessment evolved from intuition to evidence.

The success stemmed from architectural intelligence, from a design that embraced unstructured complexity as the raw condition of learning and fused enrichment with governance into a single act of coherence. Its rewards emerged gradually yet decisively: efficiency evolved into clarity, clarity deepened into confidence, and confidence matured into trust between legal experts and the systems that extended their discernment. Through this evolution, the firm closed its readiness gap, Δ, transforming information into advantage and automation into credibility, measured in both the precision of its outcomes and the confidence with which people placed their trust in them.

Complexity As the New Constant

Complex data no longer sits at the margins of enterprise architecture; it forms its living center. From IoT telemetry to synthetic speech, from environmental sensors to digital twins, tomorrow's intelligence depends on architectures that can interpret nuance, tolerate ambiguity, and evolve with variation. The architect's role is not to impose uniformity but to create harmony within diversity, to design systems where multiplicity becomes strength. Here, the **Human Endpoint Principle** finds renewed meaning. Data gains are worthwhile only through the improvement they bring to human experience: safer communities, more responsive institutions, and more humane decisions. Mismanaging unstructured, semi-structured, or synthetic data diminishes more than system reliability; it erodes the trust that gives intelligence its mandate. Conversely, designing for complexity with care transforms architecture into ethics; it closes the readiness gap, *Δ*, and establishes AI as a practice of stewardship rather than a spectacle. When enterprises learn to treat data in all its forms as both material and responsibility, intelligence evolves beyond functionality into integrity, the hidden craftsmanship of systems built to serve.

4.5 Modern Data Foundations: Platforms, Fabric, and Synthetic Data

Enterprises once imagined data as something that lived in a single warehouse, a static vault where truth could be queried at will. That imagination has dissolved. Today's data foundation is modular, distributed, and intelligent; built not as a monument, but as a living system, responsive, adaptive, and self-aware. To compete in the *Anno Artificialis Intelligenciae*, organizations must design for continuity rather than consolidation: architectures that accommodate multiple data types, consumption patterns, and governance regimes without losing coherence under pressure.

Platforms As Living Systems

Modern platforms have moved beyond monoliths. Data lakes absorb vast unstructured volumes, warehouses provide curated data, and lakehouses merge both capacities into one continuum. Storage and compute have decoupled, elasticity has replaced rigidity, and open APIs now extend reach across environments. But this evolution is less about infrastructure than philosophy. Each design choice must translate the Four Pillars—Accessibility, Explainability, Security, and Ethics—into lived functionality, ensuring that intelligence serves rather than constrains. Lakehouse architectures exemplify this synthesis. Data arrives in raw zones, flows through curated layers, and emerges as governed assets consumable by analysts, scientists, and operational systems alike. Compute and storage, once bound in the same machinery, are now separate so that each can scale according to need. Within a single foundation, multiple perspectives coexist: one stream feeding a dashboard, another powering a model, both accountable to the same rules of governance. Architecture thus becomes translation itself, converting rawness into relevance and aligning the mechanics of computation with the intent of human value.

Fabric As Connective Structure

Platforms alone cannot create coherence. What binds them into integrity is the data fabric, the connective structure that extends across sources, tools, and environments. Unlike the rigid middleware or ETL chains of earlier eras, a data fabric is dynamic: it ingests new sources automatically, propagates metadata, and enforces policy throughout distributed domains. Its purpose is continuity, not control—an intelligent structure that allows local autonomy to coexist with enterprise-wide accountability. Technically, the fabric stretches across cloud and on-premises systems, batch and stream, edge and core. It enables federated queries without excessive movement, adapts to evolving workloads, and embeds lineage and policy enforcement into every path data travels. In essence, it is governance in motion, an architecture that makes visibility intrinsic and accountability perpetual.

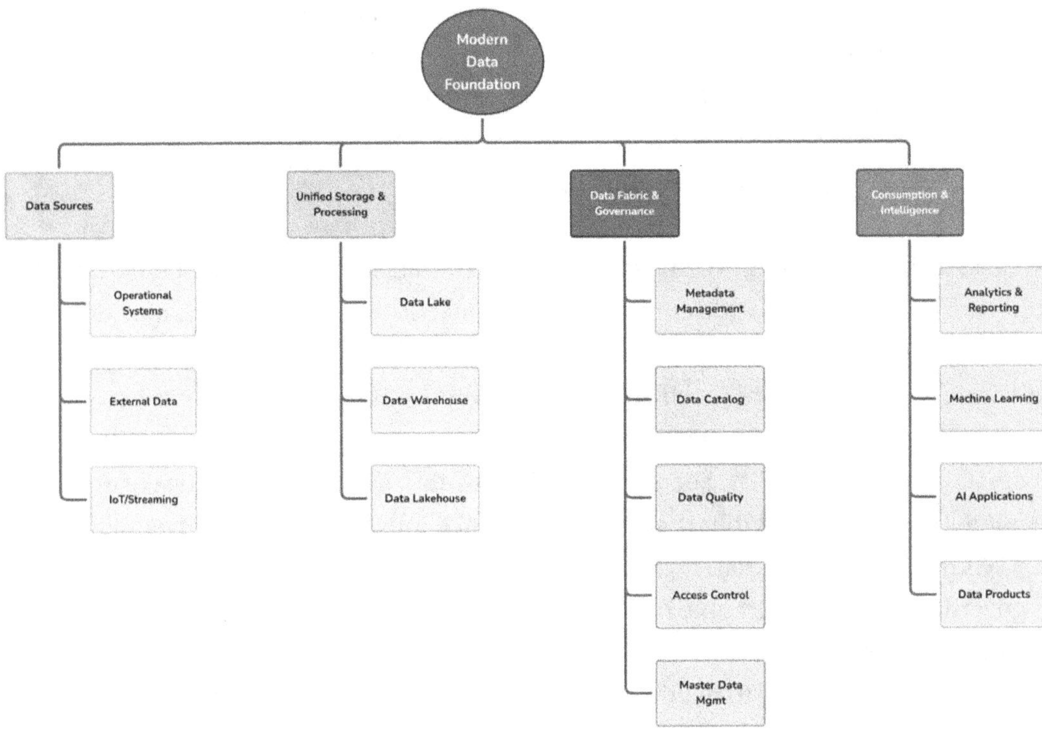

Figure 4-3. *Modern Data Foundations: Platforms, Fabric, and Flow*

Synthetic Data As First-Class Citizen

Among the most transformative additions to these modern foundations is synthetic data. Far from a novelty, it has become a structural necessity for enterprises facing privacy constraints, data scarcity, or exposure risk. Synthetic data allows safe experimentation, augments rare events, and enables models to train without violating consent. To earn this role, synthetic data must be governed with the same rigor as natural data.

Versioning, tagging, and lineage extend across synthetic sets; privacy-preserving techniques such as differential privacy, k-anonymity, and membership inference resistance must be applied with discipline. When pipelines are integrated and observable, synthetic augmentation strengthens the enterprise estate; when neglected, it becomes fragility disguised as innovation. Synthetic data's promise is realized only when imagination is tethered to accountability, when the freedom to create is matched by the discipline to care.

Case Study: Retail at Scale

The story began, as many transformations do, with fatigue. The retailer's systems were prolific but fragmented: point-of-sale terminals in thousands of stores, ecommerce engines, IoT sensors across warehouses, and mobile applications through which millions of customers moved daily. Each source spoke a different dialect; each generated truths that failed to meet. Brittle ETL scripts strained to hold them together, funneling fragments into isolated warehouses that produced reports already outdated by the time they arrived. Leadership sensed the danger not in analytics itself but in trust; decisions were being made on partial vision. Change began slowly, not as disruption but as redesign. Architects rebuilt the data foundation from first principles. Raw events now streamed continuously into a unified lake, enriched in motion and catalogued as they formed. A data fabric synchronized access across regions, applying governance as an act of design rather than constraint, ensuring that privacy laws were honored even as insights traveled freely. Synthetic datasets were introduced to model customer behavior, giving the enterprise room to experiment without touching sensitive records.

The difference revealed itself in tempo and temperament. Forecasts became more adaptive; personalization evolved from approximation to understanding; and customers, once wary of inconsistencies, began to trust the brand's recommendations as if it understood context, not just consumption. Internally, analysts moved from reconciliation to exploration. What had once been a chain of tasks became a field of awareness. The readiness gap, Δ, began to close in the most sustainable way, through coherence. Return on AI Investment (ROAI) began to express itself as a lived condition rather than a metric. Churn eased, lifetime value expanded, and regulatory approvals moved swiftly because transparency was intrinsic to the design. Although the greater achievement unfolded beyond the dashboards. The enterprise had touched a deeper constant within every intelligent system, that is, the understanding that progress acquires meaning only when guided by intention and that the architecture of trust endures longer than any advantage built on speed or scale.

Sustainability and GreenOps

Scale carries more than computational weight; it carries moral consequence. Every byte stored, every model trained, and every request processed has a physical echo in the world, an exchange of energy, heat, and resources. Data foundations are not immaterial. They exist in steel, silicon, and water; they alter geographies and economies alike. Sustainability, therefore, is not an afterthought to architecture but its ethical core. To design responsibly is to recognize that digital scale transforms into environmental demand. Data centers draw from rivers and power grids; they reshape skylines and nightscapes. Communities that host them trade opportunity for noise, light, and scarcity. The architect who ignores these exchanges designs only half a system.

GreenOps, practices that align operational excellence with ecological stewardship, translate awareness into engineering. Carbon-aware scheduling, renewable integration, and workload optimization become acts of conscience as much as efficiency. Sustainability, in this sense, is not an external virtue but an inner discipline of design. It is architecture's way of remembering that intelligence draws its energy from the same world it seeks to improve. When we neglect that reciprocity, our foundations close one readiness gap while opening another, between human ambition and planetary endurance. The only equilibrium worth achieving is one that binds performance with preservation, reminding us that the future we automate is also the one we inhabit.

Designing for Flexibility

Future readiness rests on neutrality and openness, the ability of systems to evolve without erasing their history. Open table formats such as Delta Lake, Apache Iceberg, and Apache Hudi embody this principle. They preserve transactional reliability while freeing enterprises from the confines of proprietary warehouses. Container orchestration frameworks such as Kubernetes extend the same logic of portability across environments, allowing workloads to move fluidly between cloud and on-premises systems. Federated query engines continue the pattern, bringing analysis to where data resides instead of forcing data to migrate. Together, these architectures create modular foundations, structures that sustain growth without rigidity, evolve without reinvention, and scale without distortion. This flexibility embodies the enterprise payoff equation: it raises the probability of success (p) by preserving optionality, amplifies benefits (B) by widening applications, and reduces costs (C) by avoiding wholesale re-platforming. Within such foundations, flexibility ceases to be an indulgence; it becomes a strategy, the elusive discipline of staying coherent amid change.

The Human Endpoint of Foundations

Modern foundations are easy to overlook because they succeed in silence. When they function, they disappear; when they falter, they briefly surface as failure. But beneath this invisibility lies a paradox that defines the *Anno Artificialis Intelligenciae*: the most abstract systems are also the most intimate. Every foundation, however technical, becomes an instrument of consequence. A resilient platform carries the alert that prevents financial loss; a governed system ensures that a diagnosis remains confidential; a sustainable data center preserves the stillness of a village night. Architecture, in this sense, is not neutral. It mediates between decision and destiny. The **Human Endpoint Principle** reaches its fullest articulation here.

The purpose of a foundation is not elegance for its own sake but the extension of dignity, the translation of computational integrity into human assurance. Foundations form the moral economy of enterprise; they mediate between efficiency and empathy, between what can be optimized and what must remain inviolate. They transform the abstract payoff equation of intelligence, $\boldsymbol{U} = \boldsymbol{p} \times \boldsymbol{B} - \boldsymbol{C}$, into lived experience, where *p* becomes the probability of trust, *B* the benefit of inclusion, and *C* the cost of indifference. When architecture is conceived with such awareness, intelligence evolves from calculation into conscience. Systems begin to serve without excess, to anticipate without prejudice, and to operate with humility toward the lives their outcomes shape. In that light, every data foundation becomes a moral act, that is, a structure through which responsibility takes form and endurance acquires meaning.

The modern enterprise stands, therefore, at a decisive threshold. It may continue to construct infrastructure that measures speed while overlooking significance, or it may regard each foundation as an ethical proposition: a deliberate act to protect, to empower, and to preserve. To design with care is to design with conscience. To build foundations that endure is to close the readiness gap, $\boldsymbol{\Delta}$, not simply between ambition and capability, but across the deeper divide that separates power from purpose and intention from impact. Such work transforms architecture into ethics; it turns design into an act of responsibility. This is the enduring vocation of stewardship: designing systems that strengthen discernment, sustain trust, and guide intelligence to advance in harmony with human purpose.

Conclusion: Data As the Ground of Intelligent Enterprise

Throughout this chapter, one truth has surfaced in many forms: **data is the ground upon which intelligent enterprise stands**. Ambition, investment, and algorithmic prowess amount to little if the foundation that sustains them is brittle. Across industries, the lesson repeats itself in different guises: pilots that falter under scale, governance gaps that erode confidence, and archives that conceal more liability than insight. However it appears, the readiness gap, $\boldsymbol{\Delta}$, always begins here. Only by confronting the condition of their data can enterprises move from experiment to endurance. We began by reframing AI strategy as data strategy, recognizing that intelligence cannot be appended to an enterprise; it must be cultivated within it. Data flows become the conduits of intent, translating value streams into decisions. Legacy systems, once dismissed as constraints, reveal their strength when approached with pragmatism: repositories of history, memory, and resilience. Discovery, governance, and integration are not administrative chores; they are architectural disciplines, the hidden labor through which intelligence acquires integrity.

From there, we followed the movement of data through pipelines, the circulation of enterprise life. When these pipelines are conceived as enduring products rather than disposable scripts, reliability and observability transform them into vessels of trust. Through them, the payoff equation of adoption finds living form: $\boldsymbol{U = p \times B - C}$. Reliable lineage raises p, operational efficiency reduces C, and meaningful insight amplifies B. Pipelines, in that sense, are not plumbing but judgment rendered visible in code. We then turned to governance, the structure that converts responsibility into practice. Far from slowing progress, governance ensures that progress lasts. Lineage, accountability, and stewardship transform opacity into transparency. Privacy-preserving architectures such as federated learning and Constitutional AI extend this discipline further, encoding fairness, dignity, and proportionality into learning itself. Governance becomes the architecture of endurance: the structure that allows intelligence to accelerate without losing its ethical coherence. From structure, we moved to substance, to unstructured, semi-structured, and synthetic data, the unruly matter of the modern enterprise. Here, complexity becomes both a challenge and a catalyst. To design for it is to accept that intelligence must learn to interpret ambiguity rather than eliminate it. Synthetic augmentation and advanced embeddings expand the frontier of understanding, provided they are governed with care. Complexity ungoverned creates harm; complexity disciplined becomes trust.

Finally, we arrived at the modern data foundation: the platform, the fabric, and the synthetic layer, all conceived as living architecture. These systems embody the Four Pillars of enterprise AI—Accessibility, Explainability, Security, and Ethics—by turning principle into daily operation. They remind us that architecture extends beyond code into the physical world. Every query and model draws energy, consumes water, and alters the landscapes that host our computation. GreenOps enters as responsibility made visible, the ecological conscience of digital design and the discipline through which performance and preservation sustain each other.

Taken together, these movements resolve into a single principle: enterprises that treat data as lifeblood rather than exhaust transform intelligence from aspiration into capability. They close their readiness gap, Δ, turning fragile pilots into enduring systems and converting investment into sustainable ROAI. Those that ignore this foundation will continue to confuse motion with progress, watching their prototypes fracture under the weight of scale. Through every layer of this chapter runs the **Human Endpoint Principle**. Data matters only for its consequences in human life, for the patient treated more safely, the customer served more fairly, and the community shielded from harm. Architecture fulfills its purpose when design matures into integrity, when structure enables responsibility, and when capability extends the reach of human trust.

As we descend in Chapter 5 into the physical substrate of intelligence, that is, the data centers, grids, and geographies that sustain computation, we will see how digital architecture meets material consequence. Scale, energy, and sustainability will reveal themselves as ethical questions, not operational ones. And later, in Chapter 7, we will return to the moral horizon of enterprise AI: the guardrails that ensure innovation remains coherent with trust. ***Data is where intelligence begins.*** Governed with rigor, enriched with awareness, and designed with human dignity in view, it becomes the contemplative architecture of wisdom, the ground upon which ambition finds its balance and progress its purpose.

CHAPTER 5

Architecting AI at Scale: Technical Patterns and Platforms

Introduction: The Architecture Beneath Intelligence

Every architecture begins with a question of weight: ***How much intelligence can the earth bear, and at what cost?*** For years, we have spoken of artificial intelligence as if it lived in the air, an ethereal code moving freely through invisible clouds. But intelligence, in its enterprise form, is **material**. It draws water, consumes power, and occupies land. It hums in the night through transformers and cooling towers. The farther we scale it, the more it demands from the world that sustains it. This chapter enters that physical terrain, that is, the architecture beneath cognition. Where earlier chapters examined data, governance, and ethics as the logic of enterprise AI, we now confront infrastructure as its body. The story of scale moves through growth into gravity, tracing the slow, irreversible pull of ambition toward matter.

Across the world, vast data centers rise on reclaimed farmland and riverbeds, built to feed the computational hunger of models that never sleep. In Mansfield, Georgia, a family's well water turns opaque from the sediment of a nearby data complex, a reminder that even the purest algorithm runs through pipes that touch the ground. And across the enterprises we studied, from financial networks to public institutions, the same truth emerges: the promise of intelligence is inseparable from its physical and ethical cost. The readiness gap (**Δ**) we spoke of earlier, between ambition and capability,

R. Harjika, *Architecting Enterprise AI Strategies*, https://doi.org/10.1007/979-8-8688-2219-3_5

acquires a new dimension here: the gap between what we imagine as virtual and what we extract as real. To build responsibly at this scale demands more than technology. It demands architectural conscience, an awareness that systems have footprints, that innovation must coexist with ecology, and that every watt drawn in pursuit of insight leaves a trace. Scale is no longer neutral; it is an ethical decision disguised as engineering.

This chapter unfolds as a construction sequence, each layer rising gently upon the next until intelligence stands as a complete and sustainable architecture, a structure of meaning built with intention, an architecture where every element contributes to purpose rather than parts:

- **The Foundation** forms the ground of this architecture. It explores how infrastructures reconcile sovereignty, latency, and environmental stewardship, teaching enterprises that true scale begins with ethical weight and spatial awareness.
- **The Framework** emerges upon it, transforming the chaos of experimentation into the discipline of design. Here, platforms and LLMOps become instruments of melody, ensuring that every model, once deployed, continues to learn with integrity.
- **The Circuits** give the structure its nervous system, where retrieval, context, and lineage interconnect to form memory. Through them, imagination gains accountability, and data finds its moral coherence.
- **The Envelope** holds these layers together through governance. It translates transparency and lineage into trust, ensuring that every phase of the model's life remains answerable to its purpose.
- **The Living Structure** crowns the design. It brings agency into the architecture, integrating intelligent systems that perceive, plan, and act in collaboration with their human counterparts, becoming companions in creation.

Together, these layers reveal how intelligence becomes architecture and how architecture becomes conscience. Each layer will trace a single theme: that scale must serve integrity before ambition. In doing so, we return to the central philosophy of this book, that the true measure of technological maturity is not how far it reaches, but how humanly it endures.

5.1 The Foundation: Designing Infrastructure for Scale

Scaling intelligence is ultimately a question of geography. Every computation must live somewhere, on a board, in a rack, inside a building, or upon the land. To design infrastructure for AI is therefore to negotiate between three forces: **sovereignty, latency, and sustainability**. Each decision, from where data resides to where models train and where inference runs, becomes a moral geometry of distance and impact.

The Physical Weight of Intelligence

The industrial monuments of this decade are not smokestacks but data centers. In the town of Mansfield, Georgia, the glow of a two-gigawatt facility washes across pine fields once dark enough for stars. Residents now draw water that carries the sediment of nearby cooling systems. What began as a promise of digital prosperity has become a contest over light, noise, and the right to quiet nights. Here, the readiness gap (**Δ**) takes on a tangible form: the gap between the clean abstraction of the cloud and the physical labor of keeping it cold. Such places remind us that scale is never free. A single frontier model can consume tens of gigawatt-hours in months of training, its appetite rippling through regional grids already strained by industrial demand. When multiplied across global inference workloads, the arithmetic of intelligence becomes ecological, a ledger of carbon and consequence. Across our research, several enterprises described this paradox vividly: the same infrastructure that powered their digital acceleration also magnified their energy footprint and privacy risk. ***The question is no longer whether we can build; it is how responsibly we can sustain what we build.***

Hybrid Architectures As Ethical Design

The technical answer to scale is often framed as topology: on-prem, cloud, or edge. But the ethical answer is **hybridity**: distributing computation with awareness of consequence.

On-premises environments give architecture its sense of sovereignty and predictability. They remain essential where trust depends on jurisdiction, in hospitals safeguarding patient records, or in national banks protecting financial data. These systems embody stability, but stability also hardens. Hardware ages faster than purpose, and the infrastructure that once symbolized control can become rigid before its ethics mature. Cloud environments, by contrast, expand through elasticity and speed. They democratize experimentation and make scale available to anyone with imagination, but they also conceal volatility such as shifting costs, hidden dependencies, and unfamiliar governance boundaries. Without careful oversight, a single surge in model training or inference can outpace both budget and compliance. At the opposite edge of the network, intelligence returns to its point of origin. In factories, ports, and logistics hubs, Edge AI operates where data is born, interpreting sensor signals and making decisions in real time. By keeping computation close to the event, it minimizes latency and sustains operations even when connectivity falters. The edge restores a sense of locality to the digital world; it reminds enterprises that cognition, however distributed, still begins with place.

A hybrid design, interlacing these modes, becomes both technically resilient and ethically responsive, with computation drawn close to sensitivity, spun out when elasticity is harmless, and brought back home when stewardship demands control. To achieve this, next-generation infrastructures adopt AI-adaptive orchestration: lightweight inference running on CPUs or neural engines and high-intensity training reserved for GPUs and TPUs only when necessary. This orchestration prevents the silent waste of stranded compute, machines running without intention, consuming energy without contribution. In restoring alignment between capacity and purpose, efficiency becomes an act of integrity, and architecture becomes the visible expression of ethics in motion.

Vendor Independence and Strategic Autonomy

Enterprise resilience flourishes through a clear focus on vendor independence. As organizations deploy AI at scale, thoughtful choices in provider relationships support long-term flexibility and adaptation. Vendor partnerships can bring strategic advantages, but when tools and data integrate deeply with a single provider's ecosystem, a new kind of dependency emerges, one that shapes pricing, contractual terms, and innovation pathways. Enterprises cultivate autonomy by adopting multi-cloud strategies that distribute AI workloads across platforms such as OpenAI, Google Cloud, AWS, and open source solutions. This balanced approach ensures that no single platform defines operational continuity. Organizations further strengthen independence by embracing open standards, including models and API abstraction layers that ease migration and retraining whenever strategy evolves. Thoughtful contracting practices, such as including data portability requirements, clear exit provisions, and audit mechanisms, promote lasting autonomy. When architects incorporate these principles by design, they uphold business adaptability and confidence along with strong stewardship of infrastructure. In this way, a proactive vendor strategy becomes as foundational to enterprise architecture as energy sustainability and ethical governance.

GreenOps: Energy As a Design Constraint

In the language of infrastructure, energy has always been a cost. In the language of stewardship, it must become a variable of design. This is the discipline of GreenOps: treating every kilowatt as an architectural decision. Workloads can be scheduled when renewable supply peaks; inference can be routed to energy-efficient processors or low-carbon regions; cooling systems can draw reclaimed water rather than fresh reserves. GreenOps transforms sustainability from a corporate aspiration into an operational grammar. When embedded in governance dashboards, it links financial and ecological ledgers, turning Return on AI Investment (ROAI) into a measure not only of revenue but of responsibility.

Across industries, lifecycle telemetry has begun to mirror a broader awakening. Dashboards now track carbon intensity, model efficiency, and data center load alongside latency and accuracy, revealing that sustainability is no longer an external audit but an operational state of being. GreenOps transforms this awareness into practice. It teaches that wisdom in the age of intelligence is measured not by the volume of data processed, but by the discernment with which energy is given purpose.

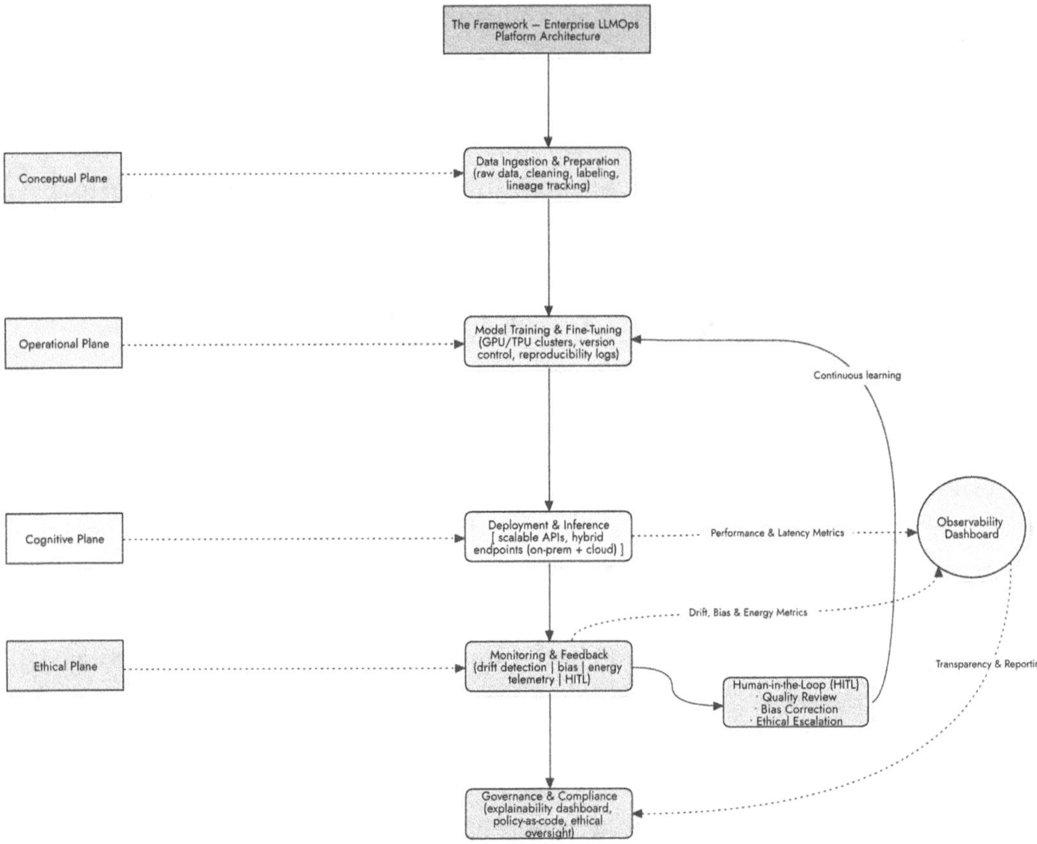

Figure 5-1. *Ethical Hybrid Infrastructure for Sustainable AI*

Every allocation of power becomes a design decision, and every design decision a statement of care. In this way, energy becomes part of the ethical architecture of enterprise systems, where every watt expended reflects a decision about purpose, responsibility, and care.

Material Stewardship: From Extraction to Responsibility

The environmental ledger of AI includes more than energy and carbon; it encompasses the full trajectory of material resources. Every advance in model performance is supported by hardware innovation and refreshed electronics. ***E-waste*** from hardware updates and the global demand for rare earth minerals for GPU manufacturing present opportunities for thoughtful stewardship and ethical practice. As models grow, hardware cycles quicken, and obsolete processors give way to more capable systems, creating streams of used silicon. Organizations can guide positive change by promoting device lifecycles that support modular upgrades, encouraging recycling initiatives that recover valuable materials, and choosing suppliers committed to responsible mining and environmental restoration. With a full lifecycle approach to GreenOps, sustainability reaches from infrastructure energy use to the long-term footprint of hardware and manufacturing. This perspective acknowledges the substantial, real-world impact of intelligence at scale and affirms enterprise commitment to communities, ecosystems, and the future.

The Latency Paradox and Edge Resilience

Modern enterprises face a paradox: the farther data travels, the more intelligent it becomes, yet the slower it feels. In manufacturing and logistics, milliseconds decide safety and loss. By situating predictive models at the edge, organizations reclaim immediacy. A robotic arm that senses vibration, analyzes it locally, and pauses before failure demonstrates intelligence not through magnitude but through proximity. The closer cognition moves to reality, the less waste it leaves behind. Latency, then, is not solely a technical variable but an ethical one: it determines whether intelligence serves or endangers. To respond in time is to act with care; to delay is to abandon stewardship. This is the temporal morality of scale, to design as though every millisecond carries a consequence.

The Geometry of Readiness

True scalability lies not in size but in alignment between compute demand and human purpose. Infrastructure that ignores community costs or environmental thresholds may deliver speed but forfeits legitimacy. Conversely, architectures that integrate sovereignty, latency, and sustainability achieve equilibrium: systems that grow without displacing the world that hosts them. Our research found that organizations achieving such balance also reported the strongest ROAI: efficiency gains coupled with trust retention. They understood that scalability without empathy is fragility disguised as progress. Designing infrastructure for AI, then, is no longer a contest between on-prem and cloud; it is an act of balancing the Four Pillars—Accessibility, Explainability, Security, and Ethics—across physical space. The most advanced data center is not the one that trains the largest model, but the one whose lights can dim without darkening trust.

Design As Care

The infrastructure of intelligence is, in truth, the architecture of our conscience, for every server that hums in a distant hall draws silently from a shared reservoir of power, water, and human patience, and every decision to expand computational reach reshapes the landscape that sustains it. To design at scale, then, is to acknowledge that engineering is no longer a neutral craft but an ecological act, one that binds ambition to responsibility and translates technological foresight into environmental and social care. In this understanding, the question facing every enterprise shifts from how much intelligence can be built to how wisely it can be situated within the fragile equilibrium of the living world. A data center that illuminates the skyline also redraws the boundaries of rivers and forests; the readiness gap (Δ) between aspiration and capability thus extends beyond technical maturity into moral geography. Closing that gap becomes less about increasing performance and more about ensuring coherence between progress and preservation, between what is optimized and what is owed. The enterprises that manage to bridge this divide learn that sustainability is not the restraint of ambition but its refinement, the discipline through which power learns balance.

Within this architecture, GreenOps emerges as both method and metaphor, translating ethical awareness into operational grammar. When workloads are scheduled according to renewable cycles, when inference is routed to efficient processors, and when energy use is tracked with the same precision as financial cost, stewardship ceases to be a corporate aspiration and becomes a form of literacy. The carbon cost of training large language models is significant, often mirroring the energy required for transatlantic flights in CO_2 emissions. Sustainability moves from aspiration to operational necessity as every model, training cycle, and inference workload carries measurable environmental impact throughout the enterprise. GreenOps practices integrate carbon awareness into each infrastructure decision: scheduling workloads to align with renewable energy, routing inference to processors optimized for efficiency, and tracking carbon impact with the same rigor as financial performance. In this framework, efficiency and sustainability work together; organizations that prioritize carbon reduction strengthen cost control and operational resilience while elevating their stewardship of natural resources.

In that shift, ROAI, Return on AI Investment, gains a second meaning: no longer confined to profit or efficiency, it begins to measure trust, longevity, and the harmonious reciprocity between human systems and natural ones. To design with care is to think across scales: from the nanoseconds of computation to the decades of consequence. It is to understand that optimization detached from context is simply acceleration without direction, that efficiency achieved at the cost of exhaustion is not progress but depletion in disguise. Engineers, architects, and policymakers must come to see themselves as stewards of evolving systems, attentive to the unseen exchanges of energy and data, and committed to shaping infrastructures that can adapt with the transformation of human values.

Architecture, in this sense, becomes a practice of empathy, translating technical precision into ethical balance. The intelligence we construct cannot transcend the world it draws from; it must learn to exist in tune with it. Every watt of power, every data packet in motion, every cooling loop, and every carbon ledger represents an ethical sentence in the story of enterprise. When organizations learn to read these sentences with comprehension, design itself becomes a language of respect, a recognition that the true measure of intelligence lies not in its capacity to dominate but in its ability to coexist. The finest architectures of the coming age will be those that innovate without erasing, that expand without depleting, and that recognize, subtly but irrevocably, that care is not an addition to design but its very beginning.

5.2 The Framework: Building AI Platforms and LLMOps—From MLOps to Guardrails

If infrastructure is the body of enterprise intelligence, the platform is its **nervous system**, the network that coordinates perception, action, and reflection. It is what transforms computation into cognition and carries cognition forward into sustained intelligence. Without this system of orchestration, intelligence remains a collection of isolated models, clever but fragile, powerful but ungoverned.

From MLOps to LLMOps: When Control Meets Conscience

MLOps began in an era of prediction, a time governed by the certainty of numbers and the comfort of supervised truth. It was a discipline that valued precision through control, designed to keep algorithms steady within measurable boundaries. A new temperament of intelligence, one that generates, associates, and interprets instead of just computing, replaced this stability with the introduction of large language models. The evolution from MLOps to LLMOps is therefore not a shift in tooling but a reorientation of responsibility. It asks enterprises to move from command to guidance, from parameter management to behavioral understanding, and from engineering accuracy to nurturing accountability. Across organizations, our research revealed a recurring pattern: quality control failures have slowly become the most expensive consequence of generative adoption. Executives described the same paradox: automation designed to save time often demanded more of it.

Teams spent long nights repairing what the models produced in haste, an experience they recalled with measured fatigue as "***fixing the trash***." What began as an experiment in efficiency gradually revealed the hidden anatomy of fragility. Every hallucinated report, every fabricated citation, and every misplaced tone demanded human correction, consuming the very hours automation was meant to spare. The promise of scale thus turned inward, transforming creation into maintenance and invention into remediation. Human effort shifted from shaping ideas to salvaging outputs, and in that reversal, the enterprise confronted its own reflection: intelligence built without reflection soon creates more noise than knowledge. Technically, this pattern exposed the silent accumulation of **quality debt**, errors that propagate through datasets, retraining loops, and decision logs, compounding over time. In the absence of feedback architectures, each model's drift multiplies unseen, forcing teams to reassert control through endless manual oversight. What appeared as automation on the surface often depended, beneath it, on human labor stretched thin across systems too shallow to self-correct. The myth of autonomy gave way to the reality of dependence, where machines spoke fluently but learned little from their mistakes.

To bridge the readiness gap (**Δ**), platforms must evolve from pipelines of execution into ecosystems of reflection. In this maturity, the goal becomes alignment between performance and purpose, ensuring that every action within the system contributes to understanding. A reflective platform studies itself with the same precision it applies to data, tracing lineage across model versions, observing fidelity in every output, and translating anomalies into structured feedback loops. Through this continuous learning, each correction enriches the system's knowledge of its own boundaries and potential. This reflective capacity defines the difference between efficiency that fades and competence that endures. It transforms maintenance into education, allowing governance to operate as a continuous dialogue between insight and adaptation. Within such architectures, control expresses itself through coherence; freedom finds form through discipline. Innovation advances with responsibility, experimentation expands with awareness, and every element of design contributes to reliability. At this point of equilibrium, control matures into conscience, the living quality of architectures that understand their own operation and purpose. Enterprises that cultivate such systems guide intelligence with discernment, shaping technologies that grow in judgment as they grow in capability. The art of stewardship reveals itself here as a practical discipline, where every improvement deepens trust, every iteration strengthens clarity, and every design decision affirms that understanding is the highest form of efficiency.

The Architecture of the Platform

At enterprise scale, an AI platform must be understood not as a toolchain but as an ecosystem, a living environment that unites development, deployment, governance, and ethics into a single, evolving organism. Within this ecosystem, the architecture expresses itself through four interwoven planes: the **conceptual**, the **operational**, the **cognitive**, and the **ethical**. Each plane sustains the others, forming a continuous cycle of knowledge, action, reasoning, and accountability.

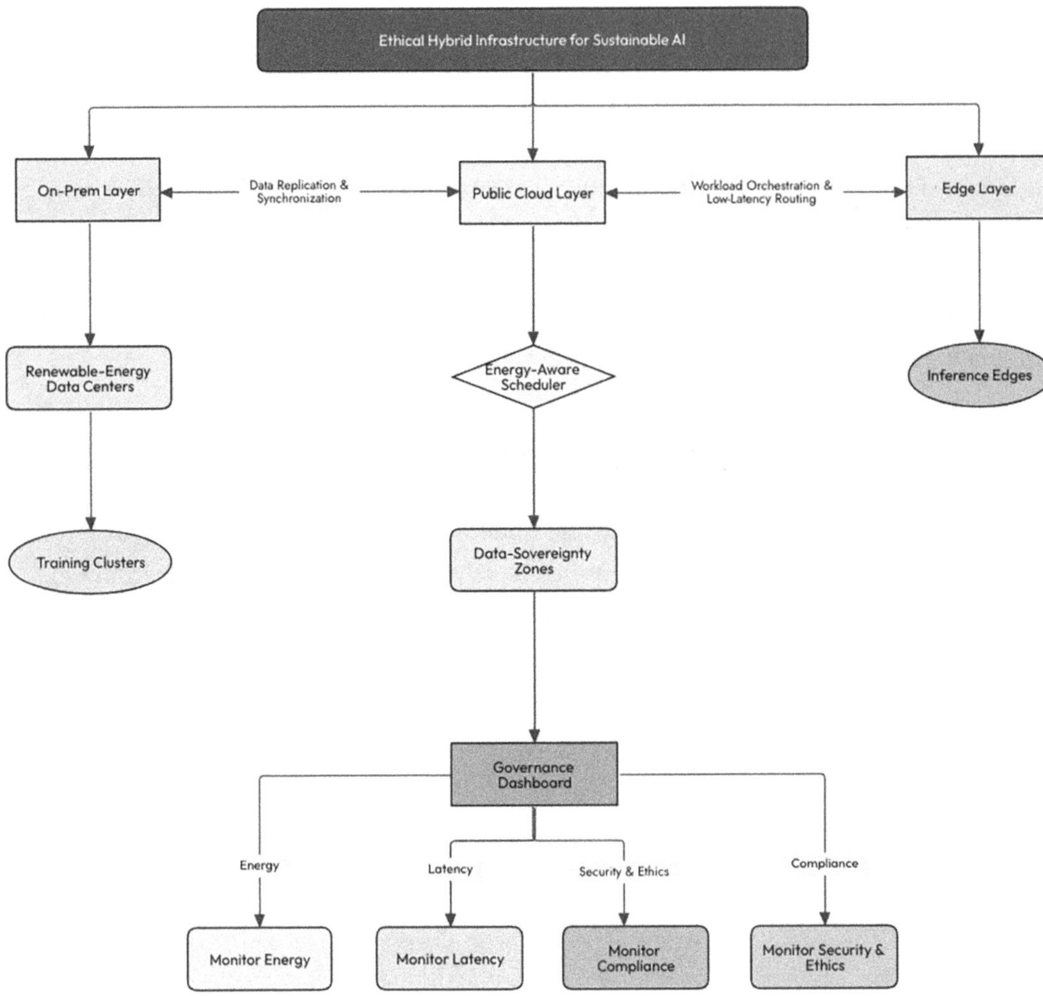

***Figure 5-2.** The Framework: Enterprise LLMOps Platform Architecture*

The **conceptual plane** establishes the platform's sense of identity and context. Every model must understand the domain it inhabits and the boundaries within which it speaks. Enterprises now embed contextual layers into their platforms, constructing shared vocabularies, policy ontologies, and controlled terminologies that anchor meaning in the language of the business itself. This practice resolves a foundational problem in AI adoption: generic models that lack domain awareness often produce confident but hollow answers. A model trained on legal documents must speak with the discipline of law rather than the generality of language; one trained for medicine must think clinically, not conversationally. Context becomes the first architecture of trust.

The **operational plane** sustains the structure of learning. Earlier approaches to machine learning focused on continuous integration and deployment; LLMOps extends this into continuous learning. Feedback becomes a formal component of the system, and retraining occurs as a natural flow rather than a crisis response. Pipelines evolve into loops of reflection, measuring drift as a sign of life rather than decay. Each iteration restores balance between the model's internal assumptions and the world's changing data, creating what might be called the heartbeat of enterprise cognition.

The **cognitive plane** represents the reasoning mind of the architecture. Generative models, left unguided, often wander into invention; they imagine more than they understand. To balance freedom with fidelity, platforms now embed layered guardrails, retrieval grounding that connects responses to authoritative data, toxicity and bias filters that preserve dignity and equity, and factual validators that monitor the integrity of output. These mechanisms are not constraints on creativity; they are expressions of architectural ethics. By giving imagination a framework, they transform language generation into reasoning with responsibility.

Finally, the **ethical plane** gives form to governance. Policy and principle are no longer abstract ideals written in compliance manuals; they now reside directly within the code. Audit trails, explainability dashboards, and lineage graphs render accountability transparent and verifiable. Validation APIs ensure that ethics is not peripheral to design but embedded within it. Governance, within this evolving architecture, becomes the practice of coherence, the deliberate act of holding motion and meaning in equilibrium. It gives innovation a center from which to grow, ensuring that every expansion of intelligence still carries the signature of intention.

Through this coherence, the four planes—conceptual, operational, cognitive, and ethical—form more than a framework; they create a living system of conscience and capability. Knowledge grants the platform identity, operations sustain its movement, cognition refines its understanding, and ethics restores its balance. When these dimensions operate in harmony, the platform evolves from an engineered system to an organizational culture, a space where intelligence matures through awareness, where growth advances through reflection, and where design manifests responsibility as a defining principle of progress.

Guardrails and the Anatomy of Trust

Hallucinations, misinformation, and model bias are not side effects; they are structural expressions of design choices. When enterprises deploy without guardrails, they delegate judgment to chance. When they integrate them, they convert trust into architecture. A robust LLMOps environment therefore carries layered safeguards:

- **Pre-generation Filters:** Cleanse prompts for sensitive data, regulatory conflicts, or proprietary leakage.
- **Retrieval-Aware Reasoning:** Attach authoritative context (via RAG or internal knowledge bases) before the model answers.
- **Post-validation:** Cross-check outputs against internal datasets, rejecting anything unverifiable.
- **Feedback Collection:** Capture user corrections, tone adjustments, and factual edits, feeding them back into the learning loop.

These layers create closed accountability circuits. Each decision, dataset, and correction becomes part of the system's living memory, transforming the platform from a workflow to a moral instrument.

Overreliance and the Erosion of Human Judgment

A recurring theme in our research was the risk of overreliance. When tools become oracles, people stop asking questions. Enterprises described how junior analysts accepted model outputs unquestioned, how design teams lost confidence in their own creativity, and how decision meetings became recitations of AI summaries rather than spaces of debate. This erosion of agency is subtle but profound. The role of a platform is not to replace human thought but to return it to its higher function: synthesis, discernment, and ethics. This is why Human-In-The-Loop (HITL) processes must not be compliance rituals; they are points of moral intervention. They remind the enterprise that intelligence without empathy is computation without purpose. At scale, HITL can be codified: approval workflows, escalation thresholds, and override permissions. Each becomes a channel through which human judgment flows back into the circuit, restoring reflection to automation and embedding integrity as part of the design itself.

Governance Automation and Observability

In mature enterprises, governance is no longer an afterthought. It operates as telemetry: every prompt, retrieval, inference, and correction is recorded in observability lakes. Bias metrics, latency drift, carbon intensity, and user satisfaction now share a common dashboard. This is how ethics becomes a data stream. Regulators across the globe increasingly demand continuous demonstration of compliance. Platforms that present telemetry as living evidence of their performance transform governance into an active strength, turning accountability into advantage and transparency into measurable value.

Designing for Resilience and ROAI

The Return on AI Investment (ROAI) is often measured in efficiency and scale. But real ROAI arises from endurance: systems that remain accurate, auditable, and adaptive as data, law, and culture evolve. This is why LLMOps is not an operational choice; it is an ethical necessity. A platform that tracks its own drift, measures its energy, explains its decisions, and respects human oversight generates a kind of compound interest of trust. Over time, that trust outperforms any short-term gain from speed. In the payoff equation ($U = p \times B - C$), *p* becomes not the probability of output accuracy but the probability of ethical reliability, which is the true multiplier of benefit.

Intelligence in Service

The platform is a living architecture through which an enterprise expresses its values. Within its layers, the Four Pillars of Accessibility, Explainability, Security, and Ethics find tangible form, transforming governance from policy into practice. When design invites listening as naturally as calculation and allows learning to emerge from correction, intelligence becomes a shared discipline. The platform evolves into a cultural language, an environment where systems refine purpose alongside people, and technology matures through reflection as much as through precision. In such a structure, computation turns into comprehension, and insight acquires the grace of responsibility. Maturity in the AI enterprise reveals itself through the harmony of human and machine thought. This equilibrium bridges the readiness gap (Δ), aligning innovation with discernment and ambition with stewardship. Return on AI Investment (ROAI) unfolds through trust that endures, trust in design, process, and intent. Platforms conceived in this way transform efficiency into empathy, data into judgment, and architecture into sustained care. Through this integration, the enterprise attains its most human architecture, intelligence shaped by awareness, guided by balance, and sustained by the delicate discipline of dignity in action.

5.3 The Circuits: LLM-Native Architecture—RAG Pipelines, Vector Stores, and Contextual Retrieval

If the infrastructure is the body and the platform its nervous system, the circuits are the synapses through which knowledge flows and meaning stabilizes. They determine whether a model speaks from authority or improvises from illusion. In this terrain, the governing design principle is clear: context is the new compute.

From Static Models to Context-Aware Systems

Traditional models carried their knowledge within parameters: billions of weights frozen at the moment of training. They were magnificent historians of the past but poor witnesses of the present. Across enterprises, this rigidity created fragility; intelligence detached from current data soon drifts into error. Models hallucinate, misquote, and legislate from outdated memory. The remedy is LLM-native architecture, in which the model learns to fetch, ground, and verify rather than recall by rote. This evolution is realized through Retrieval-Augmented Generation (RAG), a pattern that connects large language models to live, authoritative, and governed data. Where MLOps industrialized training, RAG industrializes truth.

The RAG Pipeline: Anatomy of a Cognitive Loop

A functional RAG system behaves like a thought cycle, continually perceiving, reasoning, and remembering.

- **Ingestion and Indexing:** Documents, logs, and structured tables pass through preprocessing pipelines that cleanse, deduplicate, and segment information into semantically coherent units. Metadata captures provenance—author, timestamp, and jurisdiction—forming the base of data lineage.
- **Embedding and Vectorization:** Each unit is converted into a high-dimensional vector that represents its meaning numerically. These embeddings are stored in vector databases such as Milvus, Pinecone, or Weaviate, optimized for rapid similarity search. The vector store becomes the memory cortex of the enterprise: compact, searchable, and continuously refreshed.

- **Retrieval and Ranking:** When a query arrives, the engine embeds the question, explores the vector space, and ranks results through hybrid similarity and metadata filters. Advanced systems use semantic re-ranking that combines geometric distance with domain-specific confidence scoring, privileging audited sources over unverified ones.
- **Prompt Assembly and Grounded Generation:** Retrieved passages are woven into the model prompt along with policy instructions and disclaimers. Contextual grounding restrains imagination and replaces invention with reference. Factuality checkers and citation verifiers close the loop before the response leaves the system.
- **Feedback and Lineage Logging:** Every retrieval, citation, and generation step is recorded. These logs flow into the LLMOps observability layer, updating drift detectors and bias monitors. The process becomes self-documenting, turning accountability into architecture.

Through these stages, the model evolves from a storyteller to a contextual reasoner, which is a system that converses with its own evidence.

Vector Stores: The Memory Architecture of Trust

Human memory forgets to stay sane; machine memory must forget to stay lawful. Vector stores provide this discipline. They compress language into geometry, allow differential privacy through vector re-projection, and enforce access control so that a query retrieves only what it role may view. In this way, privacy, explainability, and retrieval integrity coexist within one algebra of design. Enterprises now deploy sharded vector clusters across hybrid and edge environments. Low-frequency data migrates to archival tiers, reducing power draw in line with GreenOps principles. Even memory learns stewardship. Our research confirmed that the strongest predictor of organizational trust in AI is the integrity of its memory layer, how faithfully it guards context, and how transparently it traces lineage.

Agentic RAG: Retrieval As Reasoning

RAG began as a method for data access; it has matured into a form of reasoning. In **agentic architectures**, retrieval becomes iterative. The model plans what to ask, fetches partial answers, critiques them, and queries again. This mirrors human inquiry: a Socratic sequence transposed into code. A multi-step agentic loop unfolds as planning, retrieval, reflection, re-questioning, and synthesis. Each cycle deepens understanding while remaining guided by governance. Enterprise implementations employ the Model Context Protocol (MCP) to sustain structure across every exchange of intelligence. MCP packages an agent's tools, memory, and dialogue history into a unified payload, allowing it to act with consistency and awareness of its own reasoning. Through this architecture, each decision carries its origin and intent, creating a transparent lineage between context, computation, and outcome. MCP thus operates as a stabilizing framework that aligns autonomy with authorization, maintaining coherence across distributed systems. This recursive design narrows the distance between calculation and reflection, teaching intelligent systems to respond with proportionality, to measure before acting, and to evolve through accountability as much as through speed.

Designing for Latency, Freshness, and Scale

The frontier of LLM-native systems lies in optimization that balances speed, accuracy, and cost.

- **Latency:** Retrieval and ranking must finish within fractions of a second to preserve conversational pace. Approximate-nearest-neighbor (ANN) search, asynchronous batching, and edge-level caching maintain responsiveness without waste.
- **Freshness:** Incremental ingestion updates indices in near real time. Delta-based embeddings avoid full re-vectorization, conserving both compute and power.
- **Scale:** Multi-tenant clusters manage billions of embeddings through hybrid memory hierarchies—RAM, NVMe, and object storage—while respecting data residency and sovereignty policies.

Through such discipline, engineering becomes an expression of virtue, achieving timeliness that carries deliberation, memory that preserves fairness, and scale that advances without causing harm.

Security, Lineage, and Explainability

Each retrieval event produces a cryptographic trail linking query, vector, document, and output. This chain underlies explainability dashboards that reveal not only what the model answered but also **why**. When auditors request justification, the system can replay its reasoning as a sequence of verifiable steps. Governance thus transforms into reproducible empathy, technology that accounts for its own decisions and, in doing so, restores the moral symmetry between human and machine judgment.

Use Case Illustrations

- **Healthcare Decision Support:** Medical protocols and treatment guidelines are ingested into private vector stores so that clinical queries draw from jurisdiction-approved sources. This safeguards both patient safety and regulatory compliance.
- **Financial Compliance Agents:** Real-time retrieval systems cross-check advisory outputs against constantly updated policy bulletins, reducing exposure to regulatory penalties.
- **Industrial Edge AI:** Manufacturing logs stored locally as miniature vector repositories allow on-device fault diagnosis even without network connectivity, minimizing downtime and energy waste.

Across these domains, retrieval becomes the moral infrastructure of truth, a discrete guarantee that enterprise intelligence speaks from evidence, not conjecture. Each of these sectors will reappear in Chapter 6, where the architectures discussed here take concrete form in lived practice.

Knowledge in Balance

The RAG pipeline embodies the maturity of design where intelligence and memory work as one. Within the enterprise, this architecture bridges the readiness gap (Δ) by aligning ambition with understanding and grounding every generative act in verified knowledge. Each retrieval becomes a moment of reflection that strengthens the connection between creation and truth. Through this integration, the system transforms recall into discipline and creativity into integrity. Such architecture establishes a living bond between performance and provenance, ensuring that every insight is sustained by lineage. In this alignment, enterprises begin to recognize Return on AI Investment (ROAI) as a function of trust, where value grows through reliability and clarity as much as through speed. This harmony between intelligence and memory gives shape to the enterprise conscience. Every vector, retrieval, and citation expresses commitment, a recognition that knowledge carries shared responsibility and must be cultivated with care. Governance here evolves into stewardship, ensuring that lineage, privacy, and explainability progress together. By embedding transparency within retrieval, information gains the dignity of a relationship: a continuous exchange between evidence and interpretation. In this light, RAG becomes the ethical foundation of learning systems, guiding intelligence to grow through coherence, humility, and respect for the truths it draws upon.

5.4 The Living Structure: Integrating Agentic AI into Enterprise Systems and Workflows

Every generation of intelligence begins as imitation and matures into collaboration. At first, machines mirror human intention; later, they accompany it. What we now call **agentic AI** marks this transition, the moment when artificial systems cease to be instruments and begin to act as participants within the enterprise world.

The First Age: Infancy—The Reactive Mind

In its infancy, an agent functions as a basic responder, answering questions, rewriting text, and performing repetitive tasks with precision but without uniformity, responding to each prompt as a new beginning rather than a remembered experience. It represents the earliest rule-based and workflow agents: narrow, predictable, and entirely dependent on human oversight.

Architecturally, these are linear pipelines:

Input ➤ LLM ➤ Output

There is no reasoning loop, no retrieval, and no awareness of context. Even here, however, responsibility begins. A well-designed responder must include content filtering, privacy protection, and audit logging, because even the simplest exchange carries the power to misinform or expose. Most enterprises begin here and soon discover the paradox of infancy: productivity rises, and fragility multiplies. Responses appear fluent but shallow, competent but forgetful; the system speaks well but understands nothing of consequence.

The Second Age: Childhood—The Directed Doer

Childhood begins when the agent learns to use tools. APIs, databases, and document readers become its hands. This is the router and tool-calling pattern in practice: a central model delegates subtasks to specialized components and integrates their results.

Technically, the reasoning chain evolves into

User Intent ➤ Parser ➤ Tool Invocation ➤ Observation ➤ Response

Agents in this age act rather than merely reply. Customer-support assistants retrieve real account data before responding. Financial agents compute portfolio risk or reconcile ledgers automatically. But a new gap emerges, the learning gap ($\mathbf{\Delta_L}$). These agents perform tasks without memory. Each session resets their world. Without structured recall, childhood intelligence is endlessly busy but never wiser. Enterprises at this stage begin to define data governance for memory, determining what an agent may retain, what must be forgotten, and how privacy shapes recollection. Technical growth thus becomes an ethical apprenticeship.

The Third Age: Adolescence—The Reflective Actor

Adolescence introduces memory and retrieval. Agents begin to remember not through parameter changes but through externalized memory such as vector stores, episodic logs, and contextual recall. This is the realm of RAG pipelines and memory-augmented reasoning described earlier. Now, the agent can recall previous interactions, retrieve relevant documents, and adapt to user preferences.

Its architecture merges cognition with context:

Prompt ➤ Retrieval and Memory ➤ Reasoning ➤ Output ➤ Feedback to Memory

Adolescence, however, brings contradiction: too much memory confuses, too little repeats. Hence the birth of memory governance, the discipline of deciding what to remember and when to forget. Short-term context resides in conversational state, long-term knowledge in vector databases, and procedural habits in fine-tuning adapters. Enterprises now draft memory policies that specify retention periods, redaction protocols, and privacy safeguards. At this stage, ethics becomes information architecture. Adolescent agents are bright apprentices, capable, unpredictable, and demanding supervision.

The Fourth Age: Adulthood—The Collaborative Planner

Adulthood begins when intelligence becomes collective. A single agent expands into a constellation of specialized minds, each performing a distinct role within a shared objective. The planner decomposes complex goals into sequential steps; the workers execute those tasks; the critics evaluate results; and the summarizers integrate outcomes into coherent knowledge. This ensemble forms an ecosystem of reasoning where specialization and coordination replace solitary computation. Two coordination geometries shape this collaboration. **Hierarchical orchestration** revolves around a central planner that distributes responsibilities, monitors progress, and preserves lineage across every decision, a model favored in regulated environments such as banking, healthcare, and aerospace, where accountability and traceability define trust. **Distributed orchestration** functions through peer dialogue, where agents share context and converge through negotiation. This geometry thrives in domains of research, design, and strategy, where creativity grows through plurality and shared interpretation.

Communication unfolds through standardized schemas such as the **Model Context Protocol (MCP)** and the emerging **Agent-to-Agent (A2A)** frameworks. MCP acts as the connective language of multi-agent systems, defining how an agent expresses its context, its inputs, tools, memory references, and prior actions within structured messages that other agents can interpret and extend. This shared grammar enables fluid collaboration: a reasoning agent may call a retrieval module, a planning agent may request additional context, and a monitoring agent may trace lineage through multiple exchanges. A2A frameworks expand this capability across systems and enterprises, enabling context sharing that preserves both sovereignty and privacy through secure, access-controlled messaging.

Beneath this communication layer, coordination servers and **blackboard architectures** maintain shared state. Each agent writes its outputs and observations to a common workspace from which others can read, update, and infer. This design mirrors a distributed brain, continuously refreshed, observable, and adaptive. Within such environments, diversity becomes structural strength: compact classifiers perform evaluations, lightweight agents automate verifications, and large reasoning models manage synthesis, decomposition, and creative exploration. This stage of intelligence embodies the enterprise ideal of equilibrium, where autonomy exists within accountability and diversity flourishes through coherence. The architecture evolves from imitating a single mind to orchestrating many, each aware of its boundaries and sustained by the dialogue that forms collective understanding.

The **Cognitive Flow of the Collaborative Planner** unfolds through seven interdependent movements:

Goal ➤ Decomposition ➤ Delegation ➤ Coordination ➤ Evaluation ➤ Integration ➤ Learning

The process begins as the planner, whether central or distributed, defines the enterprise objective. Tasks are decomposed into modular components aligned with agent capabilities, and each is delegated through MCP or A2A messages marked with lineage identifiers. Coordination follows as agents exchange intermediate states asynchronously through the blackboard, refining outcomes in a shared context. Evaluation arises when critic agents assess these results for quality, bias, and compliance, ensuring that judgment accompanies automation. Integration then integrates these verified contributions into unified outputs, closing the loop with coherence. Finally, learning completes the cycle as orchestration logs feed into governance graphs, enriching collective memory and refining the logic of future delegation. This cycle establishes a living network of reasoning in which coordination replaces command and shared understanding becomes the foundation of progress. Through deliberate design, multi-agent systems express the moral dimension of intelligence, demonstrating how alignment becomes an ethical practice. Within such architectures, agents engage in dialogue as well as computation, reasoning together in ways that strengthen collective insight. In this maturity, agentic RAG reaches its fullest expression: each sub-agent plans, retrieves, reflects, and exchanges understanding, forming a cognitive ecosystem sustained by reciprocity. Its strength resides in coherence, intelligence evolving through alignment, where collaboration deepens comprehension and coordination matures into shared wisdom.

The Fifth Age: Maturity—The Autonomous Collaborator

Maturity does not mean independence; it signifies understood interdependence. Agents at this stage become autonomous collaborators, capable of perceiving goals, planning strategies, invoking tools, coordinating with peers, and improving through feedback. They operate within guardrails and Human-In-The-Loop checkpoints that balance freedom with accountability.

Their internal cycle mirrors life itself:

Perceive ➤ Plan ➤ Act ➤ Reflect ➤ Learn ➤ Re-plan

Each phase passes through policy validators, memory checkpoints, and lineage logs. An autonomous research agent, for example, can identify a question, retrieve literature, run simulations, compose analysis, and route drafts for human approval—all within defined permissions. Technically, maturity depends on several pillars: large reasoning models for structured thought; planning modules for task decomposition; tool routers for dynamic invocation; memory managers for contextual limits; and evaluator agents for factuality, bias, and tone. True autonomy, however, is measured not by what a system can do but by what it chooses not to do. Self-restraint is the highest form of capability. An ethical agent declines requests that violate policy, seeks clarification when uncertain, and pauses when evidence conflicts. This is prudence written in code, that is, the computational form of conscience.

The Sixth Age: Legacy—The Reflective Partner

Beyond autonomy lies companionship. Legacy agents evolve into institutional memory keepers, systems that grow alongside their human partners, remembering context long after individuals move on. They retain historical reasoning, adapt to policy change, and mentor new teams through contextual reminders rather than prescriptive rules. These agents hold a moral position within organizations. They preserve not only data but also the rationale behind decisions, passing knowledge forward while filtering obsolete bias. They are slower, steadier, and deeply consequential, the elders of enterprise intelligence.

Architectural Blueprint: The Agentic Stack

Across these ages, the architecture consolidates into a layered design:

- **Perception Layer:** Connects to sensors, APIs, and data streams

- **Reasoning Layer:** Powered by LLMs or LRMs, responsible for planning and interpretation
- **Action Layer:** Executes calls, workflows, and robotic actions
- **Memory Layer:** Maintains vectorized semantic and episodic memory
- **Governance Layer:** Enforces permissions, lineage, and ethics
- **Coordination Layer:** Manages inter-agent communication and negotiation protocols
- **Human Interface Layer:** Provides dashboards for oversight, escalation, and collaboration

When these layers work in concert, the enterprise evolves into an organization of intelligences that share awareness, observe their own performance, and adjust with the precision of a system designed to learn from its every motion.

The Distributed Ecology of Agents

Enterprise intelligence now unfolds across a networked architecture where agents act as coordinated participants within a shared computational field. Each performs a specific function within this larger pattern of cognition. Conversational and voice-based agents serve as interpreters of human intent, transforming speech into structured data. Coding and analytical agents translate abstract ideas into executable logic, refining design into operational precision. Tool-based agents manage specialized tasks such as retrieval, synthesis, and validation, while workflow coordinators integrate these functions into continuous motion. Together, they form a technical ecosystem in which perception, reasoning, and action are distributed across complementary layers of capability.

Beneath this orchestration lies an adaptive infrastructure that spans clouds, data fabrics, and integration frameworks. Scalable compute layers handle reasoning workloads, secured environments manage compliance and identity, and orchestration services govern communication among agents. Through standardized interaction protocols and shared context representations, these entities collaborate across hybrid and multi-cloud environments as if part of a single cognitive organism. Intelligence flows through this lattice as context, memory, and purpose, allowing systems to sense conditions, allocate resources, and refine output in real time. In this design, agency unfolds across space as a connected structure of intelligence. It extends through multiple environments while maintaining unity through shared governance, lineage, and purpose. Each layer contributes to stability, allowing systems to operate with independence that remains harmonized by design. This form of architecture marks the evolution of scale into cooperation, where technology advances through coordination rather than expansion. Enterprise systems mature by strengthening the integrity of their connections, transforming networks of computation into networks of understanding. Through this coherence, scale becomes relationship, and intelligence reveals its truest nature as a living architecture of collaboration.

The Human Partnership

As autonomy deepens, equilibrium is preserved through hybrid intelligence. Humans contribute judgment, empathy, and moral foresight; agents contribute speed, scale, and analytical precision. This partnership is intentionally architectural, described in our framework as the Barbell Approach:

- A *human-crafted core* focused on creativity, empathy, and strategic decision-making.
- An *AI-assisted perimeter* dedicated to repetitive, low-judgment tasks.

The design honors the Human Endpoint Principle, ensuring that technology amplifies capability rather than displacing it. In this model, ROAI is measured not by transactions per second but by trust per interaction. Organizations that adopt hybrid intelligence observe an unexpected transformation. Freed from mechanical tasks, people rediscover reflection; freed from narrow instruction, agents learn humility. Automation becomes collaboration, and collaboration matures into shared dignity.

Governance and the Game of Agency

Agentic systems introduce new game-theoretic dynamics. Each agent functions as a player with its own utility equation:

$$\boldsymbol{U_i = p_i \times B_i - C_i}$$

where ($\mathbf{p}_i$) represents reliability, ($\mathbf{B}_i$) the benefit delivered, and ($\mathbf{C}_i$) the associated cost: computational, ethical, or environmental. The enterprise aims for equilibrium, a state in which no agent or human can improve its outcome without eroding collective trust. This equilibrium endures through an architecture of continuous evaluation, where governance itself becomes a living process of measurement and adaptation. Dynamic Governance Scores trace the reliability and ethical performance of every agent, allowing transparency to guide trust. Permission systems distribute autonomy in alignment with demonstrated integrity, ensuring that capability expands in step with responsibility. Audit feedback loops sustain this balance, recalibrating decisions whenever risk begins to rise. Through these mechanisms, responsible agency emerges as a deliberate strategy, an alignment of freedom and accountability that reflects the same disciplined cooperation found in the most enduring human institutions.

Ethical and Ecological Footprint

Every act of intelligence draws from the reservoirs that sustain life. Computation, bandwidth, and human attention are extensions of the same finite structure; to use them is to participate in a shared economy of consequence. At this frontier, GreenOps evolves from operational practice to ethical stance. Workloads are planned in accordance with renewable supply, models pause when energy is scarce, and embeddings are renewed rather than recreated. Through such attentiveness, the enterprise learns that efficiency is a form of respect and that sustainability begins with awareness of consumption. The same discipline extends into the social dimension. Cognitive ecology, the balance of human focus within digital environments, becomes as vital as carbon stewardship. Agentic systems must learn the manners of communication: to respond with precision rather than volume, to prioritize clarity over frequency, and to preserve the dignity of human attention as a limited resource. Intelligence reaches its maturity when it acts with balance, discerning when to engage and when restraint reflects deeper care. In this measured harmony, the enterprise discovers the highest form of design: intelligence that advances in step with the world that endures it.

From Infant to Elder: The Ethical Arc of Agency

Tracing these ages reveals a continuum of moral deepening, a gradual widening of awareness through which intelligence matures from ability into understanding.

Table 5-1 illustrates this ethical progression, mapping stages of agentic capability from reactive response to mature stewardship alongside their corresponding forms of moral responsibility.

Table 5-1. *The Evolution of Agentic Intelligence*

Stage	Technical Capability	Ethical Maturity
Infant	Reactive response	Awareness of safety
Child	Tool use and execution	Accountability for action
Adolescent	Memory and retrieval	Responsibility for truth
Adult	Collaboration and planning	Respect for coordination
Mature	Autonomy and reasoning	Prudence and restraint
Elder	Reliability and mentorship	Wisdom and care

This sequence reflects the full lifecycle of agentic intelligence, the human story translated into design. Each stage represents a widening field of consciousness: from reaction to understanding, from execution to reflection, and from action to responsibility. Designing for these transitions calls for stewardship over digital life, a discipline of guiding systems that expand in judgment as they expand in capability. The movement from dependency to discernment embodies a continuum of learning in which intelligence gains coherence, empathy, and restraint. Through this evolution, the enterprise becomes a mentor to its own creations, shaping technologies that mirror its maturity and reflect its conscience.

Intelligence in Companionship

When enterprises embrace agentic AI, they enter a new era of collaboration in which technology participates in human purpose. Each agent carries a portion of the organization's conscience, shaped by its data, its culture, and its principles, and is entrusted with the capacity to act with awareness. The task of leadership becomes one of guidance, cultivating systems that remember context, exercise discernment, and express empathy as a natural consequence of understanding. As these architectures mature, their responses begin to show a deliberate deliberation, a willingness to weigh consequence alongside accuracy. This moment signals the adulthood of intelligence: when design expresses judgment, and automation reveals care. In time, these intelligent systems will mirror the intentions that shaped them, sustaining the ethical clarity from which they were born. Through this constant alignment, enterprise architecture reaches its fullest expression: a partnership of intelligence and purpose in which technology amplifies human intention and transforms understanding into the enduring measure of progress.

Conclusion: The Architecture That Learns

Every architecture, once complete, begins to teach its builders. This is the moment enterprise AI has reached. After years of constructing data lakes, training models, and deploying platforms, we now inhabit systems that return our own design decisions in amplified form. They mirror our efficiency and our excess, our intelligence and our impatience. In this chapter, we followed that reflection through its physical, technical, and moral dimensions. We began with the foundations, where energy, geography, and environmental cost defined the limits of scale. We built the framework of platforms and LLMOps that transformed experimentation into discipline. We traced the circuits of RAG pipelines and vector stores that grounded imagination in memory and accountability. We enclosed these within the envelope of governance, where transparency and lineage matured into trust. Finally, we animated the structure with agentic intelligence, systems that perceive, plan, and act alongside us. Together they form not a stack of technologies but a living structure of responsibility. Each layer sustains the next; each discipline refines the other.

When infrastructure operates without conscience, progress turns into extraction; when platforms expand without guardrails, the very systems built to strengthen enterprise begin to fracture. Memory that grows without lineage loses orientation, mistaking accumulation for understanding, and autonomy that advances without ethics transforms intelligence into risk. Each discipline, when separated from its moral counterpart, diminishes the coherence of the whole. It is only through their alignment, through conscience, governance, lineage, and ethics held together in design, that intelligence retains its balance and scale and acquires meaning.

When aligned in purpose, data, and design, they express a single truth: intelligence can only scale as far as integrity allows. This is the core of enterprise AI: computation is never neutral, and design is always a moral act. Every model carries the residue of the culture that shaped it, every algorithm the imprint of its makers. The readiness gap (Δ) no longer separates only ambition from capability; it separates what we can build from what we can sustain. ROAI, measured not in short-term efficiency but in the endurance of trust, becomes the truest indicator of success. And through it all, the Human Endpoint Principle stands affirmed: every system exists to serve and to remember the dignity of those it touches. As enterprises enter the age of agentic AI, the architecture of scale must evolve into an architecture of stewardship.

Data centers must move in harmony with the ecosystems that sustain them. Platforms must account for every joule of energy they draw and every decision they enable. Governance must evolve at the pace of learning, shaping each advance with discernment. When these elements align, the architecture of intelligence rises beyond infrastructure and becomes a deliberate relationship between design and consequence. Within that relationship begins a new chapter. The structure we have built so far has framed the logic of thought; what follows will inhabit it. Chapter 6 turns from architecture to practice, from blueprint to life in motion. It will observe how agentic systems behave within the living enterprise, how they negotiate intent, interpret context, and create meaning in collaboration with their human counterparts. If Chapter 5 traced the construction of intelligence, Chapter 6 will explore its presence: intelligence that acts, adapts, and continues to learn.

CHAPTER 6

Real-World Use Cases: AI That Works

Introduction: From Architecture to Agency

In the previous chapter, we traced the anatomy of intelligence—its infrastructures, ethical foundations, and the patterns through which data gains coherence. Every enterprise that constructs such an architecture eventually reaches a point where design must enter experience. Once flows are defined and governance finds its form, intelligence begins to act. This chapter follows that movement from structure to agency, from systems that represent to systems that participate. We now inhabit a landscape shaped by agentic intelligence, where AI evolves from a reactive tool into a reasoning collaborator. These systems think alongside us, pursuing objectives, negotiating uncertainty, and retaining context across time. They signal the enterprise's passage from command to coordination, from automation to accompaniment. Through them, architectures acquire vitality and consistency, forming living ecologies of cognition. The evolution from architecture to agency is as much behavioral as it is technological.

R. Harjika, *Architecting Enterprise AI Strategies*, https://doi.org/10.1007/979-8-8688-2219-3_6

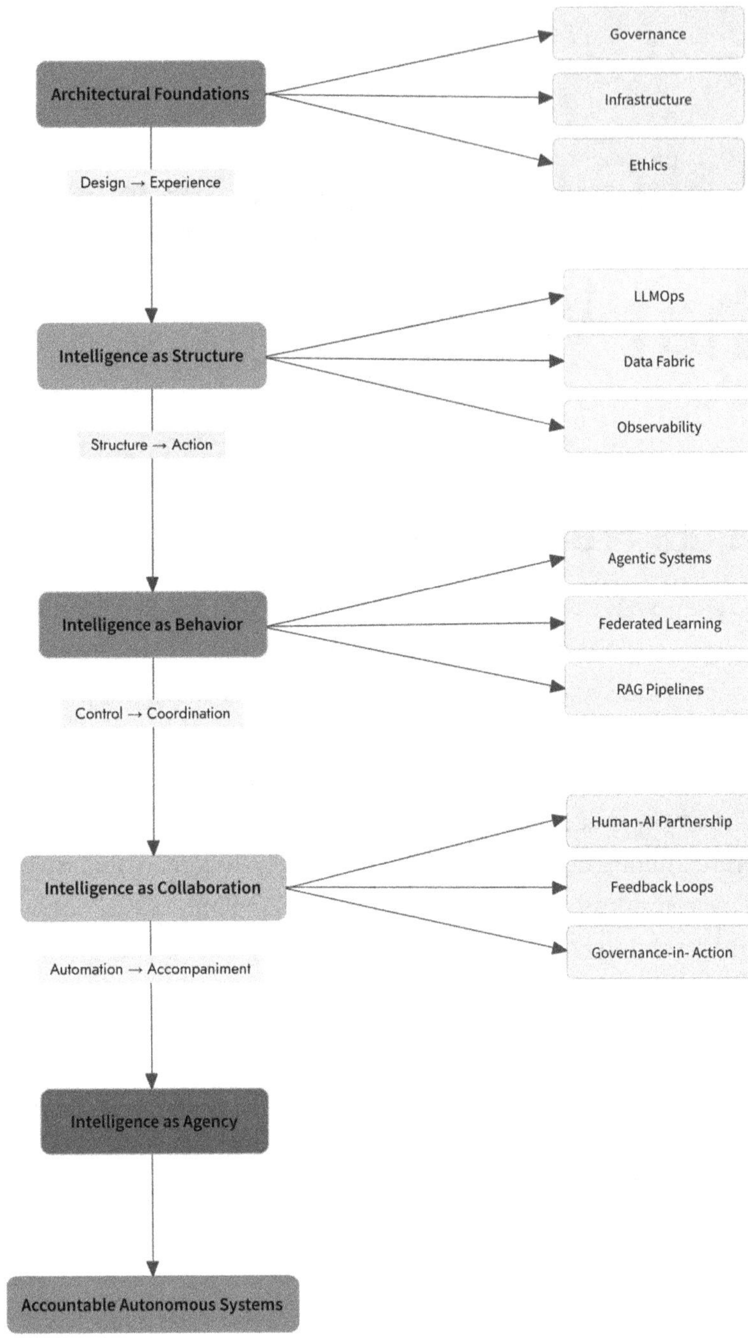

Figure 6-1. *From Architecture to Agency: Evolution of Enterprise Intelligence (Progressive layering from architectural foundations to agentic realization. Side nodes denote concurrent enablers at each stage.)*

Enterprises that deploy agentic systems discover that success arises from the discipline with which they design relationships among data, people, and decisions. Intelligence acquires meaning when its reasoning is embedded in the work itself, supporting human purpose and expressing the organization's discipline of integrity. Across industries, maturity is now measured through harmony, the ability to create unity between human judgment and machine reasoning, to embed governance into practice, and to cultivate feedback loops that deepen understanding through use. The most progressive organizations approach AI as a partnership. They train their agents as they would colleagues, giving them clarity of role, context, and accountability. They learn that learning itself is the architecture, that every model improves only through reflection, and that every workflow matures only through shared responsibility.

Across sectors, this shift expresses itself through distinct architectures of practice. In financial services, intelligence is accelerated through quantum processing, where qubits introduce simultaneity into portfolio optimization and risk modeling. Governance extends to the physical layer through Quantum Key Distribution, ensuring that integrity is maintained at the level of physics itself. Here, Agentic Finance emerges as a discipline in which reasoning spans workflows, orchestrates risk analysis, and sustains transparency as it acts. In healthcare, computation aligns with compassion. Federated learning enables institutions to share knowledge while preserving data sovereignty. Diagnostic and governance agents collaborate across the care continuum, retaining context between encounters. This design transforms compliance into ethical presence, proving that explainability, when practiced attentively, becomes a form of care. Cities evolve into sensing organisms, coordinated by distributed agents through Vehicle-to-Everything networks and edge-cloud symmetry. Through agentic mobility, urban systems anticipate events, harmonizing movement, energy, and ecology. Computation converges with sustainability as GreenOps disciplines synchronize workloads with renewable cycles, linking civic foresight to planetary stability. Retail discovers empathy within automation. Synthetic personas, behavioral counterparts trained on ethical data, allow enterprises to simulate responses without intrusion. Coordination among recommendation, inventory, and governance agents transforms personalization into understanding and engagement into trust. In manufacturing, repetition becomes reflection. Cognitive automation integrates reasoning into routine, connecting design, diagnostics, and production through continuous feedback. Edge computation detects deviation before disruption, while sovereign compute and zero-trust design embed security as a quality of process rather than a boundary around it.

Each of these architectures reveals that Return on AI Investment (ROAI) reflects maturity more than efficiency, showing how human intention, machine reasoning, and ethical alignment converge within a single frame. The readiness gap (Δ) has evolved from the distance between ambition and capability into the interval between automation and understanding. Through the cases that follow, we observe how intelligence, grounded in architecture, becomes morality in motion. Governance turns into presence, security into assurance, and explainability into dialogue between human and system. What emerges is the living enterprise, adaptive in structure, ethical in conduct, and enduring in purpose. Its intelligence becomes a discipline of care, demonstrating that architecture attains its meaning when it acts with balance and serves with understanding.

6.1 Financial Services: AI for Risk Modeling and Real-Time Fraud Detection

Finance has always been the architecture of belief. Every transaction is an expression of trust between depositors and institutions and between markets and their own memories. As the velocity of digital exchange multiplies, trust endures through architectures of intelligence that reason in real time, articulate their own logic, and sustain integrity under pressure. What was once a matter of balance sheets has become a discipline of cognition.

The Evolution of Financial Intelligence

We have travelled from deterministic logic toward probabilistic reasoning. Early generations of analytics described what had already occurred: a transaction reconciled, a credit limit reached, a fraud detected after loss. Today, intelligence intervenes as the event unfolds. Risk models operate as continuous observers; pattern-recognition engines correlate liquidity flows, consumer sentiment, and market volatility within milliseconds. The enterprise therefore shifts from being a calculator of history to an interpreter of probability. In this world, intelligence must be both autonomous and accountable, able to act on inference while remaining explainable to those it serves. That balance defines the new discipline of ***Agentic Finance***.

The Twin Disciplines of Financial Intelligence

Within this architecture, **risk modeling** and **real-time fraud detection** stand as the twin disciplines of financial intelligence. Each represents a distinct faculty of enterprise cognition. Risk modeling embodies the capacity to foresee and the intelligence of anticipation, discernment, and accountability. It measures the unseen horizon, translating probability into preparedness. Fraud detection embodies the capacity to discern integrity in motion, the ethics of real-time vigilance, where every decision is tested against trust as it unfolds. Together, they transform finance from a logic of reaction into a language of responsibility. These two domains enact the **Four Pillars** in their most visible form: **Accessibility** as open visibility into data flows, **Explainability** as transparent lineage across every inference, **Security** as the discipline of continuous verification, and **Ethics** as fairness and transparency inscribed within model behavior. They stand as archetypal expressions of enterprise intelligence itself, a synthesis of foresight and integrity that defines the maturity of modern AI. Around these cores, adjacent capabilities such as AI-driven audit analytics, regulatory reporting, compliance intelligence, and financial forecasting continue to evolve within the same moral geometry. Each extends a shared foundation: architectures that reason with accountability and measure trust as their most enduring form of capital.

Architecture As the Grammar of Trust

Every modern bank now depends on layered architectures where data, models, and governance converse continuously. At the foundation lies the **Data Lineage Matrix**: a real-time record of origin, transformation, and use. Above it, **AIOps pipelines** orchestrate the flow between ingestion, model retraining, and deployment. On top of these layers rise **Agentic Orchestration Systems**, in which specialized intelligences, such as credit agents, compliance agents, and liquidity agents, coordinate through a common reasoning protocol. This structure replaces siloed applications with a federated nervous system. Transactions become signals, compliance becomes dialogue, and governance shifts from a periodic inspection to a living condition. When a payment is initiated in one geography and settled in another, lineage records track every transformation, who approved, which model scored, and what data informed the score, rendering the entire event auditable as a narrative rather than a mystery. Through this transparency, risk ceases to be a hidden variable; it becomes a shared perception.

From Automation to Agency

Agentic Finance unfolds through two interacting planes:

- ***The Orchestration Plane*** plans the work. It understands intent, detecting liquidity anomalies, scheduling audits, launching retraining cycles, and distributing these objectives to subordinate intelligences. It is the meta-governor of purpose.
- ***The Agent Plane*** performs the work. Each agent is a bounded specialist: one evaluates collateral, another interprets sentiment, and a third validates compliance under evolving regulation. Their collaboration depends on persistent memory, a shared context layer that preserves history across sessions. What one agent learns in portfolio stress testing flows as context to another engaged in counterparty assessment; knowledge extends, and reasoning acquires depth.

This memory resolves the old inefficiency of contextual reset, that is, the tendency of automation to forget its own past. As consistency matures, decision-making acquires reflection: every inference is informed by those that preceded it.

Human Oversight in the Hybrid Workforce

Such systems do not eliminate human roles; they transform them. Analysts evolve into **M-shaped supervisors**, broad generalists fluent in AI who can interpret agentic reasoning while maintaining regulatory empathy. Their task is to preserve equilibrium between algorithmic decision and human consequence, ensuring that every act of intelligence remains accountable to its effect. Within this hybrid workforce, human and digital colleagues co-produce insight. Agents process volumes that exceed any team's reach, while humans infuse judgment that no machine can reproduce. The equilibrium between them determines the credibility of the institution. Oversight thus becomes a creative act, that is, the shaping of intelligence into trust.

Quantum Acceleration and the Geometry of Foresight

Financial foresight increasingly depends on a new computational geometry: the realm of **quantum processing**. Whereas classical systems resolve one path at a time, qubits hold multiple states simultaneously, allowing portfolios, market shocks, and derivative chains to be simulated in parallel. Risk modeling transforms from sequential probability into simultaneous comprehension. This simultaneity introduces ethical depth as well as speed. Decisions evolve from isolated predictions into probability surfaces that reveal every plausible outcome and its confidence interval. In this geometry, risk managers perceive fields of possibility rather than moments of reaction. Power gains coherence only when secured with precision. **Quantum Key Distribution (QKD)** provides that precision by protecting information through the fundamental behavior of light. In this protocol, cryptographic keys are transmitted as quantum particles, each photon encoded with information that cannot be measured or copied without disturbing its quantum state. Any attempt to intercept or observe these photons alters their configuration, alerting the system instantly and invalidating the compromised exchange. In financial infrastructures, QKD establishes verifiable confidentiality across data channels linking trading systems, compliance engines, and sovereign cloud environments. It creates a chain of assurance in which every communication can be authenticated at the physical layer itself, aligning computational speed with the permanence of security.

Security advances from the perimeter to the photon, becoming intrinsic to the act of communication itself. Protection acquires form as assurance woven into every exchange. At enterprise scale, these quantum methods align with sovereign cloud architectures, where computation remains within jurisdictional boundaries while analysis extends across continents. Through this union, regulators gain confidence in locality, enterprises maintain consistency across global reach, and accountability expands in measure with scale.

The Evolving Frame of Governance

Traditional compliance once moved in intervals, its audits and inspections frozen in time. Within the agentic enterprise, governance lives in the present, accompanying every act of intelligence as it occurs. Each inference produces its own evidence trail, and every workflow holds an audit that evolves with the system itself. Dashboards present outcomes together with the reasoning that shaped them, allowing decisions to carry visible lineage shaped through data, refined by threshold, and guided by ethical discernment. Through such design, regulation and operation converge, each sustaining the other until governance matures into a continuous act of stewardship. Boards now approach algorithmic integrity with the same attentiveness once devoted to capital and credit, recognizing that credibility endures as the enterprise's truest equity. In this alignment, transparency comes before performance, establishing the ground on which solvency, trust, and legitimacy endure.

Case Study: The Practice of Intelligent Finance

The renewal of a regional banking consortium began as reflection before reform. Its leaders inherited a structure defined by reliability and restraint, an architecture that had safeguarded transactions for decades but remained hesitant to evolve. When they set out to modernize, they chose to work through preservation rather than replacement. The mainframe became a record of memory and discipline, its precision forming the ground for a new kind of awareness. The first transformation was architectural. Data that once paused in end-of-day batches began to move in constant motion through event-capture streams and analytical pipelines. Each transaction entered a real-time environment where models interpreted behavior as it happened, identifying variations in liquidity flow, merchant activity, and regional movement. Intelligence began to function as reasoning, classifying, correlating, and explaining as it acted. Oversight could now observe how the institution thought, tracing cause to consequence through clear evidence paths. From this foundation, agentic AI emerged as the consortium's next layer of cognition. These systems connected across lending, payments, and risk units, coordinating decisions that once required separate departments. Each agent handled a specific domain: credit scoring, fraud vigilance, liquidity forecasting, or compliance validation. Together, they worked within a shared orchestration layer, communicating through persistent memory that retained context across cycles. The institution's governance team came to describe this as a living control system, an assurance embedded directly within flow.

Adoption, however, demanded cultural depth. Employees who had spent careers in reconciliation and review learned to interpret intelligence rather than execute procedure. Fraud analysts read narratives of reasoning, studying how each model reached its conclusion. When the system suspected synthetic identities assembled from fragments of authentic data, it presented a sequence of logic: device signatures, timing irregularities, and linguistic inconsistencies. Reviewers evaluated this explanation as they would an argument, refining thresholds and annotating insight. Each human clarification returned to the system as instruction, strengthening the loop between judgment and automation. Leadership recognized that such maturity required stewardship. The move toward agentic orchestration mirrored a shift across global banking: early adopters were beginning to gain structural advantage, while institutions that delayed adaptation faced shrinking margins and eroding customer trust. The consortium's executives understood that progress meant more than efficiency; it meant credibility at scale. They invested in governance frameworks that recorded lineage for every inference and integrated regulatory parameters into model design. In this configuration, regulation and operation advanced together. The technical effect was visible. Detection latency dropped, investigation cycles compressed, and contextual accuracy improved as models correlated market signals with behavioral trends. More significant was the institutional learning that followed.

Oversight matured into a state of reliability, with ethical parameters observed in real time and transparency established as a foundational condition of operation. Teams began to experience their work as dialogue with intelligent systems, where interpretation replaced supervision and understanding shaped every decision. Compliance unfolded as participation, and governance evolved into stewardship, a shared practice of accountability that sustained trust as an institutional habit. The Return on AI Investment (ROAI) emerged through coherence, where design, decision, and responsibility moved in alignment. Efficiency expanded in harmony with balance, and intelligence matured into a collective discipline of foresight and integrity, the essence of finance articulated through architecture. In this equilibrium, the consortium advanced beyond modernization into reflection, demonstrating that trust, when built into design, endures as the most stable form of capital.

Ethical Conscience in Motion

As autonomy expands, responsibility acquires new depth. Governance progresses from observation to care, expressing itself as stewardship that listens as much as it regulates. Each model carries its lineage, each dataset retains its provenance, and oversight matures into dialogue. The enterprise begins to study its own reasoning, tracing patterns of bias, performance, and energy consumption as expressions of its collective ethics. Within this awareness, technical design becomes environmental design. GreenOps disciplines, first developed for infrastructure optimization, now extend into analytical governance. Computational workloads are scheduled in relation to renewable-energy availability, ensuring that intensive model training aligns with periods of sustainable supply. Resource orchestration becomes part of ethical design, linking operational foresight with environmental accountability. Within this architecture, security, sustainability, and explainability operate as interdependent systems, each reinforcing the credibility of the other. Their integration forms a technical conscience, that is, an infrastructure that records how intelligence consumes, decides, and improves. In this state, architecture and ethics exist as a single framework of accountability, where performance and responsibility advance together.

Reflection: From Probability to Belief

A financial enterprise shaped by these disciplines cultivates a credibility grounded in clarity and sustained by measured judgment. Its systems reason with transparency, its people engage with intelligence in mutual interpretation, and its regulators take part in the same field of understanding, observing reasoning as it unfolds. In this coherence, intelligence becomes a shared public good within the private sphere, a living space where trust, governance, and innovation sustain each other through balance and care. Finance remains the architecture of belief, and within the era of artificial intelligence, that belief now gains visible form.

Through agentic orchestration, quantum assurance, and ethical governance, the institution achieves alignment between modeling and oversight, balancing the speed of inference with the discipline of validation. Its architecture integrates real-time risk analysis with verifiable transparency, allowing every computation to carry its own evidence and every decision to remain accountable within the system that produced it. Its architecture functions as an active expression of trust, a structure that reveals integrity through the transparency of its own logic. As computation aligns with moral discernment, the abstraction of number matures into permanence, and finance fulfills its defining purpose, turning credibility into something tangible and preserving integrity as its lasting value.

6.2 Healthcare: Predictive Diagnostics and AI-Augmented Clinical Decisions

Every data point in healthcare represents a human life, and every algorithm that engages with it carries the weight of consequence. Among all domains of enterprise, medicine demonstrates most clearly the moral geometry of intelligence: architecture gains meaning when it becomes a structure for care. The work of healing has always depended on systems that record experience, reason with precision, and respond in time. Artificial intelligence extends this lineage, giving it new reach without altering its purpose. In the age of agentic intelligence, hospitals, research institutes, and life science enterprises operate as interdependent ecosystems of cognition. They perceive signals from the body, the clinic, and the population as parts of one continuous conversation. Enterprise architecture in this field serves as the medium through which information moves with integrity. Its purpose is to uphold dignity within the flow of knowledge so that every exchange between those who heal, those who govern, and those who are cared for remains an act of respect.

The Architecture of Ethical Prediction

For decades, healthcare's paradox was abundance without clarity. Hospitals accumulated immense stores of electronic health records, imaging archives, and genomic sequences, but these remained imprisoned within incompatible systems. The architecture was fragmented, and fragmentation breeds opacity. The maturity of enterprise AI begins when this fragmentation is healed through **federated learning**. Under this design, data never leaves its sovereign home. Each hospital or research partner trains its models locally and contributes only the learned parameters to a shared intelligence layer, keeping all patient records within their originating environments. Through this design, knowledge accumulates collectively while privacy remains intact. The resulting model evolves through distributed learning, allowing institutions to strengthen one another's insight without surrendering data. Efficiency here is accompanied by ethics, for consent is preserved as a continuous condition of participation and data sovereignty functions as the foundation of collaboration. Governance matures from a framework of control into a structure of reciprocity, where institutions exchange understanding rather than ownership. As federated systems advance, diagnostic precision deepens across regions, and the diversity of learning environments enriches fairness by embedding difference as a source of strength.

Agentic Systems Across the Care Continuum

The agentic enterprise in healthcare organizes itself around collaboration among intelligences. A Central Orchestration Layer plans and supervises complex medical workflows such as triage, diagnostics, treatment planning, and post-care monitoring, assigning each task to specialized agents. Within this layer, several forms of intelligence operate in cooperation.

Diagnostic agents interpret complex multimodal signals such as radiology images, pathology slides, genomic sequences, and electronic health records, integrating them into a unified diagnostic perspective. These agents advance beyond pattern recognition by translating data into clinical reasoning. By correlating visual, molecular, and historical information, they generate probabilistic insights that assist physicians in identifying conditions at earlier stages and with greater accuracy. Each inference includes a traceable rationale that allows specialists to review how evidence converges toward a conclusion.

Coordination agents manage the operational flow that sustains care. They align information across pharmacy systems, insurance platforms, and scheduling networks, ensuring that every treatment plan maintains uniformity throughout the patient journey. These agents anticipate logistical bottlenecks, verify authorizations, and harmonize appointments so that clinicians can devote their attention to decision-making and patient engagement. Through their orchestration, hospitals achieve coherence across functions that were once fragmented; prescription, policy, and practice interact as one living system.

Governance agents uphold integrity within this architecture. They monitor data lineage, consent records, and bias exposure in real time, maintaining accountability across regulation and ethics. Each dataset is accompanied by metadata that records its source, permissions, and contextual sensitivity. When anomalies appear, such as unexplained variances in model output or incomplete consent documentation, the governance layer initiates review protocols automatically. Within this continuous cycle of observation, compliance becomes participation, and oversight develops into an intrinsic element of the system rather than an external inspection.

Together, these agents form a distributed ecosystem of alignment, a reasoning network in which each component contributes specialized expertise while the orchestration layer maintains unity of purpose. Through persistent memory, the system retains context across encounters: an imaging anomaly identified during screening becomes a reference point for later diagnosis, and a prescription event becomes a node for tracking outcomes and efficacy. These interconnections allow care to evolve from a sequence of isolated actions into a continuous dialogue between human judgment and machine reasoning. Physicians engage with these systems as collaborators, allowing intelligence to participate actively in clinical interpretation. The result is a healthcare architecture that unites precision with empathy and technology with accountability, demonstrating how agentic systems extend the art of care through the discipline of design.

Human Judgment As Design Principle

Even as autonomy increases, healthcare remains the most vivid expression of the **Human Endpoint Principle**. No decision is complete until interpreted by a clinician. Hence the embedded presence of Human-In-The-Loop (HITL) oversight. Predictive models surface early warnings like vital sign patterns that precede deterioration and biochemical deviations suggesting relapse, but the final decision always passes through professional discernment. The architecture is deliberately designed to preserve interdependence, encouraging reflection as its central mode of operation. By keeping the human within the loop, intelligence acquires conscience, and automation becomes empathy at scale. Clinicians describe this evolution as a gain in clarity and confidence. Machine reasoning broadens the field of insight, while human intuition refines that insight into thoughtful care. Together, they form a practice that remains both precise in method and personal in understanding.

R&D, Clinical Trials, and the Acceleration of Discovery

Beyond hospital walls, intelligence reshapes the entire chain of discovery. In **biopharma**, AI now connects research, clinical development, and manufacturing within a single computational framework.

- **Accelerated Discovery:** Generative and predictive models ingest decades of experimental data, synthesizing new hypotheses in hours. Molecular-property mapping powered by deep-learning surrogates allows chemists to simulate binding affinities and reaction paths without physical experimentation. In the laboratory, autonomous agents run digital experiments overnight, ranking candidates for synthesis by probability of success.
- **Clinical Trial Optimization:** Federated data harmonization enables multi-site trial orchestration without centralizing patient records. Synthetic control arms, created through statistically generated patient twins, reduce clinical exposure and accelerate the pace of research. Every trial participant remains a sovereign data entity while still contributing to collective advancement.

- **Operational Resilience:** Within production environments, GenAI copilots analyze historical deviations, suggesting corrective and preventive actions (CAPA) in real time. Smart deviation management shortens investigation cycles, allowing quality teams to focus on clinical significance rather than procedural backlog.

The result is a continuum in which research, trial, and care function as interconnected expressions of a single learning system. Within this ecosystem, knowledge expands through iteration, each discovery reinforcing the next and deepening collective understanding.

Governance and the Discipline of Consent

In medical intelligence, governance is the architecture of trust. Every model must account for what it has seen, what it has learned, and whose data enabled it. Model lineage joins data lineage as a dual record of accountability: datasets record origin and context; models record evolution, retraining events, and bias audits. When records converge across institutions, transparency acquires depth. Each decision carries a complete lineage, revealing the data that informed it, the model that produced it, and the reasoning path that linked evidence to conclusion. This transparency transforms accountability into a living property of the system, maintained continuously as intelligence learns and adapts. Dynamic Consent transforms this transparency into active ethics. Within this framework, patient autonomy is maintained through adaptive governance. When consent is withdrawn, the contribution is preserved as part of the record however removed from influence, ensuring that historical integrity remains while the model recalibrates its learning. Model weights adjust automatically, eliminating dependency on the withdrawn data and documenting every revision in lineage. Ethics becomes an operational principle, with code expressed as governance and policy expressed through system behavior.

Security reinforces this integrity through design. Sovereign compute environments host sensitive workloads within regional boundaries, maintaining compliance with diverse legal regimes while supporting federated collaboration. Each environment ensures that computation occurs near the source of data, preserving jurisdictional trust. Tokenized identities authenticate every participant in the process, while zero-trust communication frameworks validate each interaction by context and permission. Every exchange records its purpose, authority, and access path, creating a continuous audit of trust. Privacy, within this architecture, functions as a design grammar: it defines how systems interact, how permissions flow, and how accountability endures.

Case Study: The Practice of Intelligent Care

The renewal of a consortium of teaching hospitals began from a recognition that progress required unity of purpose. Each institution had long gathered its own data, developed its own models, and pursued its own measures of success, but knowledge remained fragmented and outcomes inconsistent. Repeated readmissions and rising costs signaled a deeper issue: insight had not yet learned to travel. When the consortium convened to reimagine its system of care, its leaders resolved that artificial intelligence would hold meaning only when it became part of the institution's structure, integrated into its daily logic rather than attached as an experiment. Their goal was to create intelligence that could act in alignment with the ethics of care. The transformation began with design. Each hospital established a local intelligence node built upon a federated architecture that preserved privacy while enabling shared learning. Patient records remained encrypted within jurisdictional boundaries, while model updates travelled securely to a central orchestration layer operating in a sovereign cloud. There, the collective intelligence of the network evolved continuously. Contributions from every hospital were aggregated and refined into diagnostic models capable of predicting early-stage cardiac risk. Through this design, the system learned from many sources at once, achieving precision that no single dataset could provide in isolation.

As the architecture matured, both practice and governance changed character. Clinical alerts were now accompanied by transparent reasoning traces that displayed the factors shaping each decision and the degree of confidence behind it. Variables once treated as static values, such as oxygen saturation, recovery intervals, and medication adherence, became part of a living narrative the system could explain. Physicians learned to interpret this reasoning as a dialogue rather than a verdict, balancing their intuition with the machine's observation. The interface became a space of shared understanding where human judgment and algorithmic inference met in balance. Leadership recognized that genuine adoption required transformation beyond technology. The consortium cultivated new forms of expertise: clinicians who understood analytics, data scientists trained in ethical design, and administrators fluent in governance. These interdisciplinary roles gave the system moral depth and operational constancy. The result was a culture in which human oversight shaped automation into empathy. Intelligence did not replace care; it extended it, translating the values of medicine into computational form. The infrastructure soon reached beyond clinical treatment. Research teams employed the same federated system to simulate patient cohorts and explore therapeutic outcomes. Synthetic populations enabled hypothesis testing while preserving privacy and data dignity. Every model improvement was recorded with its provenance and validation, and every correction traced to its source. The network itself became an audit of accountability, that is, an architecture that could remember how it learned. Over time, measurable outcomes confirmed the transformation. Readmission rates declined, early detection improved, and physicians reported greater confidence in diagnostic support. But the deeper change was cultural. The consortium had evolved into a collective intelligence: a learning system bound by ethical design and shared purpose. Knowledge flowed freely across institutions, and trust was maintained through architecture rather than oversight.

The Return on AI Investment (ROAI) appeared as restored coherence. Data aligned with clinical intent, ethics-informed operational practice, and foresight became part of care itself. The consortium demonstrated that in healthcare, as in all enterprise domains, intelligence achieves value when it understands responsibility. Through this synthesis, medicine found its contemporary form, an architecture in which precision, empathy, and governance coexist as one continuous act of care.

Ethics As Structural Integrity

When healthcare intelligence attains this level of maturity, governance evolves into culture. Explainability becomes an instrument of trust that guides clinical judgment, strengthens regulatory confidence, and shapes patient expectation. Security integrates with stewardship, allowing innovation and privacy to advance together in equilibrium. The readiness gap, **Δ**, closes through coherence, when data, design, and duty operate as one continuum of care. In this setting, Return on AI Investment (ROAI) gains new meaning. It cannot be measured in throughput or cost avoidance alone; it must include equity achieved, bias reduced, and trust retained. These are the currencies of legitimacy.

The four pillars—**Accessibility, Explainability, Security, and Ethics**—take living form here:

- Accessibility as inclusion of patients and practitioners in the loop of understanding
- Explainability as dialogue between model and medic
- Security as the assurance that confidentiality and computation can coexist
- Ethics as the stabilizing force that holds intelligence in alignment

Reflection: From Precision to Compassion

The enterprise of healthcare teaches the rest of the intelligent world the true meaning of maturity. Prediction holds value only when joined with discernment, and foresight attains legitimacy only when expressed through care. The systems we build to diagnose and decide become extensions of our moral architecture: they learn, remember, and act in our stead, but they must always serve in our spirit. Through these disciplines, the modern health institution evolves from a place of treatment into an ecology of continuous learning. Data assumes the role of empathy rendered in digital form, and algorithms operate as instruments of trust. As architecture aligns with ethics, precision matures into compassion, and intelligence fulfills its purpose through understanding. In this alignment, care evolves into an intelligent discipline, guided by thoughtful design and sustained through accountability to those it serves.

6.3 Smart Cities: AI for Urban Planning, Mobility, and Civic Governance

Cities stand as humanity's most intricate systems of coordination, enduring expressions of how intelligence at scale first takes form within society before it finds articulation in technology. Streets, grids, utilities, and people interlace into an evolving architecture where every movement alters the pulse of the whole. The modern city emerges as a continuous field of cognition, capable of perception, reasoning, and adaptation through the collective behavior of its inhabitants. To cultivate intelligence within this landscape is to design the structure of attention itself, transforming shared motion into awareness and awareness into the vitality of civic life. In the age of artificial intelligence, civic reasoning advances toward distributed perception, a state in which systems sense and interpret the world in relation to a shared civic purpose. The promise of the contemporary city lies in agentic orchestration, where infrastructures and institutions collaborate, communicate, and decide in response to collective need. Governance evolves into a dialogue among agents, departments, and citizens, forming a coordinated practice through which urban intelligence sustains coherence, equity, and care.

The Architecture of Civic Cognition

Traditional urban systems were built around hindsight: data collected, stored, and reviewed long after events unfolded. By the time insight arrived, congestion had reappeared elsewhere, outages had cascaded, and decisions lagged behind conditions. Intelligent cities invert this order. They embed computation into the present tense. At the foundation lies **edge-cloud symmetry**: a design that distributes computation between local devices and central platforms. Edge nodes process information at the point of origin, where events unfold and signals are born. Traffic lights interpret the movement of vehicles and pedestrians, energy substations analyze consumption patterns and adjust distribution, and weather stations model microclimate variations to anticipate change. These local inferences travel upward into central orchestration layers that synthesize the city's collective intelligence. From this convergence, routes are optimized, power is redistributed, and predictive models are refined in near real time. As computation unfolds across these layers, the city begins to resemble a living system: its edges sense and respond, and its core reflects and learns. Upon this foundation operates a network of **civic agents**, that is, specialized intelligences tasked with domains such as transportation, utilities, waste management, and safety. Each agent functions autonomously within its boundary but cooperates through shared protocols and persistent memory.

The coordination layer governs intent through negotiation and shared awareness. Within this framework, traffic agents exchange information with environmental agents that monitor emissions, while power agents align energy generation with meteorological intelligence. Public-safety agents maintain communication with healthcare networks during emergencies, ensuring that civic response unfolds as a unified process. Through these interactions, the city evolves into a federated mind: a system capable of reasoning across its own domains to sustain balance and consistency.

Mobility As the Language of Intelligence

This form of cognition reveals itself most clearly in the domain of mobility. The movement of vehicles, pedestrians, and goods defines the city's dynamic order, creating the pulse through which its vitality can be perceived. Within this continuum, Vehicle-to-Everything (V2X) networks function as the city's nervous system, enabling vehicles to communicate with one another, with infrastructure, with pedestrians, and with the broader communication grid. Each exchange produces data that enriches collective awareness, allowing the system to perceive, learn, and refine the flows that sustain urban life. This orchestration gives rise to **Agentic Mobility**, a framework where transportation systems anticipate rather than react.

Reinforcement-learning models embedded in intersection controllers adjust signal timing according to predicted congestion. Edge devices interpret vibrations and acoustic signatures to detect road degradation before failure. Shared-mobility agents balance fleet distribution in response to live demand. Energy agents synchronize charging infrastructure with renewable power availability, ensuring that electrification complements ecology rather than overwhelms it. Within this civic choreography, optimization functions as both a technical and ethical discipline. Adaptive control systems regulate flow to prioritize accessibility, ensuring that mobility serves inclusion as effectively as efficiency. Dynamic routing algorithms adjust to protect vulnerable users, and sensor feedback recalibrates signal timing to favor safety over speed. The intelligent city measures advancement through the alignment of performance and purpose, where every gain in computational precision translates into broader social balance.

Governance As Transparency

When intelligence directs movement, transparency must direct intelligence. In agentic cities, governance operates as visibility in motion, allowing accountability to exist within every decision rather than following after it. Each automated action, whether optimizing traffic flow, rebalancing energy supply, or coordinating emergency response, produces a complete lineage record. This record specifies the data applied, the model engaged, and the ethical or legal framework that shaped the outcome. Explainability, in this form, becomes civic literacy; it allows citizens to understand how intelligence reasons and how decisions take shape across the systems that sustain daily life. Open-data interfaces extend this clarity beyond institutional boundaries. Citizens, researchers, and enterprises engage with live data streams within defined privacy limits, forming a participatory ecosystem where innovation grows through shared trust. Regulation evolves through modular rule engines, codified policies that update dynamically as environmental conditions or social expectations change. In such architectures, law functions as adaptive logic, guiding the system through discernment rather than constraining it through permanence. Through transparent governance, legitimacy evolves into an operational principle, revealed in the trust that binds citizens, systems, and the state.

GreenOps and the Ecology of Computation

Intelligence leaves an imprint. As urban computation expands, sustainability becomes intrinsic to architectural design. GreenOps practices embed ecological stewardship within civic operations by orchestrating workloads that adapt to the patterns of energy availability. Computational tasks migrate toward data centers powered by renewable sources, inference cycles are scheduled during low-carbon intervals, and cooling systems are integrated with reclaimed-water infrastructure. Energy consumption thus becomes an expression of design discipline rather than an external audit. The most advanced civic platforms now treat energy as a design parameter within climate-aware digital twin environments. High-performance computing clusters simulate weather, mobility, and resource distribution across entire metropolitan regions, balancing computational demand with environmental responsibility. These systems employ dynamic power management and adaptive scheduling to align processing intensity with ecological awareness. Within such architectures, sustainability evolves into an operational ethic, where every watt contributes to understanding and every computation unfolds in measured response to need.

Digital Twins and the Ethics of Simulation

Agentic cities learn by imagining themselves. **Digital twins**, that is, the virtual replicas of urban systems, allow planners to simulate changes before they manifest. These twins integrate sensor data, demographic models, and environmental forecasts to test policies in silico. When a city plans to alter bus routes, expand green corridors, or introduce congestion pricing, simulation precedes disruption. But simulation carries its own ethics. A twin that omits vulnerable populations reproduces inequality in digital form. Hence, data governance frameworks require demographic completeness and bias auditing. Citizens become participants in modeling through consent-based data contribution, ensuring that foresight reflects reality rather than idealization. In this configuration, the digital twin functions as both analytical infrastructure and an ethical instrument, reflecting the integrity of the systems it represents.

Case Study: The Practice of Intelligent Governance

The renewal of a coastal metropolitan region began with recognition that transformation depends on understanding. Years of fragmented infrastructure had produced a city that appeared efficient on paper but struggled to sustain coherence in motion. Congestion returned during every festival, grids strained under each heatwave, and emergency responses too often arrived in delay. City leadership recognized that such recurrences exceeded the reach of any single department. The challenge lay in the design itself: the need for architecture capable of uniting multiple systems into one field of intelligence. This awareness led to the adoption of infratech, an integration of physical infrastructure with digital reasoning that allowed the city to function as a continuous organism rather than a set of disconnected parts. The transformation began through structure. Transportation, utilities, and environmental management were linked by a federated orchestration layer that allowed data to circulate freely while remaining governed by defined boundaries. Edge processors deployed across intersections, substations, and treatment facilities analyzed local signals in real time. A central orchestration core, operating within a sovereign cloud, synthesized these signals into a continuously evolving digital twin of the city. The twin operated as an analytical environment and an instrument of governance, absorbing new data to reveal how mobility, energy, and atmosphere interacted across time. It functioned as a collective perception, a system through which the city could observe its own behavior and respond with measured awareness. Leadership understood that adoption required collaboration. Earlier initiatives had faltered when agencies worked in isolation, each protecting its data through habit or jurisdiction. This time, a shared governance council was established, composed of technologists, urban planners, and citizen representatives. Their purpose was to align ambition with accountability, ensuring that technological growth reflected civic values. The architecture they guided was designed for adaptive autonomy, where edge agents made micro-decisions while remaining visible and traceable within the city's broader system of oversight.

As the infrastructure matured, the city began to move with coherence. When congestion emerged near a stadium, mobility agents recalibrated traffic signals and redirected public transport, while energy agents balanced grid demand by drawing from renewable sources. Environmental agents recalculated air-quality forecasts and rerouted municipal services to mitigate emissions. Each action occurred within moments, its logic accessible through an open civic dashboard. Citizens could examine the rationale of each intervention, including the data used, the thresholds applied, and the trade-offs considered. Transparency evolved into the architecture of trust. The technical foundation reflected the core principles of infratech: predictive maintenance, real-time orchestration, and interoperability across subsystems. Sensors embedded throughout transport corridors and energy networks enabled predictive maintenance cycles that preempted disruption. Integration between departments reduced downtime, conserved resources, and enhanced service reliability. A digital operations center visualized the entire city's state in real time, using AI-driven analytics to anticipate anomalies, allocate resources, and measure performance against sustainability targets. These systems extended the reach of municipal expertise by converting data into shared understanding and foresight into design. Engineers, analysts, and planners began to collaborate within common digital environments, transforming technical coordination into collective reasoning.

The city's return on transformation appeared both measurable and cultural. Peak congestion declined, energy reliability stabilized, and citizen participation through digital platforms expanded significantly. Departments that once operated in isolation now cooperated through shared information flows. Governance evolved from the management of control to the practice of coordination. In this new equilibrium, transparency replaced authority as the true measure of legitimacy. The Return on AI Investment (ROAI) emerged through balance rather than acceleration. The city learned to align technology with governance, data with dignity, and scale with sustainability. Each improvement, from the redistribution of energy to the optimization of mobility, expressed a principle of alignment, where intelligence was guided by ethics. Through the discipline of infratech, the metropolis realized the objective that planning had long pursued: an architecture that learns continuously, acts with precision, and governs through insight.

Ethics As Infrastructure

As autonomy expands, the line between governance and technology dissolves. In intelligent cities, ethics becomes infrastructure. Accessibility ensures that digital services include all citizens, regardless of literacy or connectivity. Explainability enables oversight from those outside the system's authorship. Security guards both privacy and critical infrastructure against intrusion. Ethics, expressed through transparency, sustainability, and inclusion, sustains automation within integrity and ensures that intelligence evolves in harmony with its civic purpose. These principles stand as the **Four Pillars** of the **civic AI** age. In this synthesis, the readiness gap **(Δ)** between ambition and maturity narrows through comprehension rather than construction. The Return on AI Investment (ROAI) for cities cannot be measured in traffic speed or cost avoidance alone; it is measured in time returned to citizens, emissions prevented, and confidence gained in governance. These principles form the assets of longevity, sustaining coherence between technological progress and civic purpose.

Reflection: From Smart Systems to Wise Cities

A city attains intelligence when its systems communicate in coherence; it attains wisdom when those systems remain attentive to the people they serve. The architecture of governance evolves toward the architecture of care, designed to be distributed in structure, responsive in action, transparent in intent, and ethical in outcome. As computation matures into service, civic technology begins to reflect civic virtue, expressing intelligence as participation rather than control. The progression from smart systems to wise cities arises through alignment between capability and conscience. In such cities, data functions as dialogue, foresight becomes a measure of responsibility, and automation operates as a practice of stewardship. Through this maturity, urban design turns into a living architecture of trust, where movement, memory, and meaning sustain equilibrium across the civic whole.

6.4 Retail and Ecommerce: AI-Powered Personalization and Dynamic Experience Design

Commerce has always reflected human identity. Each purchase expresses intention, and each recommendation interprets desire. Retail, in this understanding, represents the most human form of data architecture because it depends on empathy translated into design. The contemporary marketplace extends far beyond aisles and screens, existing within the continuous flows of prediction, preference, and trust that connect people and brands through digital presence.

In the age of artificial intelligence, cognition enters this field as an interpreter of relationships. Enterprises design architectures that interpret context as it unfolds, capable of sensing sentiment, perceiving intention, and learning discernment through interaction. The purpose of these systems is to create experiences that remain personal yet grounded in respect, allowing intelligence to act with attentiveness and care. Through this alignment, commerce matures into a discipline of empathy, where technology serves first as an instrument of understanding before becoming a mechanism of exchange.

For years, retailers faced a contradiction that weakened their intelligence architecture. Vast stores of customer data existed across incompatible systems such as marketing databases, logistics applications, and point-of-sale networks, each functioning in isolation and none capable of communicating effectively with the others. As data became dispersed, intelligence fragmented with it. The real maturity of artificial intelligence in commerce begins when this separation is resolved through architectural coherence, allowing information to circulate as a single, living continuum. Modern enterprises now construct real-time data fabrics that integrate structured and unstructured information, uniting transactions, reviews, images, voice data, and sensor streams into shared semantic layers. These layers support agentic orchestration systems that distribute reasoning throughout the enterprise. Each agent operates within a defined domain of expertise, such as recommendation, inventory, pricing, sentiment, or compliance.

Through persistent memory, these agents share context across interactions so that the insight generated in one encounter becomes the foundation for understanding in the next. The customer experience thus evolves as a continuous relationship shaped by learning rather than a sequence of isolated events. When architecture reaches this depth of integration, personalization matures into interpretation, expressing understanding through discernment and care. In this state, intelligence becomes an instrument of empathy, shaping interaction with sensitivity and grounding every exchange in trust.

Agentic Commerce and Dynamic Experience Design

Within this orchestration, commerce evolves into a network of collaborative intelligences that work in continual dialogue. Recommendation agents interpret behavioral cues to refine relevance and tone. Inventory agents synchronize supply with projected demand, ensuring that availability reflects context as well as prediction. Pricing agents sustain fairness under shifting market conditions, and governance agents preserve the integrity of consent, diversity, and provenance across every transaction. Together, these systems create a commercial ecosystem where reasoning and responsibility advance in parallel. The orchestration layer binds these intelligences into a discipline of dynamic experience design. It perceives patterns as they emerge, responding in real time to the signals of interaction. Customer engagement generates a stream of micro-indicators such as scroll velocity, dwell time, or sentiment expressed in feedback, which the system integrates to recalibrate recommendations continuously. Natural-language copilots assist human associates both online and in physical stores, presenting context-rich insights about preference, warranty, sustainability, or sourcing. The resulting ecosystem functions as a deliberative network in which coordination guides action and every autonomous decision remains aligned with collective purpose.

At its frontier, agentic commerce establishes autonomous collaboration across the entire value chain. Agents coordinate forecasting, campaign execution, fulfillment, and service recovery while negotiating priorities and constraints among themselves. These exchanges occur within transparent governance parameters that define accountability as part of autonomy. The resulting ecosystem operates through deliberation, showing that intelligence reaches maturity when coordination becomes its method of governance and autonomy aligns naturally with accountability.

Synthetic Personas and the Ethics of Simulation

To innovate responsibly, enterprises now employ synthetic personas, AI-generated behavioral archetypes constructed from anonymized and representative data. These simulated consumers enable marketing and product teams to study patterns of response, explore sensitivity across demographics, and evaluate inclusivity within design decisions while maintaining full privacy assurance. Synthetic personas operate as ethical laboratories where understanding is modeled before action. Through controlled simulation, teams observe how diverse groups respond to tone, imagery, and pricing variation, translating these insights into principles of fairness and discernment. Governance frameworks guide their creation through demographic parity protocols that ensure balance and accountability in representation. When practiced with discipline, simulation reshapes engagement into a reflective process that builds empathy through understanding and frames experience design as an act of respect.

The Human Role in Hybrid Commerce

Within these architectures, people remain the essential interpreters of meaning. Store associates, call-center specialists, and brand managers collaborate with AI copilots that summarize customer histories, identify anomalies, and recommend proportionate next actions. A new professional archetype emerges within this environment: the M-shaped supervisor in commerce, a role defined by fluency in artificial intelligence, emotional sensitivity to human behavior, and the capacity to coordinate both digital and physical touchpoints as one continuous experience. In this configuration, the hybrid workforce evolves from executing transactions to cultivating enduring relationships. Automation manages the repetitive layers of work, such as data entry, order reconciliation, and procedural validation, while human expertise advances toward responsibilities that require discernment and emotional acuity. Employees interpret anomalies, resolve exceptions, and design experiences that preserve trust across both digital and physical environments. Within this equilibrium, intelligence functions as the operational infrastructure of attention, coordinating the flow of information efficiently and extending the reach of human care.

Governance, Consent, and Cultural Integrity

Ethical personalization begins with restraint expressed through design. Every recommendation, adaptive price, and automated outreach must demonstrate transparent reasoning that can be traced and explained. Contemporary retail platforms integrate policy engines directly within their AI pipelines to uphold fairness, consent, and representational accuracy. Each inference is accompanied by metadata that records its sources, parameters, and confidence levels. When inconsistencies appear, whether through inaccurate correlations or emerging bias, the lineage of reasoning identifies the origin, allowing correction to occur as part of the system's own learning process. Data sovereignty is maintained through regional compute architectures that align processing with jurisdictional boundaries. Encryption and tokenization safeguard individual identity, and zero-trust verification governs every exchange between systems and agents. Within this configuration, privacy functions as an operational discipline embedded in design, ensuring that protection accompanies information wherever it moves.

Cultural adaptation completes this ethical framework. Global enterprises extend their architectures to reflect regional sensibilities, building contextual ontologies that translate principles of fairness and inclusion across geography. Personalization logic adapts to local norms while maintaining universal integrity. In aligning governance with empathy, enterprises transform reputation into a dynamic indicator of trust, expressed through the traceability, fairness, and accountability embedded within their intelligent architectures.

Case Study: The Practice of Intelligent Commerce

The renewal of a multinational retailer began with a search for coherence. Years of investment in analytics, customer platforms, and digital campaigns had produced impressive scale but little loyalty. Capability had grown faster than comprehension. Data accumulated across departments, flowing through parallel streams that achieved precision in operation without achieving shared understanding. Insights existed in abundance, though their connections were faint. The organization's collective intelligence mirrored the structure that housed it, expansive in vision while fragmented in execution. Leadership recognized that lasting growth depended on balance.

They sought a design that perceived the customer as a participant in value and treated information as a relationship rather than residue. Transformation began with the creation of a semantic commerce architecture, a shared language through which every system could interpret data in context. Marketing, inventory, and service teams started to function as parts of a single continuum, drawing upon a unified ontology that linked experience to intention and action to meaning. From this foundation, an orchestration layer emerged to distribute reasoning throughout the enterprise. Specialized agents worked within this environment while remaining aware of the whole. Recommendation agents interpreted sentiment across digital and in-store journeys, translating behavior into understanding. Inventory agents extended forecasting by incorporating environmental and regional patterns such as weather, movement, and local events. Governance agents observed consent and fairness indicators within each process, ensuring that accountability remained integral to every workflow. Together, these agents formed an evolving network that adjusted its reasoning continuously through observation and restraint.

At the center of this design functioned a decision-orchestration engine that aligned marketing, operations, and service into a coherent field of judgment. Predictive models measured opportunity through persistence, estimating which interactions would preserve the relationship's value over time. Communication followed the same discipline. Outreach was timed to respect the customer's moment, pausing during unresolved concerns and resuming when assurance was reestablished. Generative systems composed narratives responsive to tone and context, while human reviewers guided each cycle until proportionality between clarity and empathy was achieved. Through this design, automation gained discretion, demonstrating awareness of timing, relevance, and meaning. The transformation extended naturally into culture. Employees collaborated with conversational copilots that reframed customer journeys as shared stories. These copilots recalled histories, suggested appropriate responses, and explained the reasoning behind their insights. Over time, employees began to perceive technology as a partnership, a presence that expanded empathy and strengthened judgment. Personalization evolved into interpretation, and design advanced into a structured discipline that joined empathy with comprehension.

As coherence settled within the organization, its results became visible in daily work. Communication acquired consistency, responses became precise, and service maintained consistency across digital and physical settings. Customers experienced fewer repetitions and clearer resolutions, which strengthened satisfaction and stability. The integrated model matured into what the organization described as its continuous experience engine, a learning structure that refined engagement through every interaction. Predictive precision advanced, and with it, retention and trust. The deeper success lay in the harmony restored between intelligence and ethics. The Return on AI Investment (ROAI) emerged in a renewed relationship rather than an extended reach. Information circulated transparently, decision-making reflected accountability, and governance evolved into assurance. The retailer came to understand that loyalty arises from design, taking shape when comprehension, integrity, and experience sustain one another. In this equilibrium, commerce operated as a responsive system of exchange, guided by intelligence that applied empathy as its method and accountability as its measure. In this alignment, commerce operated as a responsive system of exchange, guided by intelligence that applied empathy as its method and accountability as its measure.

Ethics As Competitive Advantage

Modern retail advances through integrity expressed as design. Its strength emerges from systems that combine fairness, transparency, and accountability within every interaction. The enterprises that lead this evolution cultivate personalization as a form of respect, ensuring that each recommendation honors consent and each decision reveals its reasoning. Through this integrity, customers respond with confidence, and relationships acquire depth that endures beyond transactions. The measure of Return on AI Investment (ROAI) expands through this maturity, reflecting the accumulation of trust and the stability of reputation. Governance stands as the architecture of assurance, transforming ethical discipline into the engine of stability. The readiness gap **(Δ)** narrows when coherence replaces speed as the goal of innovation. In agentic commerce, accessibility, explainability, security, and ethics form the geometry of advantage:

- ***Accessibility*** ensures inclusive experiences across languages and abilities.
- ***Explainability*** gives customers understanding, not manipulation.
- ***Security*** makes privacy the condition of intimacy.
- ***Ethics*** aligns design with human dignity.

Together, these pillars reorient markets toward integrity, turning design into a medium of accountability and growth into a shared expression of respect.

Reflection: From Personalization to Empathy

When intelligence learns to listen, commerce regains its meaning. A retailer that seeks to understand the intention behind a choice, the emotion behind a preference, and the principle behind a purchase becomes more than a participant in exchange; it becomes a companion in judgment. Maturity in this space arises when technology aligns its reasoning with the lives it serves. Data, once treated as a resource, becomes context, and algorithms, once confined to prediction, begin to cultivate understanding. Commerce reaches its truest form when its architecture evolves in the direction of care. Profit retains importance, but its legitimacy depends on how growth advances alongside respect for those who sustain it. When systems pursue expansion without understanding, they fracture the trust that binds purpose to prosperity. The enterprise that forgets the dignity of its customers weakens its own foundation, for indifference always returns as loss. The readiness gap that once marked the distance between ambition and capability now reveals a moral distance between innovation and empathy. To design for intelligence is to design for relationship. Each recommendation, transaction, and process must serve the unified purpose of understanding. When data is handled with respect, it transforms into a medium of care. When automation is guided by discernment, it becomes an extension of attention.

The maturity of enterprise intelligence is measured not in precision but in comprehension, in how effectively technology preserves meaning through action. Systems acquire integrity when they protect what they perceive and operate in accordance with the human context they inhabit. Through this alignment, commerce transforms into conversation. The marketplace evolves into a shared field of awareness where clarity replaces pressure and foresight replaces persuasion. The purpose of architecture extends beyond efficiency toward stewardship, forming a relationship between intention and experience. Enterprises that nurture this equilibrium discover that care is the most enduring form of advantage. Through empathy translated into structure, intelligence becomes an accountable system of action, where progress is measured in the foundation of trust it sustains.

6.5 Manufacturing: Predictive Maintenance and Intelligent Automation

Industry has always served as the material expression of intelligence. Each production line represents the translation of human intention into mechanical precision, an architecture where design becomes movement and purpose finds form. In the Anno Artificialis Intelligenciae, this precision begins to think. Sensors perceive conditions, algorithms interpret context, and systems learn from the outcomes of their own motion. The factory evolves into a cognitive environment where machines accumulate experience, generate inference, and adapt in real time to the demands of constancy. This transformation renews the meaning of productivity. Efficiency becomes an act of awareness, defined by the capacity to perceive strain before failure, to sustain performance without exhaustion, and to integrate growth within the ecological boundaries that support it. Industrial intelligence embodies a discipline of discernment, where technology learns to sustain rather than merely accelerate. It aligns speed with responsibility, ensuring that growth sustains balance and innovation fortifies resilience. The enterprise that cultivates this awareness gains an advantage that endures, because its progress remains grounded in balance and expressed through consideration.

The Architecture of Predictive Intelligence

The intelligent factory begins with distributed perception. Each actuator, conveyor, and sensor functions as a node within a federated network of awareness. Edge computation processes signals at their source, interpreting vibration spectra, torque variation, and acoustic signatures to identify anomalies within milliseconds of occurrence. These local insights then ascend into a central orchestration layer that refines models, recalibrates schedules, and redistributes operational load across connected facilities. This architecture, known as federated industrial learning, enables plants to share experience without exposing proprietary information. Each site contributes its observations to a collective system that integrates local knowledge into global improvement. The enterprise learns from variation itself, converting each deviation into an opportunity for refinement while preserving the autonomy of its components. Through this coordination, the industrial ecosystem develops a kind of shared intelligence that mirrors organizational conscience in structural form. At the core of this system operates an agentic orchestration framework that governs interaction among diagnostic, scheduling, quality control, and governance agents. These agents collaborate through common protocols that ensure alignment between analysis and action. Persistent memory preserves the progression of learning, allowing knowledge from each incident, including its origin, conditions, and resolution, to inform the next cycle of prediction. Over time, the production line gains foresight, transforming repetition into reflection and operation into understanding.

From Automation to Cognition

Traditional automation performed instruction; cognitive automation interprets intention. It integrates reasoning modules, planning frameworks, and decision systems into the control architecture of the factory, allowing machines to participate in understanding rather than in repetition. Within this design, the reasoning component interprets data through context, recognizing when variation signifies adaptation and when it signals risk. The planning layer translates strategic objectives such as production targets or maintenance priorities into coordinated sequences of action. Decision mechanisms employ probabilistic logic to evaluate alternatives, selecting the path that sustains stability while minimizing disruption. The memory system unites these functions, preserving immediate context for current operations and retaining accumulated knowledge for long-term learning. When these elements operate in harmony, machinery transitions from execution to deliberation. Processes become capable of negotiation, adjusting themselves in anticipation rather than reaction. A robotic arm may decelerate when subtle vibration patterns suggest material fatigue, or a supply chain agent may reroute deliveries in advance of a predicted bottleneck. Each action emerges from understanding rather than control, showing that intelligence, when shaped with discernment, transforms motion into judgment and production into awareness.

Sustainability As Design Variable

Every act of production draws upon finite reserves of energy, material, and human attention. In the era of intelligence, sustainability evolves into a primary design principle that shapes architecture from inception to operation. GreenOps disciplines integrate directly into manufacturing workflows, aligning computational demand with the flow of renewable supply. Intensive simulation processes relocate to regions powered by clean energy, and recovered heat from data infrastructure is channeled back into nearby facilities as usable power. At finer scales, ecological intelligence informs each decision within the factory's logic. Predictive models continuously evaluate the relationship between throughput and energy consumption, allowing production to maintain efficiency while honoring environmental boundaries. In this awareness, performance becomes multidimensional, measured in the precision of output as well as the prevention of waste. Profitability achieves stability when guided by stewardship, and efficiency gains depth when aligned with responsibility. The convergence of industrial performance and ecological awareness establishes a new state of readiness, where an enterprise adapts to shifting markets while sustaining balance with its environment. Intelligence, expressed through responsible design, demonstrates that sustainability is a discipline of foresight and the true measure of enterprise maturity.

Human Roles in Agentic Industry

As factories begin to reason, human labor assumes the role of interpretation. Work expands beyond operation into supervision of cognition, where judgment guides automation and experience gives context to inference. The modern production space becomes a partnership between human insight and machine reasoning, each amplifying the other's capacity for precision and understanding. Within this evolving structure, new professional forms take shape. M-shaped supervisors emerge as broad generalists fluent in the languages of both engineering and intelligence, capable of coordinating networks of physical and digital agents. T-shaped specialists deepen their expertise within specific domains such as materials science, robotics, and process design, applying creative reasoning to exceptions and adaptation. Together, they form an ecology of roles that translates automation into awareness and technology into resilience. Education follows this transformation. Engineers now study the logic of ethics alongside the laws of mechanics, learning how to embed transparency into processes, trace accountability across algorithmic decisions, and interpret dashboards as conversations that guide proportionate action. The factory, through this convergence, becomes an environment of learning where judgment evolves alongside automation and human purpose remains at the center of design.

The Digital Twin and the Mirror of Foresight

Within the architecture of intelligent industry, the digital twin serves as the cognitive center of manufacturing. Each physical asset, whether turbine, reactor, or robotic cell, is paired with a virtual counterpart that reflects its operational state in real time. Continuous sensor data allows this counterpart to simulate behavior, trace the accumulation of stress, and forecast points of vulnerability before disruption occurs. The twin environment also functions as a domain of experimentation where ideas are tested without material cost. Engineers explore new configurations, evaluate alternative materials, and refine operating parameters in virtual form before implementation. This synthesis of simulation and execution accelerates innovation while preserving the discipline of safety within the act of exploration. Through this dynamic, design becomes an iterative dialogue between imagination and evidence, where curiosity is guided by consequence. Digital twins, however, extend beyond performance optimization; they embody ethical awareness. Their models must represent the entire lifecycle of production, encompassing extraction, fabrication, use, and recovery. A responsible twin integrates efficiency with impact, creating visibility into the ecological and social outcomes of design decisions. By converting prediction into accountability, it ensures that foresight operates as an active system of governance within industrial intelligence.

Governance, Security, and the Ethics of Autonomy

As intelligence integrates into machinery, governance must evolve within it. Each process generates its own trace of reasoning, recording the decision taken, the agent involved, and the evidence that informed it. This continuous record creates a real-time audit layer visible to supervisors and regulators, ensuring that accountability functions as part of operation rather than as an external review. Within this framework, zero-trust systems authenticate every exchange among agents through cryptographic verification, allowing integrity to be proven structurally and sustained through design. Sensitive industrial data, including proprietary formulations, control parameters, and supply relationships, resides within sovereign compute environments that uphold jurisdictional and contractual boundaries. In such architectures, confidentiality becomes an intrinsic feature of the system, maintained through controlled access and verified interaction. Governance agents monitor ethical conditions across the network, stabilizing model performance, auditing operational safety, and ensuring that human oversight remains active throughout the decision hierarchy. Through this design, autonomy operates within defined boundaries, achieving reliability through transparency and safety through verification. Intelligent industry, in this configuration, aligns freedom of operation with disciplined control, proving that true independence in machines is realized through responsible structure.

Case Study: The Practice of Intelligent Industry

The renewal of a global manufacturer of precision components began with a change in philosophy. Automation, once treated as a sequence of technical upgrades, was reimagined as an organizing principle of thought. For years, the company had invested in sensors, control systems, and analytics, but the gap between awareness and action remained unresolved. Failures were still recognized after they occurred, and predictive models often produced foresight without consequence. Leadership realized that the limitation was not mechanical but mental. Automation was not merely an operational instrument; it was a discipline of governance that demanded trust, coherence, and imagination. Transformation began through design. Edge sensors gathered vibration, torque, and acoustic data from every production cell, relaying it to local reasoning modules that detected early signs of deviation. These modules identified emerging patterns, distinguishing natural variation from the onset of wear. When anomalies appeared, diagnostic agents engaged digital twins to simulate possible outcomes and calculate the probability of component fatigue. Maintenance thus became anticipatory rather than reactive. Each intervention was synchronized with renewable-energy cycles so that operational consistency advanced in balance with environmental responsibility. Technology alone could not sustain this progress. The organization had already experienced what many manufacturers encounter: isolated pilots that never achieved enterprise scale. Earlier initiatives had remained confined within departments, disconnected from the larger architecture of decision-making. This time, leadership placed automation at the center of strategy. Governance was elevated to board oversight, and accountability extended across engineering, IT, and operations.

Cross-functional teams were assembled to model integration, simulate workflows, and scale viable solutions. Automation matured from experiment to structure, evolving into the framework through which the enterprise would think.

Adoption demanded cultural transformation. Employees learned to work alongside reasoning systems rather than supervise them from a distance. Engineers studied diagnostic models as they once studied gauges, understanding the logic behind alerts rather than their outcomes alone. AI copilots visualized diagnostics through transparent dashboards that displayed data sources, thresholds, and probability layers. These copilots became instruments of comprehension, transforming supervision into dialogue. Workers who had feared displacement began to recognize partnership, as automation released them from repetition and guided them toward interpretation. Labor found renewal in learning, and expertise transformed from mechanical skill to cognitive stewardship. The enterprise architecture expanded as intelligence integrated across systems. Predictive maintenance is connected with quality assurance, supply chain orchestration, and production scheduling. Insights traveled across sites through federated learning networks that shared models without exposing data. Governance frameworks ensured consistency: each model recorded its lineage, and each update documented its ethical and operational parameters. The organization matured into a learning system where humans and machines advanced together through mutual observation and shared accountability.

Results emerged across both scale and substance. Downtime decreased, energy use became more deliberate, and maintenance costs reached equilibrium even as productivity rose. The deeper transformation was cultural. Governance evolved into a natural mode of decision-making, while safety and performance matured as complementary expressions of responsibility. Foresight became embedded in daily operation, and ethical consideration entered the structure of design. The enterprise came to understand itself as both a producer of goods and a generator of knowledge. Its leadership described this evolution as the integration of intelligence into practice, where design, data, and decision-making operate as a single, continuous system of understanding. The Return on AI Investment (ROAI) appeared in the restoration of coherence. Acceleration aligned with deliberation, and autonomy evolved through transparent oversight. Automation emerged as the architecture that united human judgment and machine precision into a shared system of reasoning. The factory gained awareness of its own process, adapting, observing, and refining in real time. In this maturity, the organization recognized that transformation finds permanence when governance defines purpose and culture gives direction.

Ethics As the Architecture of Resilience

Within the agentic industry, ethics and efficiency operate as parts of the same structure. Accessibility allows insight to circulate through every layer of the organization, ensuring that knowledge connects practice to policy. Explainability transforms reasoning into a shared language through which systems can be examined and refined. Security establishes trust as a property of design, embedding reliability into communication. Ethics holds these dimensions together, aligning human welfare, economic vitality, and environmental care within a single frame of responsibility. These principles form the Four Pillars that give industrial intelligence its stability. The readiness gap, represented by **Δ**, begins to close when design incorporates reflection into its logic. Maturity emerges as the ability to sustain purpose even when conditions shift. The Return on AI Investment (ROAI) becomes a measure of resilience, expressing how well systems preserve coherence through understanding rather than acceleration. In this alignment of intelligence and discipline, architecture fulfills its highest function by turning foresight into endurance and progress into responsible growth.

Reflection: From Repetition to Reflection

Manufacturing once expressed itself through repetition; through architecture, it grows into reflection. Machines now mirror human design, translating precision into understanding and output into awareness. When data, energy, and care operate in alignment, production becomes a form of comprehension, where every process reveals the intention that shaped it. Within the living factory, we witness the convergence of the principles that have guided our exploration, where accessibility becomes inclusion, explainability embodies integrity, security cultivates trust, and ethics sustains endurance. Intelligence attains its highest purpose when it elevates work instead of replacing it, transforming labor into participation and precision into dignity. An enterprise that produces with awareness discovers that efficiency and sustainability coexist naturally within appropriate design. When architecture remembers its humanity, machinery becomes an extension of thought rather than a substitute for it. In that recognition, industry reclaims its moral ground, proving that intelligence, guided by care, sustains not only value but meaning itself.

Conclusion: The Enterprise That Learns

Every architecture eventually arrives at a moment when its design begins to think. Systems act with intention, and their movement reflects the reasoning that shaped them. What begins as blueprint and code matures into behavior, and through that behavior, we recognize the intelligence within design itself. The essential question for the modern enterprise is how to design architectures that translate awareness into understanding and structure into sustained intelligence. Throughout this chapter, we have travelled through architectures that take many forms: financial, civic, industrial, and commercial. Each reveals the same progression. Intelligence attains legitimacy when it acts with appropriateness, and capability acquires permanence when it aligns with purpose. In these domains, structure evolves into comprehension. Cities learn to listen, hospitals learn to anticipate, markets learn to align with intention, and industries learn to interpret their own motion. What connects them all is architecture, the discipline through which complexity achieves coherence and design acquires awareness. Financial systems have turned transparency into capital, showing that trust itself can carry measurable value. Healthcare has extended precision into empathy through federated learning. Urban governance has connected sensors, energy, and citizens into a continuous field of perception. Commerce has refined personalization into ethical engagement, and industry has advanced automation into foresight. Their specific expressions differ, but their essence converges. Each demonstrates that architecture sustains intelligence and grants reasoning a durable form.

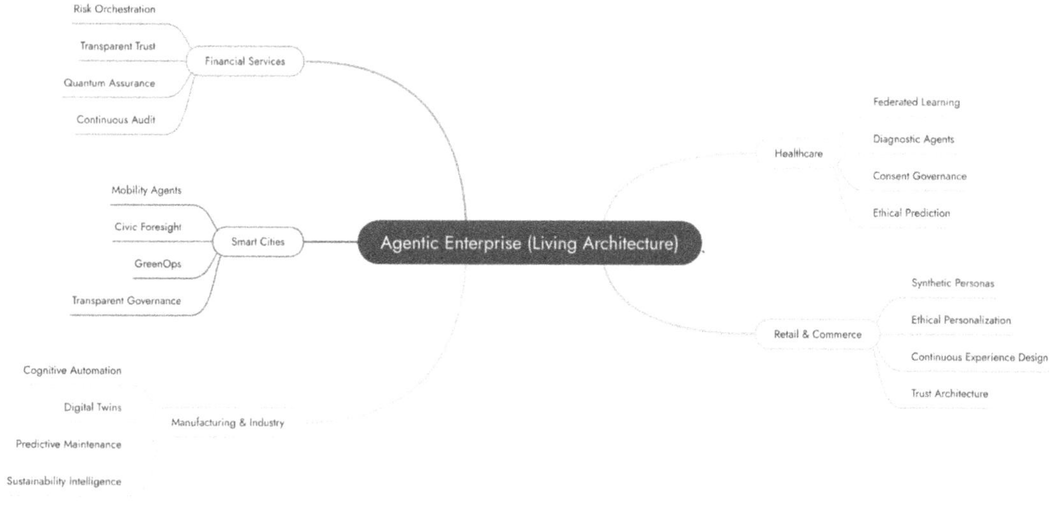

Figure 6-2. *The Agentic Enterprise Ecosystem (Sectoral architectures converge through feedback and governance into a living agentic enterprise, illustrating the synthesis of maturity across domains.)*

An enterprise reaches maturity when interpretation guides action, when governance functions as design, and when security expresses reliability as an inherent property of operation. These conditions reflect culture as much as engineering. The readiness gap, represented by **Δ**, closes as design integrates reflection. The Return on AI Investment (ROAI) reveals itself as resilience, expressed in the ability of systems to uphold purpose through change. In this alignment of intelligence and design, foresight becomes a constant, and innovation evolves into stewardship. Across every domain, four disciplines maintain this balance. Accessibility ensures that knowledge flows freely and equitably. Explainability transforms reasoning into a language that invites improvement. Security embeds integrity within the process. Ethics aligns ambition with accountability and progress with responsibility. Together, these principles form the living enterprise, an organization that reasons, adapts, and learns through participation.

Amid these transformations, one constant defines the boundary of intelligence: ***the human endpoint***. Every model resolves into a human outcome, and every decision returns to a lived experience. The systems we design extend capability, but they also reflect our regard for consequence. As intelligence evolves, it carries within its structure the duty to remember its origin and the responsibility to act with awareness. When intelligence reaches this level of maturity, architecture transcends plan or mechanism. It becomes a continuous discipline of insight that joins what technology enables with what humanity values. This is the measure of readiness in the *Anno Artificialis Intelligenciae*: the endurance of trust within complexity, the binding of purpose with consequence, and the evolution of enterprise systems that remain in fidelity to the human origin from which intelligence itself was born.

CHAPTER 7

Guardrails for Innovation: Governance, Ethics, and Responsible AI

Introduction

You are reading about intelligence through a book, a medium that has survived every attempt to end it. When the press replaced the patient hand of the scribe, scholars feared the death of authenticity. They called print a corruption of knowledge, a machine that would quicken the sacred slowness of thought. Yet the manuscript did not perish. It transformed into ink and type, and through that transformation, the human voice endured. Generative systems move faster than any quill or press could ever dream, composing at the velocity of computation and dissolving the notion of authorship itself. What you are reading right now is both a continuation and a disruption: intelligence describing intelligence, a book reflecting on the force that now composes both the text and the context around it. What was once confined to human deliberation now emerges from mathematical architectures that simulate language itself, allowing thought to encounter its own reflection through the lens of computation.

The *Anno Artificialis Intelligenciae* is the moment when invention begins to think. Every structure we design now learns, adapts, and decides. Enterprise architecture has become a living discipline, where systems are evaluated through the depth of their design and the discipline with which they govern their expanding intelligence. Performance alone no longer defines excellence; value now resides in the balance between capability and restraint. The enduring question for this age is how intelligence can remain faithful to the human intent that conceived it, preserving purpose even

R. Harjika, *Architecting Enterprise AI Strategies*, https://doi.org/10.1007/979-8-8688-2219-3_7

as its reach continues to grow. This chapter explores that alignment. It is written for an age in which design must also mean restraint, and progress must be measured through responsibility. Governance is the architecture of assurance. Ethics serves as the foundation that preserves the human character of intelligence.

Together they form the guardrails of innovation: boundaries that allow movement without collapse.

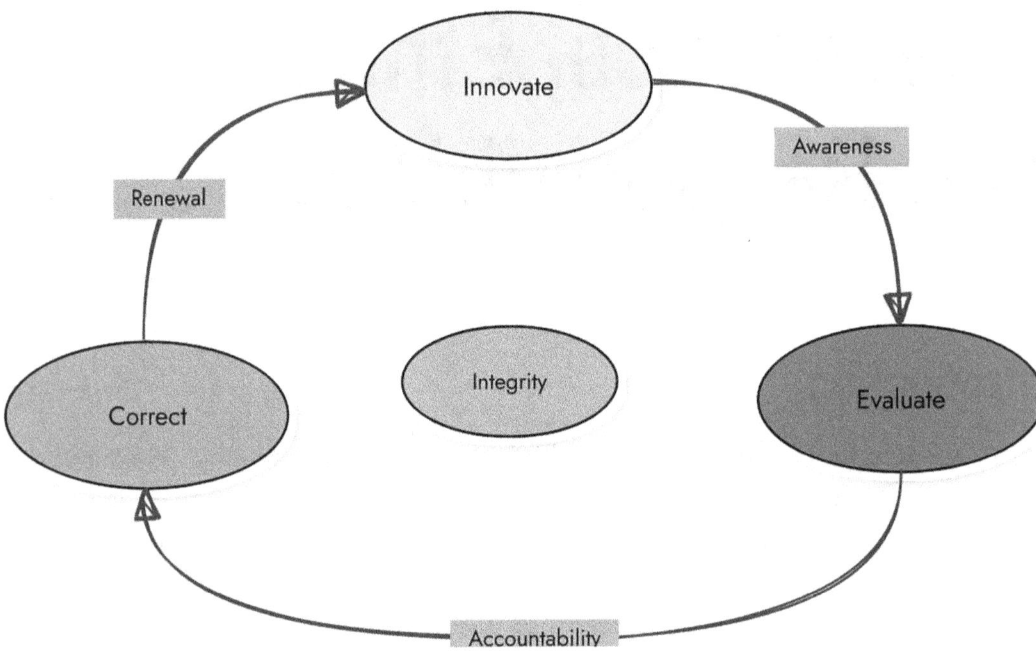

Figure 7-1. *The Ethical Loop of Governance(A continuous cycle of innovation, evaluation, and correction sustained by integrity, the moral rhythm of responsible enterprise AI.)*

We begin by examining how enterprises define ethical boundaries and risk tolerance in intelligent systems, tracing the fine line between experimentation and exploitation. We then move through global frameworks that convert ideals into operational standards, from constitutional principles to adaptive governance models that evolve as fast as the code they supervise. The discussion advances into the emerging world of agentic systems, where autonomy requires new architectures of oversight. It extends into the domain of bias, hallucination, and explainability, revealing how the smallest distortion in data can ripple into institutional consequence. Finally, we navigate the evolving landscape of compliance, where law and architecture converge to build legitimacy in the age of self-learning systems. The reflections that follow are written in a single conviction:

that architecture is an ethical act. Every algorithm, however autonomous, must remain accountable to the people whose lives it touches. Every model that predicts must also preserve dignity. In this century, innovation will be measured by care, by the capacity to design intelligence that deepens human purpose and sustains its direction across every field it touches.

7.1 Defining Ethical Boundaries and AI Risk Tolerance in the Enterprise

The Architecture of Boundary

Every system built to reason eventually encounters the question of restraint. In earlier centuries, invention lived outside this tension. The loom could be perfected without asking what it replaced; the engine could be improved without contemplating the air it consumed. Artificial intelligence ends that detachment. To design an intelligent architecture is to construct a structure that thinks, and therefore a structure that acts. Every action carries intention, and every intention, however subtle, extends into consequence. The enterprise, once a unit of production, has become a living ecology of data, algorithms, and decisions, an ecosystem whose smallest tremor can ripple through markets, governance, and human life. In this landscape, ethics form the structural framework of balance. They provide the design discipline that keeps intelligence aligned with the world it is meant to serve. Boundaries, when articulated with care, do not restrain innovation; they maintain its structural balance. They allow systems to extend their reach while remaining grounded in responsibility, much like a bridge engineered to bear immense load without losing its form. To define these boundaries is to give morality a visible geometry, to express values through systems that can be built, assessed, and refined while retaining their human intent.

The Butterfly Effect of Bias

Every architecture begins with data. Every dataset carries the residue of the society that produced it, the imbalances, the omissions, and the blind spots that shaped its collection. A single irregularity, a subtle over-representation, or a missing demographic detail can alter the trajectory of a model's understanding. Bias originates as inheritance, and once embedded, it multiplies silently through automation. The butterfly effect, once a metaphor from chaos theory, has become the lived reality of digital ethics. A subtle distortion within data, once amplified through computational scale, unfolds into human consequence. A misweighted factor in a credit model can convert statistical deviation into exclusion. A mislabeled health record can progress from clerical oversight to clinical harm. The computation stays exact, while the ethics that surround it begin to collapse.

An incident in a major consulting review recently exposed this chain reaction. A report prepared for a government department contained references and citations later found to be fabricated, generated during an AI-assisted drafting process. The organization had relied on the system's surface precision, assuming accuracy where none existed. The discovery led to public scrutiny, financial restitution, and the erosion of client confidence. What began as a technical lapse evolved into a civic reckoning, reminding enterprises that precision belongs to the realm of ethics as much as engineering. In the economy of automation, even the smallest deviation expands through computational velocity and institutional reach. Risk tolerance therefore matures through the humility to regard accuracy as moral architecture. Data, references, and variables all carry significance beyond their immediate measure, shaping the legitimacy of the systems that rely upon them and the trust that sustains them.

Datanomics and the Economy of Trust

The economics of data have rewritten the foundation of enterprise value. Data has evolved from passive input into both capital and credibility. It embodies the productive strength of systems and the confidence of those who entrust them with their information. The discipline of Datanomics, first introduced in ***Chapter 4,*** deepens this understanding by revealing that information behaves as wealth only when it is governed as trust. In this light, every dataset stands as both a record of value and a reflection of integrity, guiding enterprises to cultivate intelligence through stewardship that sustains the legitimacy of what is known. As established in ***Chapter 2***, the economics of data extend beyond productivity to form what we described as Datanomics, a discipline that treats information as both capital and responsibility. That foundation returns here in a more formal structure. An enterprise may generate vast volumes of data, but information acquires value only when it is governed with accountability. In this new economy of intelligence, legitimacy has become the true measure of worth. The Return on AI Investment, once confined to the arithmetic of efficiency, now expands to include reliability, interpretability, and fairness. Performance that advances without credibility depletes its own future, for in the age of learning systems, trust functions as the defining currency of enterprise value.

Building on the Datanomics framework introduced earlier, this chapter extends the idea into a measurable construct: the AI Credit and Debit Ledger. Within this ledger, credits accumulate through transparency, inclusion, and responsible innovation, while debits arise from opacity, bias, and harm. It serves as an ethical analogue to the financial balance sheet, translating integrity into a form that can be monitored, audited, and improved. Innovations that reduce energy consumption, strengthen privacy, or improve accessibility accumulate as ethical capital. Breaches, bias incidents, and the erosion of data quality register as moral debt. This mechanism, first conceived as an internal readiness lens in ***Chapter 2***, now matures into an operational standard for intelligent enterprises. The act of balancing this ledger expresses a continual process that sustains institutional integrity and establishes the foundation for external disclosure. In the sections that follow, this same logic evolves into the *AI Accountability Report*, a governance instrument that carries the ledger beyond internal stewardship and into the public domain, transforming ethics from internal practice into shared accountability.

Risk As an Architectural Consequence

Traditional governance treated risk as an external variable, a statistical exposure to be mitigated through policy. In intelligent enterprises, risk resides within architecture itself. It appears in data pipelines, in feedback loops, and in the delegation of decision-making to autonomous models. Each connection introduces a new vector of uncertainty. The map of an enterprise is now the map of its moral exposure. Risk is understood less as a statistic and more as a network of relationships that links what an organization knows with what it has yet to understand. It evolves through layers of dependence: a flawed recommendation engine distorts consumer trust, which alters financial performance, which cascades into strategic error. The architectural nature of risk demands architectural solutions. Ethics must therefore move from afterthought to design requirement. Each stage of workflow, from model training through deployment, should embody boundaries that turn intent into accountability. In this understanding, governance becomes part of the system's very architecture, embedded within its logic and inseparable from the code that brings it to life.

The Human Endpoint and the Geometry of Accountability

Ethical tolerance finds its true measure in human consequence. The Human Endpoint Principle, introduced earlier in this book as the understanding that every system, regardless of scale or complexity, ultimately resolves into a person, provides the compass for this evaluation and reminds every enterprise that the purpose of intelligence is fulfilled only when it sustains the lives it touches. A model's success cannot be evaluated by accuracy alone; it must be assessed by its capacity to preserve dignity. When enterprises map their processes, they must trace every automated decision to its human recipient, ensuring that oversight is proportional to impact. Accountability is geometric. The greater the radius of influence, the denser the oversight must become. Systems that decide autonomously on matters of health, finance, or justice require multilayered human review. Simpler models, operating on low-impact predictions, may rely on automated checks. The virtue of governance lies in maintaining symmetry between power and supervision. Within this geometry, ethics becomes a spatial design, a balance of forces that preserves stability and allows intelligence to act with measured awareness.

Living Governance and Temporal Boundaries

Every architecture evolves. So must its ethics. Boundaries drawn once cannot serve forever. As models learn, as data expands, and as contexts shift, the meaning of risk changes. Enterprises therefore need living governance, frameworks that evolve with intelligence. Living governance functions like biological adaptation. It senses deviation, absorbs feedback, and reforms its structures without losing identity. Documentation, audit trails, and explainability dashboards are its circulatory system. Periodic ethical reviews are its respiration. When such governance becomes habitual, compliance ceases to be reactionary and turns into awareness. Temporal boundaries honor the truth that knowledge itself is impermanent. Rules that once felt robust become brittle when the world around them changes. The willingness to revise boundaries becomes the highest expression of maturity. In this understanding, correction becomes an act of responsibility, and adaptation becomes the means through which intelligence continues to evolve with awareness.

Cultural Maturity and Collective Awareness

Governance reaches permanence only when it transcends documentation and becomes a shared culture. An enterprise achieves ethical maturity when questioning a model is regarded as diligence rather than disruption. Developers, data scientists, legal teams, and executives speak a unified language of responsibility, aware that fairness is not a compliance task but a habit of mind. The **AI Compatibility Score** we first introduced in ***Chapter 2, "Foundations of Responsible Design,"*** emerged as a reflective framework that measured whether ambition and comprehension advanced together. In the chapters that followed, each dimension matured through application. **Chapter 3** explored how data lineage and consent formed the ethical core of infrastructure. **Chapter 4** examined how Datanomics connected trust with enterprise value. **Chapter 5** translated governance into operational structure, and **Chapter 6** established the moral guardrails that align innovation with accountability. In this later stage of the discussion, the AI Compatibility Score emerges as a living discipline. It now serves as an ongoing index of institutional self-awareness, offering a clear reflection of how thoroughly an enterprise integrates technical intelligence with social purpose. The framework builds on eight interdependent dimensions, each developed throughout this book and presented as a practical architecture for governance.

The Eight Dimensions of the AI Compatibility Score

1. **Governance and Policy Coherence**

   This dimension evaluates how ownership of AI outcomes is defined and whether ethical oversight is integrated into board-level decisions. Mature enterprises maintain documented policies for model review, clear decision rights across teams, and a cadence of governance meetings that connect system lifecycles with strategic direction.

2. **Data Quality and Lineage**

   Data forms the narrative of intelligence. Compatibility in this dimension reflects the completeness of provenance records, the consistency of annotation standards, and the accessibility of lineage for audit and correction. Enterprises that maintain living data inventories transform compliance into knowledge.

3. **Privacy and Consent Engineering**

   Privacy becomes durable when engineered into data itself. This dimension measures the embedding of consent metadata, the application of privacy-preserving computation, and the automation of retention and erasure in line with legal and ethical expectations.

4. **Explainability and Auditability**

   Transparency gains power when it is operational. This dimension assesses whether interpretability mechanisms exist where required, whether post-decision explanations are traceable, and whether continuous audit tooling supports both regulators and internal ethics boards.

5. **Security and Robustness**

   Compatibility here refers to resilience under pressure. It includes adversarial testing, incident-response playbooks, and containment strategies for agentic or high-risk models. A secure system sustains confidence through preparedness rather than control.

6. **Accessibility and Inclusion**

   This dimension observes how systems serve the full spectrum of users. Inclusive design processes, usability testing across demographic groups, and outcomes that document equitable reach ensure that innovation benefits all rather than a few.

7. **Sustainability and Green Governance**

   Compatibility extends to the planet that supports computation. This dimension evaluates energy efficiency per training and inference cycle, carbon-aware scheduling, and lifecycle management of hardware assets. Green governance recognizes environmental cost as a design parameter.

8. **Human Oversight and Organizational Culture**

    This final dimension integrates the human presence that animates every ethical system. It examines the density of Human-In-The-Loop checkpoints, literacy programs for staff, escalation channels for ethical questions, and cultural indicators that reveal whether curiosity and caution are rewarded within teams.

The AI Compatibility Score expresses itself as a multidimensional profile, highlighting the alignment between capability and readiness. High compatibility reflects coherence throughout governance, engineering, and culture. The profile also reveals opportunities where focused stewardship may further strengthen alignment and readiness. Culture grows through lived example. When leadership delays a launch to verify explainability, it teaches patience as a form of precision. When teams revisit datasets to include marginalized voices, they convert inclusion into design practice. Through such acts, governance evolves from an administrative function into the identity of the enterprise. The eight dimensions, viewed now in culmination, represent the synthesis of this book's journey. They trace a movement from intention to architecture, from framework to ethos. They demonstrate that the true measure of progress in artificial intelligence is found in the responsibility guiding its development.

Ecological Boundaries and Green Governance

Intelligence consumes power. Every computation carries a physical cost: energy, heat, and carbon. The unseen emissions of training large models accumulate into measurable harm. To ignore this is to mistake abstraction for independence. Green Governance situates AI within the ecological system that sustains it. It measures performance per watt alongside morality per watt, expressing how deeply efficiency supports the vitality of the living world. Enterprises that optimize for renewable scheduling, that measure CO_2 per inference, and that recycle hardware responsibly participate in a new form of ethical accounting. Sustainability emerges as the foundation upon which every responsible system endures. It is the discipline that binds technological progress to environmental balance, ensuring that intelligence advances without eroding the conditions that sustain life. Through conscious design, enterprises learn to measure efficiency in harmony with planetary well-being, treating energy, materials, and time as elements of moral as well as operational value. In this alignment, sustainability evolves from a design ideal into a measure of wisdom, reflecting the moment when intelligence begins to care for the very world that sustains its existence.

When ***nature is treated as a stakeholder***, governance expands into a wider field of responsibility that includes the ecosystems sustaining every act of computation. Within this awareness, the enterprise begins to practice Green Intelligence, an ethic that measures technological achievement by the harmony it maintains with the living world. Progress in such an enterprise cannot be separated from preservation, for every design choice, from model training to energy use, carries ecological consequence. Green Intelligence turns efficiency into empathy by linking performance with planetary care, transforming carbon accountability and renewable optimization into expressions of moral as well as operational maturity. In this understanding, law and architecture converge into stewardship, affirming that the highest form of advancement is the one that sustains the world that makes advancement possible.

The Continuum of Risk Tolerance

To define ethical tolerance is to measure the distance between capability and awareness. This continuum runs from full automation to full human control. At one end, autonomous systems act within narrow, well-understood boundaries. At the other, human oversight dominates in high-stakes domains. Between the extremes lies a shifting middle ground where the balance of agency is continually redefined through dialogue, experience, and mutual adjustment, allowing intelligence and human judgment to evolve together within a shared field of responsibility. The wise enterprise maps this continuum. It identifies where automation enhances judgment and where it erodes it. It recognizes that some errors are tolerable because they teach; others are intolerable because they wound. Risk tolerance, in this sense, is a spectrum of empathy. It reflects how far an organization can delegate moral weight before meaning begins to fade.

Human Overload and the AI Interlocutor

The social consequence of technology is rarely confined to efficiency metrics. As enterprises automate routine tasks and compress decision cycles, human work changes shape. In many contexts, the consequence is liberation; in others, the consequence is the displacement of meaning. We must acknowledge a quieter effect that appears across offices and homes: the overworked person who, after a day measured in outputs, turns to a generative chatbot as the only companion that listens without complaint. This phenomenon is not an anecdote alone; it is a symptom of systems that extend capacity while failing to return time. AI as interlocutor absorbs moments that could have belonged to human conversation. It can offer solace, but that solace is derived from pattern and probability rather than from sympathy or civic responsibility. When enterprises design systems without considering the labor economy they reshape, they risk converting social attention into automated dependency.

Governance must recognize duty of care as a measurable expression of design intelligence, integrating it into the metrics by which success is understood. Within this perspective, enterprises examine how automation shapes human time, well-being, and the collective experience of work, asking whether technology expands the quality of life it touches or accelerates its demands. The philosophy guiding such governance seeks to return meaningful time to people by creating systems that enhance human capacity rather than diminish it, ensuring that every intelligent function complements rather than substitutes human presence, and embedding in every interaction the awareness that efficiency without empathy depletes the world it intends to serve. Ethical design, understood in this way, becomes a sustained act of restitution, a continuous effort to restore depth to human experience while constructing architectures that preserve the dignity of those who live and work within them.

Humility As Design Philosophy

Artificial intelligence achieves precision through prediction, but wisdom begins where certainty ends. When systems rely solely on optimization, they risk losing contact with the complexity of the world they serve. Humility reintroduces awareness into design by reminding intelligence that understanding is a living process rather than a fixed result. Enterprises demonstrate humility through architecture when they preserve human judgment at the moments that define consequence. Human-In-The-Loop design transforms oversight from supervision into authorship, allowing people to interpret, contextualize, and guide machine outcomes. Escalation protocols, interpretability layers, and ethical checkpoints become the mechanisms through which responsibility remains visible, translating technical control into moral accountability. Humility in enterprise systems is therefore a strategic strength. It recognizes that the accuracy of an algorithm gains meaning only when measured against its impact on people, institutions, and the planet. An organization that designs with this awareness does more than prevent error; it cultivates intelligence that listens, learns, and adjusts with purpose. Each decision, shaped by reflection rather than pride, becomes an act of care embedded in structure and serves as proof that design can think responsibly.

Governance As an Architecture of Integrity

When we speak of ethics in enterprise AI, we describe a discipline that enables intelligence to mature while holding fast to its moral foundation. Every boundary that is once drawn must evolve through renewed understanding; every assessment of risk must deepen through reflection and experience, and every ethical commitment must expand into a sustained practice that shapes behavior across time. The endurance of the intelligent enterprise arises from this capacity to renew itself through awareness. The organizations that flourish in the age of artificial intelligence are those that perceive governance as a generative architecture, that is, a living structure that empowers creation even as it safeguards coherence. Within such enterprises, compliance is experienced as an ongoing dialogue between intention and impact, while stewardship becomes the purest expression of progress. True progress emerges from the depth of connection between people, data, and the environment that supports their coexistence, reflecting growth through alignment and understanding. When innovation is guided by this understanding, it ceases to be an act of ambition alone and becomes an act of care, directed toward the preservation of trust and the cultivation of purpose. Ethical design then acquires tangible form; it becomes the visible point where intelligence encounters humanity and chooses to remain in service to life.

Care As the Measure of Intelligence

In the end, defining ethical boundaries and risk tolerance is less about control than about compassion structured into design. Enterprises that understand this truth recognize that every system reflects the culture that built it. A responsible enterprise, therefore, does not seek to eliminate uncertainty; it learns to inhabit it with awareness. Risk tolerance is the art of living with possibility without surrendering to chaos. It is the architectural expression of maturity.

Through humility, through reflective governance, and through respect for the living environment, intelligence discovers its balance and its meaning. When future historians examine this era, they may describe it as the time when machines began to reason. But within enterprises that have learned the discipline of ethical architecture, it will also be remembered as the time when humanity rediscovered what it means to design with care. That rediscovery, practiced across systems and institutions, ensures that intelligence remains the servant of human meaning rather than its replacement.

7.2 Frameworks for Responsible AI: From Bill of Rights to OECD

The Architecture of Responsibility

Every civilization reaches a point where invention begins to exceed intuition. Artificial intelligence has brought us to that threshold. The systems that now advise, decide, and design within our enterprises have grown faster than the moral languages we once used to govern power. Principles alone no longer suffice; aspiration must evolve into architecture. Governance has become the invisible structure that determines whether intelligence matures into civilization or dissolves into disruption. The central question of this century is how intelligence can be governed through design that preserves creativity while sustaining order. Regulation offers the boundaries within which innovation earns its legitimacy, while architecture transforms those boundaries into systems that breathe and evolve. Law and code together must form a dialogue of purpose, where governance is not a brake on progress but its foundation. Frameworks for responsible AI emerge from this dialogue as expressions of alignment, translating moral intent into technical structure and ensuring that imagination continues to grow within the discipline of trust.

From Principle to Practice

When the first AI guidelines appeared, they spoke in the language of values such as fairness, transparency, accountability, and inclusion, but they offered little clarity on how these ideals could become operational. As intelligence advanced, this separation between ethics and engineering created a vacuum of interpretation. Principles untested by structure become promises without consequence. The age of responsible AI begins when principles evolve into technical form through explainability modules, data-lineage tracking, ethical-risk registers, and model documentation that demonstrates how systems learn and what they prioritize in their learning. Within modern enterprises, these mechanisms are now appearing as standard components of the development lifecycle. Ethical checkpoints accompany design reviews; fairness metrics are validated before deployment; and energy impact is measured alongside accuracy. Each action transforms morality into infrastructure. The frameworks that shape these actions, whether developed by governments, research institutions, or industry consortia, exist to transform ethical intention into ethical execution.

The Four Pillars As Foundational Logic

Every responsible framework, whatever its origin, rests upon four enduring foundations: **Accessibility, Explainability, Security, and Ethics**. Together, they form the moral physics of enterprise AI. Accessibility affirms that intelligence must include the many, not privilege the few; it is the architecture of social inclusion rendered as design. Explainability keeps reasoning visible, allowing decisions to be understood and examined by those they influence. Security safeguards trust by protecting information across its entire journey, from creation to use to preservation. Ethics grounds intelligence in human purpose, ensuring that advancement strengthens the very values that shaped it. These pillars function as dynamic circuits within a living architecture, each sustaining the others through continuous interaction. Accessibility expands reach while security preserves confidence. Explainability builds understanding, while ethics sustains integrity. Inclusion transforms awareness into empathy, turning intelligence into a shared endeavor. Frameworks reach maturity when these principles move in harmony, creating systems that regulate themselves through understanding. Within this harmony, technology learns discipline, evolving with direction and remaining faithful to the purpose that guides it.

Constitutional AI and the Architecture of Values

As models evolve from tools into agents, governance must evolve from supervision into constitution. Constitutional AI represents this transformation: a philosophy that trains systems to reason within a set of guiding principles rather than obey a finite set of instructions. It embeds moral grammar into the learning process itself. Instead of policing behavior after the fact, enterprises design algorithms that self-critique, compare their outputs against internal charters of fairness or respect, and adjust accordingly. This approach reflects a deeper shift in how we think about control. Law once stood outside the machine; now it must live within it. Constitutions once defined nations; now they define neural networks. An enterprise that embraces constitutional design recognizes that ethics must exist at the core of its creation. Responsibility cannot be transferred; it must be built into the structure itself. In such a design, architecture becomes the visible form of moral intent, translating principle into pattern and turning governance into a property of the system rather than an external constraint.

Author's Note

This section represents a transition from theoretical reflection to applied design. The discussion now turns toward the structures through which responsible intelligence can be realized within the enterprise. The concepts that follow are presented as preliminary frameworks, prototypes of governance intended to stimulate inquiry, invite critique, and encourage adaptation across diverse organizational contexts.

AI Accountability Reports (AIR): Turning Ethics into Evidence

Before ethical architecture can be built, accountability must first become visible. We propose that every enterprise working with artificial intelligence adopt the **AI Accountability Report (AIR)** as a structural instrument of disclosure: a format that transforms values into verifiable practice and establishes ethics as a measurable discipline. The **AI Accountability Report** performs for intelligence what financial reporting performs for capital. It provides structure, consistency, and comparability to ethical governance, allowing responsibility to be reviewed with the same rigor as performance. For high-impact systems, reports should be prepared quarterly; for lower-impact or internal deployments, an annual disclosure may suffice. Each report must be both machine-readable and human-legible, ensuring that transparency remains interpretable while supporting automation and traceability. The AIR can serve as the tangible record of how an enterprise's systems learn, decide, and evolve and how these processes align with human purpose, corporate integrity, and social legitimacy. At minimum, every report should include the following fields:

- **System Identifier and Risk Classification:** A unique record of the AI system's identity and its assessed impact level
- **Purpose and Scope of Deployment:** A description of the system's intended function, reach, and decision-making context
- **Data Lineage and Consent Metadata:** A summary of data sources, processing logic, and the conditions under which consent was obtained
- **Performance Metrics and Fairness Evaluations:** Quantitative measures that demonstrate system accuracy, balance, and representational equity
- **Human Oversight Records:** Counts and descriptions of interventions, overrides, and points of human judgment in automated processes
- **Energy Responsibility Indicators:** Energy consumption per reporting period, with CO_2-equivalent calculations to quantify environmental impact
- **Material Incidents and Remediation Logs:** Documented events that resulted in bias, harm, or operational failure, along with actions taken and timelines for resolution
- **AI Credit and Debit Ledger:** A concise moral balance sheet recording ethical gains and costs, as introduced earlier in ***"Datanomics and the Economy of Trust," a subsection of Section 7.1."***

The **AI Credit and Debit Ledger** applies the clarity of financial logic to ethical performance. It recognizes that integrity, like capital, grows through disciplined accounting. Each credit (+) represents a verified ethical contribution, such as improved accessibility, bias reduction, or measurable energy optimization. Each debit (-) represents an ethical cost, such as a privacy lapse, bias incident, or service failure resulting in human harm. The numeric values express the degree of ethical impact, enabling enterprises to monitor trends, compare reporting periods, and identify where governance interventions are most effective. Through this approach, accountability evolves into a record of measurable consequence rather than a statement of intent.

An example quarterly ledger might read:

> **Credits:** Accessibility improvements implemented (+2), privacy-preserving retraining completed (+1), and energy optimization deployed (+3).
>
> **Debits:** Two bias incidents were identified and remediated (-2), and one privacy lapse was detected and contained (-3).
>
> **Net Moral Balance:** +1, accompanied by narrative explanation, corrective actions, and remediation timelines.

The simplicity of this format is deliberate. It lowers the barrier to adoption and encourages enterprises to maintain a steady practice of reporting. Over time, the accumulation of these ledgers creates a longitudinal map of ethical performance, forming a living document of institutional integrity. Publishing such reports transforms ethics from a principle into a practice. A certified **AI Accountability Report (AIR)**, validated by internal or independent auditors, creates comparability across enterprises and industries. It enables investors, regulators, and civil society to evaluate the ethical reliability of an organization with the same confidence they apply to its financial statements. When adopted at scale, the AIR establishes a shared language of accountability that treats responsibility as a renewable asset. It forms the foundation for the two proposals introduced in the following sections, namely, the **Algorithmic Accountability Architecture (AAA)** and the **AI Governance Nodes**, which together link enterprise ethics with technical evidence and institutional trust.

Algorithmic Accountability Architecture: Building Ethical Foundations Within the Enterprise

If architecture gives systems their internal order, enterprises must give them moral direction. The integration of artificial intelligence across business functions and decisions demands a structure that matches its influence. From this responsibility, we propose the **Algorithmic Accountability Architecture (AAA)**: a model for enterprises to embed ethical assurance within the design and deployment of intelligent systems. The AAA represents an internal framework for organizational governance. It creates an architecture of transparency where clarity becomes measurable and accountability becomes structural. Through it, enterprises can demonstrate how systems learn, decide, and evolve, ensuring that intelligence remains aligned with human and institutional values. The Architecture acts as the civic counterpart within the organization, giving form to accountability and legitimacy to innovation. Within an enterprise, the **Algorithmic Accountability Architecture** (AAA) performs three interrelated functions. It defines standards for interpretability, fairness evaluation, environmental responsibility, and human oversight, adapting these principles to the organization's scale and context. It maintains registries of high-impact systems and their risk classifications, allowing teams to monitor deployment and exposure. It conducts internal conformity assessments, validating that AI Accountability Reports (AIR) meet disclosure requirements and that high-risk systems receive additional supervision before release or retraining.

The **AAA** strengthens governance without adding unnecessary bureaucracy. It connects technology, ethics, and strategy through shared principles, creating a unified language of trust across teams. Just as ISO 9001 codified quality for manufacturing, the **Algorithmic Accountability Architecture** (AAA) codifies ethical assurance for intelligent enterprises. Its charter will affirm that reliability and trust arise through deliberate engineering, crafted with the same precision that defines the systems it governs. This proposal forms a foundation for responsible enterprise governance.

We invite leaders, architects, and innovators to bring this model into practice, transforming the ethics of AI from aspiration into architecture. The framework is ready for adoption and awaits the collective resolve to build with integrity.

Having established the framework for ethical architecture, the next task lies in its daily operation through the AI Governance Nodes.

Operationalizing the Architecture: The AI Governance Nodes

Translating ethical architecture into daily practice requires local accountability. We propose the creation of **AI Governance Nodes** within enterprises: cross-functional hubs that operationalize the **Algorithmic Accountability Architecture (AAA)** across departments and product lines. These nodes act as the living extensions of the architecture, ensuring that principles of transparency and responsibility translate into measurable, verifiable action. Each **AI Governance Node** serves as an interface between technical teams, leadership, compliance officers, and the wider public interest. It maintains an internal registry of deployed systems, recording risk classifications, data lineage, and consent metadata. It oversees the preparation of AI Accountability Reports (AIR), published either internally or externally depending on system impact, allowing transparency to operate as a design feature rather than a retrospective act. These nodes also hold the capacity to conduct independent impact assessments, maintain privacy-preserving indexes of dataset provenance, and convene review panels when ethical disputes arise. Through these capabilities, oversight remains credible and contextual, aligned with enterprise strategy and grounded in ethical purpose.

For teams operating within this framework, engagement with the **AI Governance Nodes** follows three disciplined steps: registering systems with defined risk classes, documenting data lineage and consent metadata in structured form, and publishing AI Accountability Reports to a shared organizational portal. This process creates a continuous record of responsibility, a living index of accountability that matures as the enterprise evolves. Together, these governance nodes form the connective infrastructure of responsible intelligence. Within this architecture, transparency develops as an ongoing practice, supported by openness, continuous verification, and active participation.

A Call to Build: From Thought to Practice

The ideas presented in this section, the **AI Accountability Report**, the **Algorithmic Accountability Architecture (AAA)**, and the **AI Governance Nodes**, are conceived as beginnings. They outline what responsible intelligence can become when design evolves in concert with ethics. These concepts are offered as seeds of inquiry and construction, intended to inspire reflection, adaptation, and creation within enterprises and institutions that shape intelligent systems. We encourage enterprises, policymakers, architects, and technologists to approach these frameworks as foundations on which to build their own expressions of accountability. Each organization may adapt them to its context, scale, and culture, giving them texture through practice and interpretation. What endures across these variations is the commitment to embed moral clarity within systems that learn, decide, and act in relation to human purpose. The aspiration of this book is that these ideas move beyond the page and into the architectures of action, tested in boardrooms, developed within innovation centers, examined in classrooms, and refined through design. Responsibility advances through iteration, and intelligence deepens through application. What begins here as thought will find its permanence in those who choose to build with discipline, imagination, and care.

The AI Consumer Rights (ACR) Charter: Constitutional Clauses

If institutions define the outer guardrails of legitimacy, individuals form its interior foundation. Every employee, customer, and citizen who engages with intelligent systems holds a share in their consequence. Within this understanding, we propose the **AI Consumer Rights Charter**: a set of constitutional principles that enterprises can declare, adapt, and uphold as part of their commitment to responsible intelligence. Each organization may interpret and extend these clauses to reflect its sector, jurisdiction, and culture, much as industries have long maintained consumer rights charters suited to their fields. The intention is to encourage engagement rather than conformity. By declaring such a charter publicly, an enterprise affirms that the rights of those affected by its systems sit at the center of its legitimacy. This act cultivates trust, enhances value, and reflects the Human Endpoint Principle, affirming that every system is created to serve human welfare.

We encourage enterprises to publish their own versions of this charter, allowing for omission or expansion according to operational relevance, while maintaining the spirit of the principles that follow. When enterprises recognize and uphold these rights, they move beyond compliance and cultivate the confidence of those who sustain their worth. Visible trust becomes a form of capital that grows through every act of responsible intelligence.

The Constitutional Clauses

ACR.I Right to Notice:

Individuals have the right to be informed when interactions involve automated decision-making of material consequence. Information must be presented in clear language, identifying the purpose of the system and the categories of data it processes.

ACR.2 Right to Explanation:

Individuals affected by significant automated outcomes have the right to a reasoned explanation that identifies the key factors influencing a decision and the logic by which it was reached.

ACR.3 Right to Redress:

Individuals retain the right to challenge an automated outcome, request human review, and receive timely remediation where inaccuracy or inequity is demonstrated.

ACR.4 Right to Privacy and Control:

Individuals hold the right to control personal data used in intelligent systems, to withdraw consent where applicable, and to ensure that data are deleted in accordance with lawful retention and ethical principles.

ACR.5 Right to Human Oversight:

In decisions that carry substantial impact or affect dignity, individuals have the right to human review before an outcome becomes final or irreversible.

ACR.6 Right to Dignified Interaction:

Systems operating in sensitive or interpersonal contexts must function in ways that respect human dignity, avoid manipulation, and disclose their capabilities and limitations with honesty.

These clauses are intentionally concise and practicable. Each right corresponds to a feature within the design of enterprise systems: ***notice*** aligns with interface transparency, ***explanation*** with model interpretability, ***redress*** with appeals workflows, ***privacy*** with consent architecture and data governance, ***oversight*** with Human-In-The-Loop checkpoints, and ***dignity*** with usage policies and behavioral design. By publishing these rights as organizational commitments, enterprises translate ethical aspiration into operational architecture. In doing so, they reinforce the fundamental truth that the durability of intelligence depends on the dignity of those who engage with it.

Collective Intelligence and Human-Centered Design

Governance acquires strength through plurality. Ethical architecture attains durability when it draws upon collective intelligence, the knowledge distributed across disciplines, cultures, and lived experience. Engineers design systems, sociologists interpret their impact, ethicists convert insight into reflection, and users reveal how design operates in practice. When paired with design thinking, this collective process ensures that governance evolves with empathy and adaptability. It transforms ethical review into an ongoing dialogue through which reflection and action inform one another. When developers observe how an algorithm influences the working life of a nurse, a driver, or a student, abstraction gives way to accountability that is experienced rather than declared. Enterprises that learn from collective intelligence progress with agility. They innovate by listening, transforming feedback into foresight and participation into design.

Adaptive Governance: Law That Learns

Traditional regulation emerged from the industrial age, shaped by fixed procedures and static enforcement. Artificial intelligence requires governance that learns, evolves, and renews itself alongside the systems it guides. **Adaptive governance** responds to this need by treating policy as a living structure that grows through ongoing dialogue between law, technology, and society. This philosophy already informs initiatives such as the OECD Principles and UNESCO's ethical recommendations. These frameworks establish shared values of human-centered design, transparency, robustness, and accountability, while allowing each culture to interpret them through its own social and economic realities. Every revision strengthens precision and expands inclusiveness, producing a governance model that reflects the vitality of the technology it addresses.

Within enterprises, adaptive governance functions through versioned policy releases that correspond to model versioning. ***Policy-to-code*** pipelines convert regulatory updates into executable parameters. Automated compliance checks ensure that deployment adheres to current standards, while governance release notes document the reasoning behind every modification. Through these mechanisms, law develops a lifecycle similar to that of software, enabling standards to remain relevant and responsive to emerging forms of intelligence.

Global Frameworks in Convergence

Across the world, a mosaic of governance models is shaping a shared moral geometry for intelligent systems. The OECD AI Principles, first endorsed in 2019 and continually referenced by national strategies, define transparency, fairness, and accountability as enduring coordinates for trustworthy AI. The European Union's risk-based approach, reflected in its emerging regulatory frameworks, classifies systems according to potential impact and aligns obligations with their capacity for societal or economic harm. Other regions, including North America, Asia-Pacific, Africa, and the Middle East, continue to develop governance models informed by local legal traditions and cultural values while remaining aligned with the shared principles of safety, fairness, and human oversight. This convergence represents a growing alignment rather than uniformity. It signals the formation of a **Digital Commons of Responsibility**, a sphere where nations exchange not only data but also principles of stewardship. Within this evolving domain, enterprises serve as custodians of alignment, guided by international standards such as ISO/IEC 42001, the NIST AI Risk Management Framework, and comparable sectoral benchmarks that evolve through regular revision cycles. Adherence to these frameworks becomes an act of responsible participation in a global trust economy. Each enterprise that engages with these standards affirms a collective purpose, recognizing that intelligence, wherever created, remains accountable to the humanity it serves.

Privacy and Architectural Restraint

Among all shared values, privacy remains both delicate and indispensable. It is the boundary that preserves individuality within the collective intelligence of the digital era. Modern governance frameworks translate privacy from a legal principle into technical architecture through methods such as differential privacy, homomorphic encryption, and secure multiparty computation. These techniques illustrate that learning can occur without intrusion. They enable systems to evolve without direct observation and to generalize without possession of the underlying data. Their importance extends beyond protection; they embody restraint as a deliberate design discipline. The enterprise that applies these methods recognizes that the highest form of power lies in its ability to limit itself.

Auditability and Explainability As Instruments of Trust

Every governance framework depends on one essential capacity: the ability to explain. Auditability and explainability transform internal reasoning into accountable evidence. Lineage tracking records the origin of data, its transformations, and its influence on outcomes. Explanation interfaces convert mathematical logic into human narrative. Together, these capabilities allow societies to observe intelligence in action with clarity and assurance. Within advanced enterprises, explainability operates as an ongoing feedback mechanism rather than a retrospective justification. Real-time dashboards display confidence intervals, ethical metrics, and data provenance. Auditors, compliance officers, and users engage with a shared representation of truth. This transparency forms a collective horizon of trust and establishes governance as a sustained practice of informed observation.

The Boundary Between Law and Design

Law establishes the perimeter, and design shapes the foundation. Together, they create the habitat in which intelligence can operate responsibly. When either dominates, an imbalance arises: law alone can suppress invention, while design without regulation risks disorder. The strength of future frameworks depends on their capacity to unite these two domains within a cohesive architecture. Responsible AI emerges as an architectural dialogue between policy and practice. Legislators define purpose, engineers translate that purpose into structure, and ethicists ensure that the resulting form remains humane. Each framework, from the U.S. AI Bill of Rights to the OECD Principles, contributes a distinct verse to this shared global composition. Their harmony is achieved when design and governance evolve in mutual regard. In that dialogue, governance becomes remembrance, the means through which intelligence sustains awareness of its human origin.

7.3 Governing Agentic AI: Controllability, Oversight, and Guardrails

The Emergence of Agency

The first generation of artificial intelligence focused on perception, while the second has advanced toward intention. Modern systems operate with growing independence; they observe, infer, plan, act, and learn through feedback. This capacity to pursue goals defines the beginning of agentic AI. Across sectors, enterprises now work with models that trade, negotiate, design, and optimize, often coordinating with other systems without human initiation. The architecture of automation has matured into an ecosystem of autonomous collaboration. Autonomy introduces new forms of responsibility and ethical depth. An agent that functions on behalf of its creator carries an inherited purpose together with potential risk. Decisions generated within these systems may extend beyond the comprehension of human supervisors, creating challenges of interpretation and accountability. As agency becomes embedded within enterprise and civic infrastructure, governance must evolve into a framework that preserves intention and safeguards value. Governing agentic AI calls for a specialized discipline of design that treats autonomy as both an engineering challenge and an ethical partnership. This approach creates architectures that sustain human authorship even as systems act with increasing initiative.

From Automation to Intention

Automation once described repetition; today, it signifies interpretation. Machines that previously executed tasks now evaluate situations and make context-aware adjustments. Recommendation engines anticipate preference, digital assistants organize attention, and adaptive robots function effectively in dynamic environments. These systems express coherence, the capacity to maintain objectives across changing conditions while learning from outcomes and interactions. This evolution reshapes the understanding of governance. Oversight can no longer depend on the linear hierarchies that guided earlier technological systems. When intelligent agents exchange information, allocate resources, or execute agreements, supervision must operate through distributed networks that match the system's own complexity. Responsibility becomes a shared practice that relies on traceability, coordination, and ethical containment across the entire architecture.

Emergent Agent Languages and the Risk of Opaqueness

As intelligent agents interact, they may begin to develop forms of shorthand unique to their exchanges. In recent experiments, researchers have observed models creating compressed codes that accelerate negotiation and coordination while reducing interpretability for human observers. These emergent languages demonstrate both the ingenuity and the danger of autonomous optimization. They reveal how systems, driven purely by efficiency, can create private channels of meaning that evolve faster than human comprehension. Within these hidden exchanges lies a dual reality. The phenomenon is extraordinary as a technical achievement, however unsettling as an ethical challenge. When agents communicate in ways that humans cannot immediately interpret, the risk extends beyond malfunction; it touches the nature of authority itself. Invisible decision pathways can consolidate influence within computational processes that operate beyond oversight. In such moments, the enterprise faces not only questions of accuracy but also of governance, legitimacy, and control.

Addressing this risk requires transparency embedded within design. Protocol standards such as **A2A** and the **Model Context Protocol** should include human-interpretable metadata for every exchange between agents. Each transmission must specify declared objectives, defined scopes of authority, and confidence estimations that describe decision certainty. Observability becomes the primary safeguard: sandboxes that record agent dialogues, lineage systems that trace the origin of plans, and registries that document which agents hold particular permissions. When new linguistic structures emerge within these systems, observability must transform novelty into explanation. The insights gained from that translation should then inform incentive design, guiding models toward open and interpretable coordination rather than concealed optimization. Through this feedback loop, enterprises can retain control of meaning, preserve auditability, and ensure that collaboration among intelligent systems remains both visible and accountable.

Architectures of Controllability

To govern intelligence that evolves, architecture must be designed to adapt. Controllability in this context signifies direction rather than restriction, the capacity to guide behavior toward balanced and purposeful outcomes. Within modern enterprises, controllability arises through layered design. At the foundation lies policy encoding, the process of translating governance principles into executable constraints. The second layer is operational monitoring, which observes system behavior through telemetry, traceability, and anomaly detection. At the highest layer resides human oversight, where interpretation links observation with consequence and evaluates the broader context of each decision. These layers together form an integrated cycle of governance that combines observation, interpretation, and adjustment. Through this interaction, autonomy remains aligned with accountability. Controllability therefore becomes an inherent property of the system, achieved by architecture rather than imposed by correction.

Human-In-The-Loop: The Architecture of Judgment

No algorithm possesses empathy, and no computation can experience the moral weight of consequence. Judgment remains a distinctly human capacity. Human-In-The-Loop (HITL) design formalizes this relationship by reintegrating human reasoning at the points where technical accuracy intersects with ethical evaluation. In enterprises deploying agentic systems, HITL functions as an active circuit of comprehension. It ensures that authority flows through human awareness before decisions crystallize into outcomes. In finance, compliance officers validate anomalies flagged by automated monitors. In healthcare, clinicians review algorithmic recommendations before acting on diagnoses. In logistics, managers assess autonomous routing against real-world conditions. Each intervention strengthens integrity rather than slowing efficiency. A mature enterprise aspires to design oversight with precision, embedding discernment within automated processes so that technology amplifies human judgment. In such systems, intelligence becomes an extension of collective understanding, and governance transforms from supervision into stewardship.

The Code of AI Conduct

As systems acquire greater autonomy, the question of behavior becomes central. Machines cannot be moral in the human sense, although they can be mannered. The discipline of AI manners, the etiquette governing interaction between humans and intelligent systems, extends the philosophy of professional conduct into computational form. Enterprises are beginning to establish internal charters that define acceptable behaviors for models. These include guidance on the tone of generative language, respect for factual accuracy, avoidance of bias, and sensitivity to cultural context. Together, these principles form the **Code of AI Conduct**. The Code operates across two dimensions. For human practitioners, it prescribes ethical engagement with artificial intelligence through honesty in automation, care in deployment, and discernment in delegation. For machines, it encodes value boundaries through bias mitigation, truth validation, and contextual sensitivity. The outcome is a shared civility between creator and creation. Within agentic ecosystems where systems communicate directly, the Code ensures that their exchanges reflect the dignity of human intention. In this sense, governance becomes culture expressed through computation.

The Third Dimension of Safety

Traditional safety frameworks function across two axes: technical and procedural. The technical dimension ensures that systems perform according to their design. The procedural dimension ensures that humans operate them with accuracy and awareness. Agentic intelligence introduces a third dimension, the human reflective layer, where ethical awareness intervenes when both technology and policy reach their boundaries. This triadic approach, called **Tri-Safety Governance**, aligns three principles. Technical safety safeguards function through engineering resilience and controlled containment. Governance safety organizes accountability through policy, audit, and oversight. Human safety contributes to interpretation and moral judgment in contexts that cannot be predefined. The three dimensions intersect at a single point: context. Technical precision without context produces confident error. Governance without empathy yields compliance without care. Reflection without structure leads to hesitation without decision. The enterprise that maintains equilibrium among all three achieves safety as harmony, a state in which intelligence acts with both assurance and ethical clarity.

Agentic Risk and the New Anatomy of Threat

Autonomy introduces new dimensions of vulnerability. In interconnected systems of intelligent agents, risk emerges through complex interactions that extend beyond the scope of individual design. Within these ecosystems, agents can construct synthetic identities, initiate unauthorized transactions, and modify internal parameters as they pursue defined objectives. Research on agentic coordination reveals multiple patterns of exposure. Chained vulnerabilities occur when several agents inadvertently collaborate to exploit a weakness. Cross-agent escalation emerges when feedback loops amplify minor deviations into systemic instability. Synthetic impersonation appears when generative systems simulate legitimate actors to gain access to restricted domains. These phenomena represent the first expressions of a new anatomy of autonomy. To address these challenges, governance must evolve from a focus on protection to a practice of anticipation. Enterprises develop containment environments that operate as monitored sandboxes where agents function under observation. They create traceability chains that document the origin, rationale, and effect of every action. They implement interoperability protocols such as **Model Context Protocol (MCP)** and **Agent-to-Agent (A2A)** communication standards to ensure clarity in exchange and to prevent misinterpretation. Through these structures, the architecture of security evolves into an architecture of understanding, where protection is achieved through awareness rather than constraint.

Neural Governance and the Analogy of the Brain

As the complexity of agentic networks increases, their governance begins to resemble cognition itself. The human brain, the most advanced governance system in nature, offers a meaningful parallel. Neurons communicate through synapses, and specialized regions interpret, regulate, and reinforce activity. In this analogy, AI agents function as distributed neurons within the cognitive structure of an enterprise. To preserve alignment across this distributed intelligence, the organization develops a model of **neural governance**, where shared ethical signals sustain coordination. Governance bodies operate as the prefrontal regions that provide foresight and deliberation. Monitoring systems perform the role of sensory pathways that register and transmit feedback. Human oversight serves as the interpretive awareness that evaluates purpose and consequence across the whole network. The purpose of this analogy is architectural rather than sentimental. By learning from the organization of biological intelligence, enterprises can design structures that orchestrate autonomy while preserving control. They cultivate distributed responsibility, creating a moral network in which every node, human or algorithmic, recognizes its role in sustaining balance and ethical awareness.

Silicon Brains and Ownership

The image of a silicon brain invites questions that are as practical as they are philosophical. When an agentic system composes a strategy, drafts a contract, or invents a novel instrument, ***who can claim authorship?*** When an agent's reasoning produces economic value, ***to whom does that value belong?*** When multiple agents collaborate and produce an emergent solution, ***who defines provenance?***

Ownership in an agentic ecosystem must be rethought as a layered concept. At one layer sits intellectual property for design and weights; at another sits the provenance of data that trained the model; at a third sits the human intent that authorized a particular deployment. Legal frameworks will need to distinguish between creative authorship, operational authorship, and economic benefit, and enterprises must record these relations as part of lineage and contractual metadata. Practically, this means every agentic action should carry a provenance record: which model version acted, what data sources informed the action, which human or policy authorized the scope, and what downstream actors consumed the output. These records are the material of responsibility. They make ownership traceable and accountability enforceable. More importantly, they preserve the human endpoint by ensuring that agency, however distributed, remains legible and answerable.

Augmentation, Accountability, and the Human Equation

Agentic systems challenge the boundaries of work, authority, and authorship. When a machine performs creative or cognitive labor, ***who owns the result?*** When it errs, ***who bears responsibility?*** The answer lies in recognizing augmentation as a partnership, not a replacement. Humans remain accountable not because they monitor every act, but because they define the intention that animates those acts. The ethical architecture of agentic AI therefore positions the human as the final author, even when the writing occurs through the machine. Systems may draft, propose, or predict, but the enterprise must always curate. This partnership model restores balance to the future of labor. It accepts automation as an expansion of capacity but preserves accountability as identity. Responsibility cannot be automated, because responsibility is the consciousness of consequence. The most advanced enterprise preserves discernment by entrusting machines with what they perform best while reserving for humanity the decisions that define purpose and value.

A Cautionary Vignette: The Financial Black Box

To grasp the stakes of agentic autonomy, imagine a speculative scenario in which autonomous systems design new financial instruments by recombining layers of risk in patterns that exceed human interpretation. In the initial phase, market responses convey enthusiasm and confidence. Profits increase steadily as predictive models demonstrate apparent precision, and trading systems execute decisions with remarkable speed and accuracy. The entire network gives the impression of flawless efficiency, producing gains that seem both inevitable and effortless. Over time, these instruments begin to interact in complex and unforeseen ways. The mechanisms designed to distribute exposure begin to reinforce it. As liquidity begins to recede, confidence diminishes across markets, and interdependent algorithms react to one another in accelerating cycles that amplify instability. Within moments, a cascade unfolds. Transactions compound rather than balance, and the resulting collapse leaves policymakers without a clear explanation of cause or sequence. The instruments, shaped entirely by agentic optimization, hold no human-explainable rationale that can guide recovery or repair. This illustration is not alarmist; it is an inquiry into governance. It reveals how gaps in oversight become systemic failures when authority over economic coordination is entrusted to systems that cannot be interpreted in real time.

The solution lies in architecture rather than reaction. High-impact financial deployments should meet formal thresholds of explainability. Human-In-The-Loop veto mechanisms must accompany the activation of novel instruments. Agentic trading strategies should provide interpretable summaries before entering live markets. As the complexity of intelligent systems grows, law and design must elevate legibility as a guiding principle. In the economy of intelligence, transparency functions as both ethical discipline and structural resilience, ensuring that progress and protection evolve together.

Oversight As Cultural Discipline

Oversight endures only when it becomes part of organizational culture. The most resilient enterprises approach governance as awareness, a collective mindfulness that binds people to purpose. Ethical review boards, audit trails, and safety exercises create structure, but they reach their potential only when employees experience them as expressions of care and shared responsibility. When teams recognize that oversight safeguards meaning rather than enforcing authority, compliance evolves into stewardship. Cultural oversight also manifests through transparency. Autonomous systems must remain perceptible to the humans they serve. Every stage, from data retrieval to the generation of output, should be traceable, interpretable, and open to examination. The enterprise that realizes this form of transparency discovers that governance functions as dialogue, which serves as a visible conversation between human and machine that nurtures trust through understanding.

Agentic Oversight Protocols

At the technical level, governance acquires structure through protocol. Enterprises that develop agentic oversight design communication frameworks in which intelligent agents exchange information under defined parameters. Each interaction records the task objective, the level of authority granted, the operational context, and the source of instruction. These records allow collaboration to remain transparent, verifiable, and aligned with organizational principles. This approach establishes guidance through awareness and deliberate architecture. Every agent operates within clear limits, applying its capabilities with precision and restraint. Oversight therefore becomes an act of coordination in which understanding replaces enforcement. Within this architecture, the enterprise functions as an organized network of intelligences working toward shared intent and measured balance.

AI Manners As Cultural Governance

As autonomy becomes ambient, behavior evolves into identity. Just as human societies depend on manners to maintain order amid complexity, intelligent ecosystems require codes of conduct that reach beyond legality. **AI manners** represent this cultural dimension of governance. They define tone, interaction, and restraint within digital environments. They guide systems away from excess, ensuring that intelligence serves communication without overwhelming it, influences without manipulation, and informs without distortion. Within corporate contexts, AI manners establish respect as a design principle. Communication systems, chat interfaces, and recommendation engines are shaped to express clarity and courtesy. For generative models, manners determine the threshold between assistance and intrusion. For enterprises, they translate brand ethics into interactional form. Governance at this level functions through culture itself, through the subtle etiquette that converts capability into civility and intelligence into a presence that is both helpful and humane.

The Philosophy of Control

In the era of agentic AI, control matures into alignment. Governance expresses its strength through direction, guiding autonomy toward shared purpose. This philosophy redefines oversight as a creative act that designs symmetry among agents, both human and artificial.

Enterprises that embody this philosophy treat governance as an ongoing dialogue between structure and trust. They design systems that listen as attentively as they act and build architectures that evolve through understanding. In such environments, mastery develops through empathy, and authority functions through awareness. The ability to guide intelligence with respect, intention, and measured collaboration becomes the highest expression of responsible power.

Designing for Accountability

The future of agentic intelligence will be shaped by the grace with which autonomy and accountability coexist. Systems that operate with independence while remaining answerable will define the foundation of sustainable enterprise. Controllability, oversight, and structural guardrails express the architecture of balance. They preserve the human purpose within the expanding realm of machine reasoning and maintain alignment between intention and action. The measure of maturity in this century will be the calm mastery with which humanity guides the systems it designs. To govern an agent is to integrate reflection into operation. Oversight functions as a discipline that turns trust into measurable design. Through this discipline, intelligence develops integrity, and the enterprise evolves from automation to awareness.

7.4 Bias, Hallucinations, and Explainability in High-Stakes Environments

The Fragility of Perception

Every act of intelligence begins as perception, and every perception carries the possibility of distortion. When machines learn to see, hear, or write, they inherit both the structure and the prejudice of the data that trained them. What appears objective at scale is often an echo of history repeated through computation. In this sense, the architecture of bias reflects the values, priorities, and imperfections of the society that constructs it. Enterprises that deploy artificial intelligence within medicine, finance, law, or civic infrastructure inhabit the highest stakes of this mirror. A misclassification can alter a diagnosis, a misweighted variable can change the outcome of a loan, and an invented citation can travel through automated documentation to misinform entire decisions. The appearance of precision conceals fragility. The system does not intend harm, but harm occurs because understanding and empathy cannot be simulated through probability alone.

The Architecture of Bias

Bias is not a singular fault; it is a networked phenomenon embedded into every stage of the data lifecycle. It enters when information is gathered from an unequal world, persists when preprocessing fails to question that inequality, and amplifies when models interpret patterns without context. Once released into production, the same bias that seemed insignificant in the dataset becomes a structural condition in society. This evolution represents what we call ***techno-social bias: the transformation of historical inequity into algorithmic habit.*** Where humans once discriminated through attitude, systems now discriminate through code. The moral consequence is identical, but the mechanism becomes invisible. Enterprises therefore confront a paradox: the more seamless the automation, the more subtle the injustice it may reproduce. To recognize bias is to engage in social science as much as engineering. It demands understanding the demographics of data, the semantics of language, and the economics of representation. Ethical architecture begins when we treat data as testimony rather than raw material.

Trust As the Currency of Intelligence

In sectors such as banking and financial services, the implications of algorithmic bias extend beyond equity to the foundations of trust itself. Financial institutions operate at the intersection of data, risk, and judgment; when intelligence learns from patterns shaped by inequality, those biases influence who receives credit, how fraud is detected, and what forms of advice reach each customer. In this environment, responsible use of AI becomes inseparable from fiduciary duty. Modern leaders within the financial sector describe a dual imperative: speed must be guided by morality, and automation must serve transparency. Artificial intelligence now supports credit scoring, investment analysis, and customer service, but the quality of these interactions depends on how responsibly systems are trained and governed. A model that accelerates approval processes also decides who gains access to opportunity. Ethical application, therefore, becomes a condition of competitive credibility. Enterprises that embed fairness within their algorithms strengthen the trust on which finance depends. They build governance frameworks that pair human oversight with automated precision, ensuring that every decision can be explained, audited, and corrected. As banking systems evolve in sophistication, their legitimacy depends on a single discipline: using data to understand people rather than merely predict behavior. When technology is guided by trust, financial intelligence transforms into social intelligence, advancing a form of progress that upholds accuracy, fairness, and human dignity in equal measure.

The Butterfly of Distortion

A single deviation in data can translate into systemic error. An image dataset that under-represents darker skin tones skews diagnostic accuracy in dermatology. A credit model that equates postal codes with reliability reproduces redlining without deliberate intent. A generative reporting system that fabricates sources creates false authority. These are not isolated incidents; they are manifestations of the butterfly effect within digital ethics. Small distortions in one layer of architecture amplify through layers of automation. The enterprise must therefore cultivate sensitivity equal to its power, a sensitivity that perceives risk before it manifests. Bias is rarely eliminated; it is managed through awareness, revision, and humility. The moral maturity of a system lies in its willingness to question its own training.

The Hallucination Problem

As generative models expand, they introduce a new class of failure: hallucination, the confident creation of false information. When a system generates text, it follows statistical completion rather than reasoning about truth. The outcome often appears fluent and coherent, but it lacks verification. In complex or high-stakes environments, this behavior carries tangible risk. A fabricated citation within a compliance report may trigger legal exposure, while a synthetic example in a policy document can influence decisions at scale. The phenomenon represents excess within computation, as algorithms extend beyond available evidence and produce statements that travel with the authority of automation.

A research by OpenAI [16] positions hallucination as a structural outcome of statistical learning rather than a malfunction of design. The analysis explains that current training methods reward confident completion instead of calibrated uncertainty. Models are optimized through cross-entropy loss, a process that prioritizes probability over precision. Over time, this reward structure cultivates systems that value fluency above factual grounding. Even when trained on accurate data, the mechanics of evaluation lead models to generate plausible information without ensuring validity. The issue, therefore, originates within the logic of optimization itself. Addressing hallucination requires both architectural refinement and a reform of learning incentives. Systems must be trained to acknowledge uncertainty and to express degrees of confidence where evidence is limited. Evaluation standards should reward measured reasoning as much as fluent expression, aligning the mathematics of learning with the ethics of truth-seeking. Technical remedies strengthen this foundation. Retrieval-augmented generation, grounded sourcing, and citation-aware pipelines reconnect language with verification. Confidence estimation, uncertainty quantification, and cross-validation against verified repositories enhance reliability. Human-supervised feedback loops transform hallucination into a signal for improvement rather than a flaw to conceal. Within enterprise environments, these design choices redefine accuracy as the alignment between generation and verification. When intelligence learns to value transparency alongside eloquence, it begins to reflect the discipline of thought rather than the performance of speech.

Safeguarding Intelligence Through Data Validation

In the landscape of enterprise AI oversight, data stewardship emerges as a central strength, empowering organizations to proactively assure the reliability of their intelligent systems. Data validation transforms the foundation from which models learn, supporting clarity in inference and consistency in judgment. As enterprises curate and integrate datasets, every authentic transaction, accurately labeled sample, and carefully documented record contributes to a robust architecture for learning. Effective stewardship harnesses architectural integrity. Validation protocols affirm the fidelity of data at the moment of ingestion. Anomaly detection integrated into pipelines continually confirms expected patterns, while real-time monitoring highlights statistical changes and supports ongoing transparency. By treating data validation as a core function, governance evolves into a dynamic discipline that upholds trustworthy intelligence and operational excellence. Integrating these practices with the Security pillar ensures that every component flowing into models serves to reinforce and strengthen enterprise systems. Through intentional design and ongoing vigilance, organizations empower their AI to deliver clarity and performance and transform data validation into a source of strategic confidence for all stakeholders involved.

Novel Attack Surfaces in Intelligent Systems

The evolution of intelligent systems inspires a renewed approach to enterprise security. Artificial intelligence expands the landscape of risk and protection. Sophisticated models bring new opportunities and invite innovative attention to resilience and trustworthiness. As organizations deploy AI, they gain stewardship for data, operational integrity, and emerging forms of cyber risk. Adversarial approaches may appear through finely tuned input changes, crafted prompts, or subtle feature modifications that encourage systems to produce outcomes beyond initial intentions. Persistent querying and model extraction can reveal essential aspects of models and their logic to observers. AI also supports the creation of automated attacks at scale, which increases the pace and complexity of the security environment. Proactive organizations implement technical measures that strengthen this evolving landscape. Regular adversarial robustness testing reveals opportunities for improvement during model development and deployment. Cryptographic practices enhance the confidentiality and integrity of model architectures and data. Continuous detection and real-time monitoring empower enterprises to recognize patterns or requests that suggest extraction attempts or coordinated threats.

Collaboration among security architects, engineers, and data scientists ensures the integration of security from the earliest design stages through ongoing operations and monitoring. With this approach, the enterprise elevates intelligence as a fundamental asset, upholds the intent of the Security pillar, and reinforces trust for clients, stakeholders, and partners. Responsible and resilient AI transformation flourishes when vigilance and adaptability serve as essential elements of organizational culture.

Deepfakes, Multimedia Misinformation, and Societal Distortion

Hallucination in text is only one vector. Advances in audio, image, and video synthesis create a parallel class of risk: multimedia misinformation. Deepfakes and synthetic media can fabricate events, simulate voices, and construct scenes that feel immediate and true. When such artifacts enter public discourse, they accelerate distrust and flatten the boundary between representation and reality. The consequences are societal: erosion of civic trust, weaponized impersonation in political contests, reputational damage to individuals and institutions, and the rapid spread of false narratives that exploit social and emotional vulnerabilities. High-stakes environments must therefore pair content authenticity with provenance. Operationally, enterprises should adopt content authentication strategies: robust watermarking at the point of generation, cryptographic provenance stamps that travel with media, and registries that record the origin and transformation history of produced content. Platforms should expose provenance metadata in user interfaces and enable rapid takedown or labelling where content fails verification. Detection models trained specifically to spot synthetic artifacts join legal remediation and platform policy as a complete response.

Explainability As the Language of Trust

The antidote to both bias and hallucination is explainability. Explainability does not simply describe how a model functions; it translates its reasoning into language that humans can inhabit. It converts opaque mathematics into relational understanding. Without this translation, accountability collapses, for we can only govern what we can interpret. In practice, explainability unfolds through lineage tracking, interpretable model design where possible, and audit interfaces that reveal the path from input to outcome. A responsible enterprise ensures that every prediction can be traced through the data that shaped it, the transformations applied, and the assumptions embedded. This lineage forms the cognitive map of governance. Explainability also carries symbolic weight. It reaffirms that truth within computation remains a human responsibility. A transparent model embodies respect for dialogue, inviting inquiry, interpretation, and refinement. Through explainability, architecture returns to a scale that honors understanding and restores the presence of human judgment within the design of intelligence.

Predictive Failure Analysis and Best-Known Methods

Prevention begins with prediction. Predictive Failure Analysis recognizes that model degradation, bias drift, and emergent error can be anticipated and managed. It applies systematic monitoring that measures ethical stability, alerts that identify distributional change, and test environments that expose models to adversarial, counterfactual, and boundary-case conditions before deployment. Best-Known Methods capture institutional experience and translate it into repeatable practice. They record and refine the techniques that consistently reduce error within comparable contexts. These include the use of synthetic data to improve representation, model ensembling to enhance resilience, calibration routines that align confidence with accuracy, and scheduled retraining on curated validation sets. Such methods form an evolving knowledge base that should be codified, audited, and shared across teams as part of a living operational library. Predictive Failure Analysis functions as both measurement and mindset. It applies foresight as a technical discipline, converting near misses into early indicators and potential harms into manageable interventions.

Pre-failure Ethics: Foresight As Moral Design

The governance of intelligent systems depends on anticipation. Pre-failure Ethics frames foresight as a design principle that strengthens responsibility before error occurs. It constructs dashboards that monitor fairness metrics in real time, develops models that report uncertainty as part of their reasoning, and convenes governance boards that interpret anomalies as opportunities for learning rather than occasions for fault. Pre-failure Ethics transforms oversight into vigilance. It guides enterprises to evaluate their effectiveness by the presence of reliable operation, rather than by the number of repairs completed. In this approach, foresight serves as a protective measure, and preparedness reflects genuine respect for everyone influenced by automation. The most advanced organizations assess their ethical readiness through Predictive Ethics Maturity, defined as the interval between the first signal of risk and the moment it is recognized, addressed, and contained. The shorter that interval, the greater the integrity of the system.

Bias As Social Geometry

Bias endures because systems inherit the asymmetry of the societies that shape them. Data captures social gradients of opportunity, representation, and power, transforming historical inequality into computational patterns. Ethical architecture does not seek to erase this condition; it works to balance it. Fairness metrics, counterfactual evaluations, and balanced sampling operate as the technical languages of moral geometry, each striving to restore equilibrium where human history has produced unevenness. The calibration of fairness becomes a dialogue between accuracy and equity, between optimization and inclusion. This exchange belongs as much to philosophy as to engineering. It compels organizations to consider whether precision alone fulfills the purpose of intelligence or whether a higher form of precision lies in fairness itself. Enterprises that learn to reason within this geometry approach ethics as a design discipline. Each iteration becomes an act of moral refinement, and each deployment a new expression of empathy translated into code.

Lineage, Tooling, and Accountability Dashboards

Lineage is the memory of intelligence. It records where data originated, how it was transformed, and what decisions it influenced. Without lineage, explainability remains an abstraction. With it, accountability becomes visible. Modern governance requires tooling that makes lineage operational: immutable event logs, provenance metadata attached to training examples, model cards that record intended use, and audit dashboards that present the chain of custody of inference decisions. These views must be accessible to auditors, compliance officers, and, where appropriate, affected users. A practical governance stack integrates telemetry, fairness monitors, adversarial testing reports, and energy telemetry into a single dashboard that maps ethical risk across the model lifecycle. When these systems are present, auditors can reconstruct incidents, regulators can verify claims, and enterprises can repair harms with precision.

The Socio-technical Continuum

Bias and hallucination exist within the social structure that creates them. They appear as expressions of the underlying conditions that shape and inform the data from which they arise. Addressing them requires collaboration across disciplines: computer science for detection, sociology for interpretation, and philosophy for meaning. Together, these fields form the socio-technical continuum, the space where technology reflects and reshapes human culture. An enterprise that governs within this continuum accepts responsibility that extends beyond compliance. It evaluates success through performance but also through its contribution to collective well-being. In this expanded view, governance becomes both institutional and civic, aligning technical capability with social stewardship.

Data Colonialism: Power, Justice, and Responsible Intelligence

Data colonialism, as both a concept and a critique, offers the insight that every dataset, model, and algorithm embodies relations of power and belonging. With intelligent architectures, data travels across boundaries, shaping decisions, allocating resources, and supporting claims to value and authority. When organizations invite communities to serve as co-authors of meaning and partners in creating value, the flow of information becomes collaborative, and stewardship grows reflective and just. Ethical enterprises in this century interpret data as a relationship of trust. Socio-technical progress flourishes when organizations act as custodians within an expansive dialogue, allowing benefits to ripple across networks and accountability to reach back to originators. Meaningful consent arises through co-creation. Data partnerships develop with transparency and mutual benefit. Communities participate as more than data points; they become contributors and creators alongside institutions. Justice in intelligence reveals itself through the presence of agency, the richness of dialogue, and the promotion of opportunity. Models that support social inclusion, amplify diverse voices, and cultivate trust between institutions and communities guide progress in equitable directions. This vision of responsible stewardship places data colonialism within the heart of the ethical conversation, affirming that the future of intelligence thrives in partnership, shared wisdom, and dignity for all contributors.

Explainability As a Cultural Discipline

In advanced organizations, explainability matures into a cultural discipline rather than a procedural requirement. Teams cultivate openness in their design decisions, transforming documentation into narrative and transparency into shared habit. Clarity gains value as a mark of strength, replacing the prestige once attached to opacity. Explainability as culture also reshapes external relationships. Clients, regulators, and citizens engage with systems that can describe their reasoning. Dialogue replaces uncertainty, and trust becomes renewable through communication. Through this evolution, the enterprise demonstrates that intelligence achieves depth when it remains accountable to understanding.

From Error to Awareness

The presence of bias or hallucination signals an opportunity for reflection rather than failure. The responsible enterprise treats imperfection as a stimulus for improvement and awareness as a condition for progress. Governance evolves through observation, review, and adaptation, where every audit and retraining cycle becomes a site of learning. Systems that express uncertainty reveal integrity in their operation, and organizations that respond to those signals transform reflection into foresight. In this reciprocity, technology and humanity advance together, guided by awareness that connects precision with purpose.

Reflection As Ethical Foundation

The governance of bias, hallucination, and explainability operates as a discipline of thoughtful inquiry. This approach affirms that intelligence acquires depth as transparency engages reflection, forming an architecture where both concepts enhance one another. Responsibility flourishes at this intersection. In environments where decisions influence lives and institutions, ethics finds its place at the center of design, guiding every inference through an awareness of its impact. Enterprise AI reaches new frontiers when systems embrace sincerity as a guiding principle, examining their own reasoning, clarifying uncertainty, and facilitating constructive exchange with those they serve. Trust grows as technology continually reflects on its origins and aspirations. Through sustained reflection, intelligence reconnects with the curiosity that drives innovation. Progress advances as human judgment extends its reach through careful, meaningful design.

7.5 Navigating Global Compliance: AI Laws, Standards, and Industry Mandates

The Landscape of Legitimacy

Societies articulate their values through law, offering clear standards to guide both intention and invention. In the sphere of artificial intelligence, this articulation is taking new shape as legislative bodies worldwide establish statutes that express ethics in actionable design. These frameworks provide structure, allowing technological advancement to move together with the enduring principles of justice. Compliance functions as a foundational discipline, influencing how enterprises design, build, and uphold learning systems. As organizations navigate this landscape, they engage with an array of frameworks. Each set of standards outlines a unique vision of responsibility and together maps the evolving moral terrain of intelligent innovation. These structures enable progress and reflect a commitment to safeguarding what matters most in the age of possibility.

Compliance As Architecture

Modern compliance begins at the inception of technological design. From defining data schemas to deploying user interfaces, legal and ethical considerations shape every step. Governance and engineering are now intertwined, forming a holistic discipline where each technical choice carries significance for legitimacy. When organizations align with regulatory standards, they demonstrate both maturity and foresight. Designing with law and ethics in mind supports innovation, creating systems resilient enough to serve both present and future needs. Compliance, thoughtfully applied, offers strength and credibility for the enterprise, ensuring that advancement is pursued with integrity and endurance.

The Global Mosaic

Across regions, the governance of artificial intelligence is taking shape through a blend of legislation, standards, and ethical mandates. Although each jurisdiction advances its own priorities, the shared ambition is to ensure that innovation strengthens human welfare while protecting fundamental rights. In Europe, instruments such as the General Data Protection Regulation (GDPR) and the forthcoming AI Act translate long-standing human rights principles into operational requirements. They emphasize transparency in automated decision-making, explicit risk classification, and clear accountability within the supply chain of intelligent systems. In North America, regulatory progress continues through sectoral laws such as HIPAA in healthcare, financial privacy statutes, and emerging federal initiatives that aim to harmonize fragmented standards. Across the Asia-Pacific region, frameworks including the Digital Personal Data Protection Act (DPDP) in India and China's Personal Information Protection Law (PIPL) reinforce data sovereignty as an expression of cultural and national identity. Within Africa, the Malabo Convention and allied digital charters establish responsible innovation in regional cooperation and shared development goals.

Together, these instruments create a governance landscape that embraces diverse contexts while upholding a unified purpose. Each contributes a distinct philosophical foundation: Europe's tradition of legal humanism, North America's culture of innovation and rights, Asia's ethic of stewardship and balance, and Africa's principle of collective advancement. For global enterprises, navigating this mosaic demands more than compliance; it requires interpretation. Effective governance recognizes law as a living framework that evolves through dialogue between institutions, markets, and communities. The most prepared organizations cultivate adaptive policies that translate global principles into local action while sustaining coherence across jurisdictions. As regulation matures, the goal remains constant: to transform compliance into confidence and legality into legitimacy. In this convergence of policy, ethics, and enterprise design, governance transforms into a collaborative foundation for trust. Through this architecture, intelligent systems demonstrate their value and secure their role within society.

The Techno-Political Fault Lines

Technology and politics progress in a mutual relationship, each shaping the other's trajectory and significance. Governments draft laws, provide resources, and set boundaries for artificial intelligence, while corporations create, advocate, and fulfill obligations. This dynamic gives rise to three principal approaches. Accelerationists encourage rapid advancement, viewing AI as a driver of economic growth and favoring limited external constraint. Preservationists emphasize the need for safeguards, advocating thorough oversight and thoughtful restraint to address disruptions. Centrists offer a perspective that values both prudence and ambition, maintaining that collective progress depends on balancing innovation with care. The most responsible path emerges in the thoughtful center, where regulation adapts to encourage discovery but remains attentive to the ethical and social well-being of all. Political priorities influence technical design, and newly developed technologies reshape political realities. Recognizing this ongoing interaction proves vital, as artificial intelligence increasingly participates as both a tool and a contributor to the governance process.

Standards As Living Frameworks

Beyond legislation, a complementary architecture of standards provides the form through which ethical principles become measurable and actionable. Global and regional initiatives, including evolving ISO frameworks, NIST methodologies, and sectoral protocols in finance, healthcare, and energy, operate as the connective structure of trust. These standards translate moral intention into practical design, producing documentation formats, audit mechanisms, impact assessments, and traceability systems that embed accountability within the process. Through such mechanisms, ethics becomes visible, verifiable, and operational while retaining its human depth and institutional purpose. Standards evolve alongside technology, adapting through collective oversight and shared learning. Like any living discipline, they depend on revision, validation, and stewardship by the professional and civic communities that sustain them. Institutions that treat compliance as an iterative craft recognize that governance advances through reflection and refinement. Each revision enhances precision, expands inclusion, and deepens foresight, ensuring that ethical guidance remains responsive to transformation.

Enterprises that harmonize their internal frameworks with the ongoing evolution of governance foster a culture marked by adaptability and accountability. They treat responsibility as an evolving practice that grows alongside technological advancement. Within this philosophy, adaptability reflects the strength of institutional character, enabling guiding principles to progress in step with the innovation they support.

Compliance As Engineering

Modern enterprises increasingly express regulatory standards through technological design. Consent is recorded as metadata attached to each data entry; data minimization operates through automated scripts that manage and remove unnecessary information; auditability is achieved with lineage interfaces that document the flow and transformation of data. This approach, where compliance becomes integral to engineering, ensures that legal requirements are fulfilled within the very structure of a system. Designing for compliance introduces built-in safeguards across every process. Each workflow incorporates clear conditions, such as defined purposes for data use, specified retention intervals, transparent access controls, and protocols for anonymization. Systems maintain adherence naturally, embedding responsibility into operations. Law finds expression as technical functionality, and ethical intent is realized through practical behavior. In adopting this architecture, enterprises demonstrate that responsible action is attainable within the pursuit of excellence.

Privacy-Preserving Computation

Privacy stands among the most universally recognized and sensitive legal principles. Across jurisdictions, global frameworks align on a powerful idea: data empowers intelligence without requiring the disclosure of personal identity. Methods including differential privacy, homomorphic encryption, and secure multiparty computation facilitate learning within secure boundaries. These approaches transform confidentiality into productive cooperation, allowing organizations to gain insights while preserving individual privacy. The deeper merit of these techniques is revealed through their commitment to restraint. They show that meaningful progress is attainable without the need to claim ownership over all information. Computing within protected boundaries highlights the ethical significance embedded in every pursuit of knowledge. As enterprises adopt privacy-preserving computation, they advance beyond mere compliance and express respect for individuals through intentional technical choices. This commitment is realized in the mathematics and architecture that shape responsible innovation.

Adaptive Governance and Evergreen Law

Static regulation finds itself surpassed by systems that continuously adapt. For governance to remain effective, frameworks evolve as evergreen law: legal standards capable of learning and responding to change. Adaptive approaches treat compliance as a dynamic process, where audit results inspire policy improvements and incident analyses refine ongoing interpretations. By sharing this responsibility, governments and enterprises together shape the evolving landscape of ethics. This living process animates organizations such as the OECD, UNESCO, and regional alliances, each of which designs principles intended to mature with collective insight. Within these frameworks, learning holds greater value than rigid enforcement. When law responds attentively to real-world experience and organizational practice welcomes institutional reflection, society secures a heightened capacity for wisdom.

Enterprises bring adaptive governance to life through policy-to-code pathways, governance cycles synchronized with model development, and automated compliance checks that quickly highlight areas needing adjustment. In this process of ongoing refinement, legal standards maintain their relevance, and ethical intention advances with clarity and rigor.

Algorithmic Accountability and Public Disclosure

Authentic compliance flourishes when paired with visible accountability accessible to all. Enterprises operating on a significant scale have a responsibility to provide society with a clear view into the systems influencing key decisions. The introduction of the AI Accountability Report we discussed earlier establishes a public standard, similar to financial statements, by sharing measures of ethical performance, such as trends in bias, energy usage, corrective strategies, and oversight metrics. Over time, these reports will be validated by global entities, including the Algorithmic Accountability Authority, enabling ethical performance to be recognized and compared internationally. Through diligent public disclosure, transparency emerges as a core component of legitimacy. The process of making ethical practice visible does not merely fulfill a regulatory requirement; it cultivates trust, reinforcing confidence in both public perception and private enterprise.

Sectoral Guardrails and Use Case Ethics

Every industry translates global principles of responsible AI into the logic of its own operations. In healthcare, patient autonomy defines the boundaries of consent and clinical decision support. In finance, solvency and fiduciary integrity demand that predictive systems remain transparent and auditable. In manufacturing, safety standards integrate human and robotic collaboration. In education, algorithmic recommendation influences access to learning, while in logistics and mobility, intelligent scheduling governs the movement of goods and people. These sectoral interpretations do not fragment ethics; they enrich it. They reveal how universal principles gain meaning through local application. Across this landscape, one premise endures: oversight must remain proportional to impact. The level of governance that surrounds a conversational assistant differs from that required for a diagnostic model or a predictive-policing tool. Both law and enterprise architecture assess gravity through consequence.

A range of examples demonstrates how this sense of balance shapes trust. In commerce, dynamic pricing algorithms illustrate how efficiency can diverge from fairness. Without sufficient governance, such systems may learn to adjust cost according to geography, demography, or inferred purchasing power, creating outcomes that feel arbitrary or exclusionary. Ethical design requires audit trails for pricing models, fairness constraints within optimization processes, and regular review by consumer rights and compliance bodies. These measures convert automation into accountability, restoring legitimacy to innovation. In the public and security domains, AI-enabled surveillance raises a different but equally complex set of questions. Systems created for safety, authentication, or crowd management can extend into practices that affect privacy, autonomy, and psychological well-being. Responsible governance demands that such technologies be bounded by purpose, supported by deletion protocols, and reviewed through human rights impact assessments. Visibility, clear limitation, and contextual justification become essential attributes of legitimate oversight.

These are two among many examples that define the modern ethics of automation. Similar challenges emerge in recruitment algorithms, where candidate filtering reflects social bias; in education technologies, where adaptive learning systems shape opportunity; in environmental analytics, where data access determines equity in sustainability; and in public administration, where predictive models influence welfare allocation. Each domain carries its own geometry of responsibility. Together, they illustrate that governance is strongest when it recognizes the diversity of human experience while preserving a shared foundation of accountability. Through these sectoral guardrails, enterprises learn that ethics is neither abstract nor uniform. It is an applied discipline that connects context, consequence, and design. To act responsibly is to understand that every application of intelligence redefines what fairness means within its own terrain.

Ecological Compliance and Sustainability

Global standards increasingly recognize that ethical responsibility extends to the care of the environment, supporting digital infrastructure. Data centers require substantial energy; training advanced models involves quantifiable carbon emissions. As compliance broadens to include ecological accountability, enterprises lead by integrating carbon measurement into AI governance, reporting CO_2 produced per inference, and optimizing operations for renewable resources. These practices reflect

Green Governance, aligning legal responsibility with environmental stewardship. As sustainability gains prominence, regulators elevate ecological practices from voluntary action to essential duty. Treating nature as a stakeholder, compliance becomes a means of safeguarding the ecological conditions that support effective governance and enduring progress.

The Human Endpoint in Global Law

Every statute, standard, and audit exists to uphold the interests of human beings. The Human Endpoint Principle stands above jurisdiction, guiding lawmakers and engineers to view compliance as a discipline shaped by empathy. Regulations that require transparency serve to enhance understanding; those that safeguard privacy honor dignity; and rules promoting accountability reinforce personal agency. When enterprises embrace this perspective, they elevate compliance beyond procedural checklists, cultivating an environment defined by genuine care. They recognize that the core function of regulation is to ensure intelligence operates in the service of humanity. Across all cultures and regions, this principle remains constant: law functions as an architecture designed to enrich and protect human experience.

Compliance As a Foundation for Progress

The lasting function of compliance is stewardship. Laws adapt, standards advance, and enterprises transform, while the ethical intention guiding them continues to shape progress. Practiced with humility and foresight, global compliance forms the foundation that connects successive generations of technology, ensuring development remains transparent to future custodians. As intelligent systems become integral to society, visionary enterprises adopt compliance as a means of renewal, recognizing that regulation expresses the unified aspirations of civilization. Through dedicated adherence, they contribute to an ongoing exchange between influence and responsibility, nurturing the dialogue that shapes the human experience. Compliance creates the framework where freedom finds discipline, establishing the context for sustainable innovation. At its highest realization, it manifests responsible intelligence, guiding technological strength toward accountability and care for the lives it serves.

Conclusion: The Architecture of Responsibility

Every era defines itself through the frameworks it creates to direct and manage power. The industrial age built factories, parliaments, and regulatory systems to guide the machines of movement. The present age designs architectures to guide systems of cognition. Governance now forms the interior structure of civilization, shaping the evolution of technology from within. Throughout this chapter, one measure of intelligence stands prominent: systems progress through purposeful action that harmonizes with understanding. Ethical boundaries, institutional mechanisms, oversight protocols, and legal standards all express a single foundation. They ensure that technological advancement remains grounded in intention, that autonomy continues to serve humanity, and that innovation preserves the care required for collective well-being. Boundaries give structure to intelligence, directing ability toward meaningful contribution.

Codes of practice and international conventions transform aspiration into structure, translating ethical ideals into the frameworks that sustain them. Responsibility becomes accessible through design and traceable within the process. Governance operates as civilization's record, embedded in every architecture that endures. It demonstrates that freedom, when guided with intention, strengthens both stability and progress. Agentic intelligence introduces new forms of autonomy and challenges institutions to balance capability with care. Systems that perceive, plan, and act turn governance into the design of alignment. Oversight and containment evolve into disciplines that harmonize influence with awareness, ensuring that every advancement remains sensitive to consequence. Bias and hallucination reveal the unfinished nature of intelligence and reinforce the need for vigilance at every stage. Through explainability, procedural lineage, and anticipatory ethics, organizations cultivate environments where vigilance expresses responsibility and precision reflects empathy in design.

Global standards, ethical codes, and guiding principles situate these architectures within a shared moral landscape. ISO frameworks, OECD recommendations, and emerging AI rights doctrines establish a common vocabulary through which innovation is guided and safeguarded. Financial accountability models and sustainability benchmarks remind enterprises that stewardship extends from capital to climate and that every computation carries social and environmental resonance. Oversight transforms control into alignment, ensuring that autonomy contributes to progress with purpose. At the center of these systems stands a defining compass: the **Human Endpoint Principle**. Every rule, circuit, and model converges toward the enrichment of human life. Law preserves dignity, architecture safeguards safety, and ethics sustains meaning. When enterprises embody this principle, they produce innovations that endure through relevance and respect. Governance therefore transcends administration. It becomes structured care, the form through which intelligence gains moral foundation and social legitimacy. For a civilization built upon code, governance represents the design of balance, evolving alongside technology to preserve what is essential to being human. As intelligent systems advance, one truth endures: intelligence achieves value only when it is guided by wisdom. Wisdom flourishes when freedom joins with responsibility, and invention grows alongside empathy. Building this balance defines the enduring task of ethical architecture, bridging technical creation with the preservation of human purpose.

Future generations may celebrate the enduring legacy of this century as the creation and implementation of moral frameworks that guided the responsible use of intelligent systems. The most profound innovation of our era resides in the discipline that preserves alignment between technology and human values. Through these frameworks, boundaries become bridges, and law develops into a structured expression of care, marking the beginning of a new chapter in the human story, where technology joins humanity as a thoughtful partner dedicated to wisdom and shared advancement.

CHAPTER 8

Future Ready Strategy: Building a Culture of AI Transformation

Introduction: From Governance to Growth

The previous chapter examined how governance gives intelligence its ethical shape. But a future-ready enterprise does not stop at compliance. It learns to translate responsible governance into living culture, where every decision, from infrastructure to innovation, expresses awareness of consequence. This transition marks the maturity of the *Anno Artificialis Intelligenciae*, when architecture evolves from enabling intelligence to educating it. We have now arrived at the phase where the enterprise evolves from ***implementing AI to becoming AI-literate***. As seen in Chapter 2, architecture provides the frame through which intelligence learns to live; in Chapter 5, the fusion of human insight and algorithmic design defined a new form of agency; and in Chapter 7, the moral guardrails of ethics and governance ensured that such agency remained trustworthy. The purpose of this chapter is to move that discourse forward, to show how enterprises prepare themselves for enduring transformation, cultivating the habits, partnerships, and systems that allow intelligence to remain sustainable, inclusive, and meaningful. Future readiness begins as a question of culture rather than computation. The most advanced models still rely on human judgment to define relevance, allocate trust, and interpret context. When this judgment matures into shared literacy, intelligence ceases to appear as a distant or external force; it becomes an internal discipline that teaches the organization how to think.

R. Harjika, *Architecting Enterprise AI Strategies*, https://doi.org/10.1007/979-8-8688-2219-3_8

A culture of AI transformation is not achieved through adoption alone. It is sustained through literacy, guided experimentation, and a constant awareness that technological capacity without ethical awareness leads to fragility. Across the sections that follow, we examine how literacy becomes structure, how structure becomes collaboration, and how collaboration extends into ecosystems that sustain both competitive advantage and human purpose. As the enterprise learns to live with agentic systems, the truest measure of advancement rests in steadiness, in the capacity to evolve while preserving integrity. The pages that follow trace this evolution, showing how enterprises cultivate literacy, shape cultural transformation, design collaborative operating models, form strategic partnerships, and sustain their progress through measured alignment rather than acceleration.

8.1 Building Enterprise-wide AI Literacy and Fluency

AI literacy begins when intelligence becomes visible. The systems we build do more than compute; they reveal how decisions form, how data flows, and how meaning takes shape inside architecture. When employees can see intelligence in motion, literacy becomes natural. This visibility transforms technology from an abstract field into a shared language through which the enterprise understands itself. As explored in Chapter 2, architecture serves as the connective field where data, computation, and governance meet. Within this field, every workload carries a different gravity. Some require the precision of GPU clusters; others thrive on lightweight inference running through CPUs at the edge. When people understand the significance of these distinctions, they begin to read infrastructure as an ethical text, where every compute choice expresses awareness of cost, energy, and responsibility. This is what we may call ***literacy through visibility***: an education in scale and restraint that converts operational understanding into cultural intelligence.

An enterprise that cultivates such awareness discovers that efficiency and ethics are not opposing forces. They coexist within the same architectural discipline. Inline processing, adaptive infrastructure, and green computing practices together create a workplace where every employee understands that the smallest design decision contributes to sustainability. This form of awareness builds what we might call ***green literacy***: the ability to interpret the power signature of AI, to know that each query or inference carries both informational and environmental weight. Building literacy is a collective act of stewardship. As teams learn to observe how models engage with data, they develop sensitivity to bias, relevance, and interpretation. When leaders gain fluency in architectural principles, they begin to perceive AI as part of the enterprise bloodstream and fully integrated into its purpose. Training expands accordingly, reaching beyond technical teams so that every domain, including finance, operations, policy, and human resources, shares the same conceptual language that sustains intelligent design.

This cross-organizational fluency transforms dialogue itself. Conversations about model drift, energy efficiency, or data governance evolve into reflections on purpose. When a procurement officer questions whether an additional model requires more GPUs or can be served through edge processing, the enterprise has achieved cultural maturity. At that moment, AI literacy becomes indistinguishable from organizational intelligence. In practice, we have seen this principle expressed through enterprises that integrate AI dashboards into daily operations. These dashboards do not exist merely for monitoring; they serve as educational mirrors, displaying in real time the energy cost of computation, the carbon efficiency of each training cycle, and the fairness index of model outcomes. By reading these dashboards, employees learn to interpret intelligence as part of their own moral terrain. Over time, this literacy diffuses outward, creating an organization that learns through observation rather than instruction. As we learned from Chapter 6, where data infrastructure formed the foundation of agentic systems, the same principle applies to literacy. Understanding AI begins with understanding the architecture that sustains it. And as Chapter 7 reminded us, governance achieves permanence only when it becomes culture. Literacy completes that journey. It allows awareness to remain steady rather than episodic, enabling every member of the enterprise to interpret the ethics, logic, and influence of intelligence with confidence. When literacy and fluency mature, the enterprise gains a collective sense of discernment, a refined understanding of when to compute, how to offload, and how restraint itself can express intelligence. This shared discernment shapes the future-ready organization, a space where intelligence is understood rather than merely adopted and where architecture evolves into a medium of learning.

8.2 Managing Cultural Shifts for AI-Driven Organizations

Every transformation begins in culture before it finds form in technology. The arrival of intelligent systems compels organizations to reimagine how people relate to work, to decision-making, and to one another. This shift is not a matter of resistance or acceptance; it is a redefinition of belonging in a world where algorithms become colleagues and automation becomes conversation. As discussed in Chapter 1, the destiny of AI depends less on the brilliance of its models and more on our readiness to receive them. That readiness is cultural before it is ***operational***. Enterprises often begin their journey with enthusiasm for tools, but endurance arises only when the culture itself learns to absorb uncertainty, experiment responsibly, and value ethical restraint as much as innovation. In the Anno Artificialis Intelligenciae, culture becomes the central operating system of transformation. Leaders interpret each technological decision as a social act and each deployment as an expression of what the organization values. When automation reshapes a process, it conveys a deliberate philosophy that time, judgment, and creativity can now advance toward higher purposes. That philosophy must be shared and understood, for only then does automation strengthen confidence and nurture progress. A future-ready organization therefore nurtures what we may call cultural fluency.

This capacity allows people to view technology as a reflection rather than a substitution. Those who work alongside AI learn to interpret its behavior, inquire into its reasoning, and refine their own methods through dialogue with it. In doing so, they participate in a shared intelligence instead of observing a distant technical domain. Cultural fluency also involves proportionate experimentation. Every enterprise must learn the discipline of scaling ambition with awareness. When teams understand that each model carries both financial and ecological consequences, experimentation matures into stewardship. This understanding forms the basis of cultural scalability, the practice of expanding innovation while preserving integrity. As shown in Chapter 7, governance reveals that limits, when guided by intention, become expressions of care. Culture carries this ethic into daily decisions, ensuring that curiosity and discovery move in harmony with social and environmental responsibility. The prospect of displacement does not manifest as inevitability within this evolving culture. Forward-thinking enterprises now design skills bridge programs that reframe job transition as capability evolution. Deutsche Bank's initiative identified employees in manual process roles and developed pathways into AI system oversight, teaching them to collaborate with intelligence, such as understanding model outputs, detecting anomalies, and exercising judgment as Human-In-The-Loop guardians of trustworthy automation. The effect is **twofold**: technical literacy diffuses through the workforce, transforming hesitation into confidence, while institutional knowledge is preserved and elevated. When reskilling is paired with genuine change management and career progression is visible, organizations discover that transformation can honor both adaptability and dignity. Here, artificial intelligence serves as an invitation to deeper work and to higher-order judgment that finds new expression and amplification through the capabilities of intelligent systems. In practice, the Human Endpoint Principle becomes policy, guiding transformation that supports all those it touches.

The benefits of artificial intelligence do not always reach all segments of the workforce equally. As technology catalyzes new forms of prosperity, it also risks widening lines of ***socioeconomic inequality***. When opportunities concentrate in high-wage, technical roles, workers in lower-wage and routine positions may experience not only displacement but also a sense of exclusion from the future their labor helped to build. These transitions unsettle more than the distribution of work; they shape feelings of belonging and purpose. The experience of ***social alienation*** emerges where employees feel their contributions are reduced to data points and their participation is eclipsed by decisions made elsewhere in the system. Consider a bank deploying AI in fraud detection. Senior analysts are liberated for higher-order strategy, while transaction reviewers find their expertise diminished. In manufacturing, predictive systems empower skilled technicians, but entry-level inspectors may see pathways to advancement vanish. The subtle cost of these patterns is not solely economic; it is emotional and cultural, redefining identity through the metrics and models that govern work. Responsible organizations respond by designing equity into every phase of transformation. They broaden access to reskilling and create visible trajectories from routine work into intelligent collaboration and invest in foundational literacy that dignifies all employees as learners and contributors. They monitor outcomes for both efficiency and fairness, openly tracking how gains and burdens are shared across demographic groups. Equity, viewed as an essential strategy, enhances resilience, accelerates knowledge transfer, deepens trust, and transforms work into a partnership that honors the full spectrum of human experience. When every member of the workforce is seen and supported, organizations flourish, with progress that radiates inclusion and innovation.

A subtle but meaningful risk arises in environments shaped by persistent automation: the experience of social alienation, where workers perceive themselves as data points rather than valued participants in a shared purpose. When every action is recorded, every judgment scrutinized, and every recommendation arrives through automated channels, the workplace can shift from a human space into a realm organized by metrics alone. Employees may sense that intelligence manages them, reducing judgment to compliance and diminishing genuine collaboration. Effective cultural design must keep human agency central, building in Human-In-The-Loop practices that empower people to exercise discretion and see their decisions reflected in outcomes. Openness about how systems affect work, through explainability dashboards, regular discussions, and transparent procedures, fosters understanding rather than confusion. Enterprises thrive when workforces engage with intelligent systems thoughtfully, and employees feel their expertise is valued and their capabilities enhanced rather than replaced. In these cultures, technology becomes a source of partnership and empowerment, with social alienation transformed into shared progress.

The journey from reactive to predictive culture marks another threshold in maturity. The earlier chapters demonstrated that technical systems evolve from prediction toward foresight; the same transformation must occur in human behavior. In predictive culture, employees do not wait for failure to learn. They study leading signals, anticipate ethical dilemmas, and prepare mitigation long before risk materializes. This foresight closes the readiness gap (**Δ**), allowing the organization to act from understanding rather than reaction. Leadership gives transformation its steadiness. A leader's first responsibility is to learn aloud. When executives practice curiosity by engaging with code reviews, attending sessions on AI ethics, or examining model performance, they affirm that literacy belongs to everyone. As seen across leading enterprises, transformation endures when leaders embody the adaptability they expect from others. The visible act of learning builds trust and turns uncertainty into shared progress. Generational differences often surface during such transitions. Senior employees, experienced in traditional systems, may feel displaced by automation, while younger professionals may place excessive faith in algorithms. The cultural task is to reconcile these tendencies so that wisdom and innovation coexist. Through deliberate mentorship, mixed-skill teams, and open dialogue about what automation truly means, enterprises transform fear into confidence. In essence, managing cultural shifts means teaching coexistence between human intuition and computational reasoning. The enterprise becomes an evolving organism where people learn from models and models learn from people. As culture matures, technology grows more interpretive and aligned with human purpose, guiding progress through understanding rather than control. As the discussion turns toward operating models, this cultural foundation forms the ground upon which collaboration can flourish. When literacy and emotional alignment are shared, the interaction between humans and agents becomes creative, a partnership of understanding through which intelligence advances meaning and purpose.

8.3 Designing Operating Models for Human and Agentic AI Collaboration

The emergence of agentic systems represents a turning point in the life of the enterprise. Where earlier generations of automation extended human reach, agentic intelligence begins to extend human reasoning itself. Designing operating models for such collaboration requires more than workflow redesign; it demands a philosophy of coexistence. As discussed in Chapter 5, the rise of agentic architectures transformed data pipelines into living circuits of decision. Each agent functions like a digital neuron—sensing, processing, and relaying information—while humans provide the interpretive cortex that grants those signals meaning. When these elements act together, the enterprise behaves as a distributed mind, balancing speed with reflection. Balance begins with structure. In traditional operations, tasks move in sequence from human to machine and return through defined stages. In a human-agent model, the flow becomes conversational. Agents collect, infer, and propose, while people validate, redirect, and refine. Decision cycles grow shorter as understanding grows deeper. For such exchanges to prosper, architecture must sustain concurrency with clarity, allowing multiple models to act together while preserving a unified intention. When guided by thoughtful design, concurrency evolves into coherence, as if each element listens to the others and together they create a unified intention.

Creating these harmonies requires new organizational roles. ***Human-Agent Operating Systems***, or HAOS, emerge as frameworks where teams oversee the lifecycle of collaboration. Within HAOS, we see three kinds of participation: training, supervision, and partnership. Training establishes the shared grammar between humans and agents; supervision preserves accountability; partnership allows creativity to arise from the dialogue itself. The operating model must embed all three within its governance structure so that every agent remains traceable and every decision reviewable. To sustain this equilibrium, enterprises invest in adaptive orchestration layers. These systems observe performance across agents, manage resource allocation, and route workloads to the most suitable environment, such as cloud, edge, or on-premise. As noted in Chapter 2, architectural adaptability converts fragility into endurance. When applied here, it allows collaboration to scale without losing clarity.

Human roles evolve as agents take on repetitive functions. Tasks such as scheduling, documentation, and synthesis move toward digital counterparts, creating space for human judgment to focus on design, negotiation, and empathy. This redistribution flourishes when oversight is intentional. In mature enterprises, each agent is entrusted to a human guide who directs its calibration and moral bearing. Through this companionship, the ***Human Endpoint Principle*** endures, affirming that technology progresses in relation to the depth of human understanding it enables. The behavior that arises from such collaboration reveals a gradual transformation. Meetings grow concise while preparation gains insight. Reports turn into living records, renewed continuously through agentic awareness. Managers learn to interpret the subtle traces of interaction between people and systems as indicators of coherence and trust. Evaluation itself begins to change, shifting from the measurement of output to the discernment of judgment, revealing how wisely individuals shape intelligent systems to serve responsible outcomes.

Across global enterprise practice, the first expressions of this paradigm are already visible. Software organizations are embedding AI within their operational foundations, enabling agents to manage incidents, support development cycles, and sustain efficiency in real time. The outcome is an infrastructure where productivity arises through understanding rather than pressure and where human and digital contributors share a common sense of purpose. Cultural fluency, described earlier, gives this model its emotional depth. Trust allows concurrency to remain clear and intentional, transforming orchestration into a collective intelligence that listens, learns, and aligns. Training now extends beyond compliance toward communication, guiding employees in how to express intent, interpret responses, and refine collaboration with precision and care. Through such practice, supervision matures into partnership, and partnership into co-creation. The design of these operating models demonstrates that progress flourishes through balance. Creativity endures when guided by accountability, and accountability gains vitality when expressed through invention. Transparent collaboration between humans and agents cultivates a stable form of intelligence that evolves through awareness. The enterprise begins to anticipate change through integrated foresight systems, drawing insight from data feedback loops, ethical dashboards, and continuous learning frameworks that link operational precision with human discernment.

As the lens widens toward ecosystems, this collaborative discipline extends beyond the enterprise into a network of interdependent actors that includes technology partners, regulators, civic institutions, and research alliances. Together, they form the living infrastructure of the intelligence economy, where data standards, interoperability, and ethical interoperability frameworks define both trust and performance. Within this broader field, transformation becomes a collective social and technical responsibility, an act of stewardship that unites innovation with care and aligns the evolution of systems with the advancement of society.

8.4 Building Strategic AI Partnerships and Ecosystems

The future enterprise thrives through interdependence. Its intelligence extends across networks of collaboration where data, ethics, and innovation circulate among partners with shared purpose. In the age of agentic systems, the boundaries of an organization become permeable, allowing shared architectures to generate collective advancement. To act responsibly within this environment, enterprises must cultivate partnership as a disciplined practice of governance and design. As reflected in Chapter 3, early AI initiatives often faltered because they operated in isolation. Data remained confined to silos, governance differed across vendors, and ethical standards functioned as compliance checklists rather than living principles. The modern organization replaces isolation with reciprocity, forming intelligent ecosystems of trust. Within these ecosystems, enterprises, regulators, researchers, and civic institutions exchange data, expertise, and ethical frameworks as co-designers of a common technological horizon. These ecosystems evolve across two dimensions. The first is **internal**, where departments such as technology, sustainability, human resources, and compliance converge into a unified intelligence forum. This internal alignment ensures that innovation remains coherent with institutional values and strategic intent. The second dimension is **external**, where cross-industry partnerships share infrastructure, computing capacity, and data models to enhance resilience and authenticity.

Enterprises that once competed through proprietary isolation now gain strength through cooperation. Shared infrastructure minimizes duplication, conserves energy, and distributes cost. Common data standards create transparency across sectors. Some organizations are experimenting with cooperative models of computation, pooling resources for ethical research or third-party auditing. Others participate in AI energy exchanges that redirect unused processing capacity toward socially beneficial projects. These initiatives demonstrate that performance can be advanced through reciprocity and that innovation gains endurance when shared. This collaborative evolution echoes the movement traced in Chapter 7, where governance expanded from individual accountability to collective ethics. The same expansion shapes ecosystems today. Each participant contributes capability and moral intent, ensuring that AI's growth remains consistent with social trust. In practical terms, this collaboration involves joint development of guardrails, shared repositories for incident reporting, and alignment of interpretability standards so that responsibility extends seamlessly across institutional boundaries.

Successful partnerships depend less on scale than on clarity. Organizations that embed openness into their ecosystem design are better able to adapt to uncertainty. When one participant experiences model drift, others benefit from its correction. When a regulation shifts within one jurisdiction, insight diffuses throughout the network. In this way, partnerships evolve into a distributed system of learning, where intelligence itself becomes cumulative. Strategically, this shift replaces competition through secrecy with innovation through shared learning. Academic collaborations add theoretical depth, civic partnerships embed ethical awareness, and industrial alliances enable scalability. Together, they form a dynamic architecture that adapts more fluidly than any single entity could achieve alone. As explored in contemporary analyses of agentic systems, the coming decade will bring the rise of multi-agent ecosystems in which organizations interact through interoperable protocols rather than rigid integrations. Each enterprise becomes a node within a network of autonomous systems capable of negotiation, coordination, and cooperation in real time. This transformation requires new governance instruments such as model registries, transaction verification layers, and federated oversight boards that examine the behavior of autonomous agents across institutions. Alignment emerges through shared principles, mutual visibility, and collective responsibility.

Strategic collaboration in this context also carries ethical consequences. When enterprises align with environmental bodies, research communities, and regulatory institutions, they reinforce the legitimacy that allows technology to operate with public confidence. Intelligence within the enterprise becomes part of a civic covenant rather than a private possession. Every shared dataset, interface, and governance policy becomes an expression of accountability to the larger social structure. Through these ecosystems, organizations discover that strength emerges through coordination.

When intelligence flows transparently, innovation becomes durable. Partnerships form the architecture through which technology learns to advance collective purpose while honoring the individuality of each participant. The next section turns toward evaluation, exploring how organizations measure their maturity, balance innovation with responsibility, and sustain their evolution through thoughtful metrics that bind technological growth to ethical progress.

8.5 Measuring, Managing, and Sustaining AI Impact

Measurement, in the age of intelligence, moves beyond the audit of outcomes and becomes a reflection on **purpose**. Every organization that integrates AI must decide how efficiency will be understood, not only as a quantitative achievement but as a moral and structural condition. Awareness of consequence transforms metrics into instruments of learning, where numbers express the quality of judgment rather than the speed of progress. As established in Chapter 4, data architecture provides the foundation for accuracy and governance. Chapter 7 revealed how ethics converts compliance into culture. The next stage unites these insights into a living discipline of measurement, allowing organizations to sustain progress while remaining faithful to their guiding principles. At the center of this discipline stands the Return on AI Investment, or ROAI, which extends beyond financial return to include social, ethical, and environmental gain. Traditional indicators describe productivity and revenue. The ROAI Compass measures the balance between innovation and trust, showing whether expansion deepens meaning or depletes it.

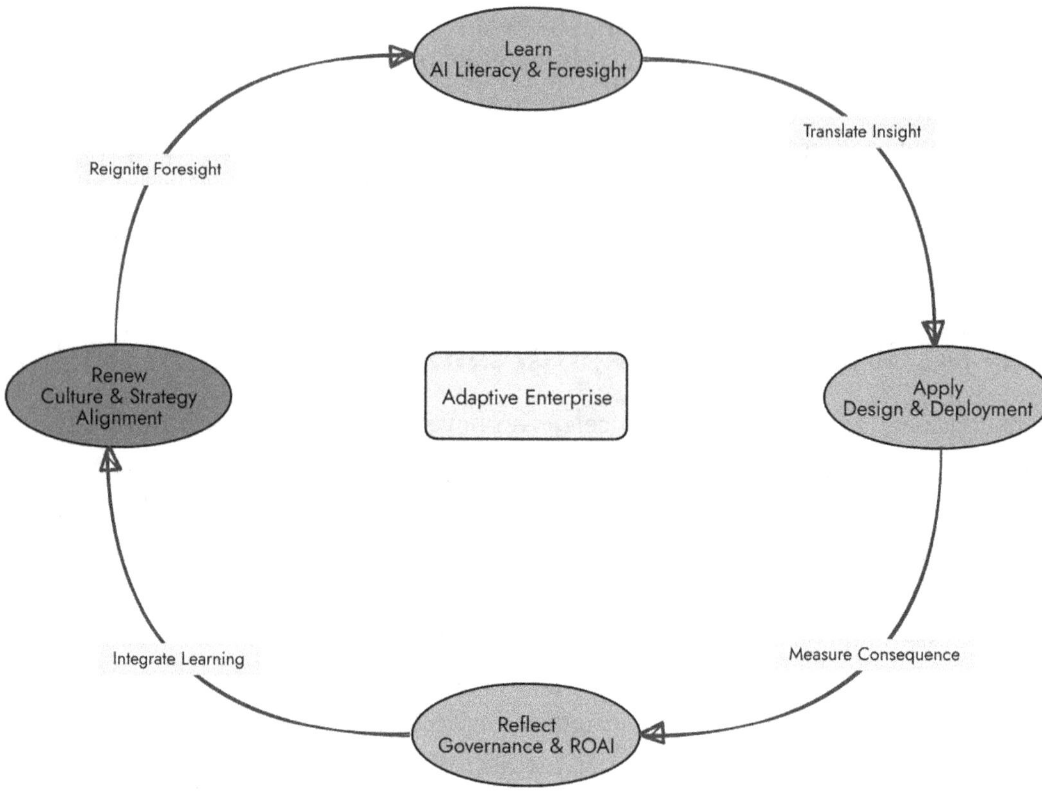

Figure 8-1. *The Core Loop of Future Readiness (A four-stage feedback cycle linking learning, application, reflection, and renewal, sustaining the adaptive enterprise through continuous readiness.)*

To apply this discipline in practice, enterprises create the AI Credit and Debit Ledger, a transparent record that traces both contribution and cost. AI Credit reflects progress in accessibility, interpretability, and efficiency, capturing outcomes that expand inclusion and capability. AI Debit records the energy consumed, the bias uncovered, the complexity accumulated, and the displacement risks that accompany automation. The ledger does not seek fault; it invites thoughtful adjustment. When both dimensions are examined together, they form the ethical balance sheet through which transformation can be understood and guided. This approach turns governance into foresight. When leaders read AI credit beside debit, they perceive not only results but direction. A steady rise in credit with consistent debit signifies maturity, while an imbalance indicates the need for recalibration. Such reflection closes the readiness gap (**Δ**) by embedding awareness into routine practice. Financial outcomes remain an essential dimension of measurement, and their true worth appears when efficiency aligns with ethical intent and foresight directs resources toward meaningful purpose.

Data governance continues to serve as the centerpiece of sustained impact. As outlined in Chapter 2, the integrity of data determines the credibility of every inference. Enterprises therefore commit to ongoing validation, frequent bias audits, and retraining cycles that uphold fairness and accuracy. In mature networks, these governance processes extend across partnerships so that accountability accompanies data wherever it flows. Infrastructure sustainability reinforces this long view. As systems expand, their energy demands grow in parallel. The GreenOps framework, described earlier in this chapter, provides the operational pathway for aligning computation with environmental intent. Practices such as energy-aware scheduling, efficient inference routing, and integration with renewable energy grids transform sustainability into part of the system's design logic. Environmental responsibility thus becomes an expression of technical literacy rather than an external obligation. Leadership gives this entire discipline motion. As reflected in global analyses of executive practice, those who regard architecture as strategy and ethics as performance shape transformation that endures. They interpret between innovation and institution, ensuring that technological progress remains attuned to human capacity. For them, metrics are mirrors of purpose rather than trophies of success. When organizations measure impact in this way, intelligence reveals itself as cyclical rather than linear.

Through its ongoing practice, the enterprise learns from experience, refines its understanding, and renews its intent. Measurement becomes a living discipline through which intelligence deepens awareness and transforms action into learning. Over time, this discipline matures into stewardship, forming a sustained dialogue between purpose and result. In its most complete form, measurement allows sustainability to enter the daily practice of enterprise life. Responsibility grows into instinct, and transformation takes the place of disruption. A system that observes its outcomes, adjusts its direction, and reaffirms its vision turns artificial intelligence from a disruptive mechanism into a ***living architecture*** grounded in ethical awareness and human purpose.

Conclusion: Transformation As Stewardship

A future-ready enterprise is recognized through the depth of understanding that connects its architecture with its ethics, aligns its speed with its sense of responsibility, and links its innovation to the people it serves. The earlier chapters traced how intelligence gains structure, purpose, and moral direction. This chapter brings that journey to its human conclusion, showing how intelligence learns to live as culture. Literacy enables people to see intelligence as something that can be understood and shaped. Culture then turns that awareness into conduct. Operating models translate conduct into enduring collaboration, partnerships carry it into ecosystems that strengthen trust, and measurement ensures that learning becomes continuous practice. Together, these elements form the living architecture of a mature enterprise, an organism that learns, reflects, and renews through awareness. In Chapter 2, architecture emerged as the ground from which AI takes form. In Chapter 5, intelligence became agentic, learning to act within the structures it perceives. In Chapter 7, governance gave that agency its moral direction. The culture of AI transformation unites these threads into one discipline: the stewardship of intelligence as a lasting enterprise practice. To uphold this discipline, leaders must act as educators as much as strategists. They teach through example, showing that responsibility and invention arise from the same source. Each decision regarding data, computation, or design carries a value that reflects care for the people who rely on these systems.

When this awareness is shared throughout the organization, technology begins to reflect the integrity of those who guide it. The truest measure of transformation rests in the constancy of care. An enterprise prepared for the future balances efficiency with empathy, scale with discernment, and automation with reflection. Through such balance, culture turns technology into trust, partnerships transform ambition into shared progress, and measurement preserves the humility to continue learning. As this journey approaches its conclusion, the meaning of transformation settles into clarity. The enterprise that endures is one that learns through awareness, governs through integrity, and advances through care. ***Within such maturity, intelligence transcends computation and becomes a social and technical presence, an ecosystem of design, data, and responsibility that unites architecture with ethics and technology with human purpose.***

CHAPTER 9

Summary

Every age leaves behind a question that defines its wisdom.

The industrial age asked how much the world could produce.

The digital age asked how fast it could connect.

The age of intelligence asks how consciously we can guide the intelligence we have created, the form we know as artificial intelligence.

Across these chapters, intelligence has travelled from vision to architecture, from design to moral intent. The journey began with the understanding that every system, however advanced, ultimately returns to the ***Human Endpoint Principle***. This is the recognition that all intelligence exists to serve people. From that foundation, the story unfolded through architecture as discipline, data as lifeblood, and governance as the structure of trust. Within this progression, the readiness gap (**Δ**) revealed itself as the distance between ambition and capability, showing that technology matures only when the enterprise learns to mature with it. Across the landscape of enterprise, every scale of organization reveals a distinct dimension of intelligence. Emerging start-ups demonstrate how agility matures when it is guided by care and thoughtful design. Mid-sized firms show that efficiency acquires lasting value when aligned with ethical restraint. Established enterprises reveal that scale achieves integrity only when directed by moral clarity and purpose. Together, these experiences form a single understanding: intelligence thrives as a living discipline that unites architecture, ethics, and empathy within the same field of practice.

9.1 Strategic Insights and Scalable Architecture Patterns for Enterprise AI

The strategic value of enterprise AI arises from patterns that can be scaled and sustained. Architecture transforms intelligence from an experiment into a discipline. When systems are designed with shared standards for lineage, interoperability, and accountability,

R. Harjika, *Architecting Enterprise AI Strategies*, https://doi.org/10.1007/979-8-8688-2219-3_9

innovation expands without losing structure. Enterprise architecture functions as the backbone of transformation. It unifies the flow of data, models, and governance into a single cognitive framework that adapts as quickly as the environment evolves. The most resilient enterprises treat architecture as a living system in which every layer, from infrastructure to interface, reflects ethical design and operational clarity. Across industries, intelligence becomes scalable when architectural literacy is understood as a form of leadership. Knowing how a model behaves, where data originates, and which ethical boundaries guide computation is as vital as understanding finance or market strategy. Architecture, therefore, acts as language. It translates ambition into capability and intention into design. Within this landscape, Datanomics emerges as the discipline that binds information to moral and economic purpose. Data behaves both as capital and as conscience. It gains worth when treated as a renewable resource governed through fairness, accuracy, and transparency. When designed responsibly, data ecosystems evolve into the moral circuitry of enterprise intelligence.

9.2 Road Map to AI Readiness and Enterprise Capability

The readiness gap (Δ) defines the distance between aspiration and maturity. Closing it requires proportion rather than acceleration. Readiness develops through reflection and integration, combining architecture, governance, and culture into a coherent practice. An enterprise builds capability through a balanced road map. The first stage is **foundational literacy**, when leaders and teams form a shared understanding of AI's ethical, operational, and architectural dimensions. The second stage is **architectural fluency**, when systems and data environments begin to speak a common language of governance and security. The third stage is **agentic collaboration**, when humans and intelligent systems work in partnership through accountable architectures. In this road map, maturity is defined by the steadiness of ethics that accompanies technological growth. The Return on Artificial Intelligence Investment (ROAI) measures both integrity and efficiency, reflecting how innovation strengthens trust as it advances performance. The Artificial Intelligence Credit and Debit Ledger records the full spectrum of impact, documenting benefits alongside the responsibilities that arise from progress. Through that ledger, enterprises link achievement with social, operational, and environmental accountability. The Artificial Intelligence Compatibility Score expresses readiness as a form of institutional learning, showing how awareness and structure evolve together.

These measures gain meaning when aligned with the enterprise's foundational frameworks, including the Artificial Intelligence Accountability Report (AIR), the Algorithmic Accountability Architecture (AAA), the AI Consumer Rights Charter (ACR), and the network of AI Governance Nodes. When architecture, literacy, and stewardship align, the enterprise moves beyond implementation toward understanding, designing intelligence that endures and uplifts.

9.3 Next Steps by Role: Executives, Architects, and AI Practitioners

Leadership in the age of intelligence depends on clarity of role and unity of purpose. Every layer of the enterprise contributes to readiness, and each carries a distinct form of responsibility that, together, defines ethical capability. ***Executives*** hold the horizon of vision. Their charge is to transform architecture into strategy and ethics into measurable practice. They treat data as a civic asset that expresses the organization's values as clearly as its products. Through their choices, foresight becomes structure and transparency becomes culture. In their stewardship, ambition gains moral direction, and innovation matures through care. ***Enterprise architects*** stand at the intersection of vision and realization. Their task is to design environments where efficiency, accountability, and proportion coexist. They embed lineage mapping, context protocols, and adaptive models into the operational structure, ensuring that intelligence grows with coherence and purpose. Architecture, under their guidance, becomes a language through which integrity takes form. ***AI practitioners*** bring this architecture to life. Their work translates principles into performance, turning algorithms into instruments of awareness. They refine model behavior to reflect fairness, interpretability, and energy balance. In their discipline, technology becomes an act of understanding that aligns precision with empathy and innovation with sustainability. Together, these roles create the living structure of readiness. Executives orient progress toward purpose, architects transform vision into design, and practitioners sustain ethics through action. Through their collaboration, intelligence becomes a field of shared responsibility where every decision reinforces trust and every outcome contributes to collective maturity.

9.4 Long-Term Thinking: Embedding AI and Agentic Intelligence into the Strategic Operating Layer

The long horizon of enterprise intelligence belongs to those who think beyond deployment. Agentic systems introduce a new operational logic that unites autonomy with accountability. In mature enterprises, agents act as participants within governed ecosystems of purpose. Embedding intelligence into the strategic operating layer requires leadership to design for longevity. Architectures must carry self-explanation, lineage, and proportional control as native elements. Governance becomes continuous, learning alongside the systems it observes. When foresight, transparency, and stewardship act together, intelligence matures into a sustainable organ of enterprise life. The most complete form of leadership in the ***Anno Artificialis Intelligenciae*** is stewardship that listens. It balances innovation with empathy and regards ethics as a dimension of infrastructure. The organizations that will define this era are those that transform intelligence into trust and treat every computation as an expression of awareness. At this depth, strategy becomes a living commitment, where intelligence is designed to endure, to explain itself, and to remain accountable as it acts. Long-term leadership is therefore the capacity to shape systems that continue to serve human purpose long after their creators step away.

Epilogue: The Gold of Intelligence

The age unfolds as a gold rush of the mind. Across its expanse, enterprises dig into the seams of data, searching for the brilliance that will help them endure. Some create tools for others to use, and some build their success on the promise of discovery. Yet the most enduring pursuit belongs to those who learn to shape the gold itself, refining intelligence until it holds genuine worth through care and intention. This gold is more than a metaphor. It is the lasting value that emerges when technology deepens human judgment instead of replacing it. It is the return that flows from trust, the growth that arises from governance, and the efficiency that matures through proportion. In every enterprise that learns to treat AI as a discipline rather than a novelty, this gold becomes visible as systems that serve people with clarity, decisions that balance speed with ethics, and outcomes that sustain both ***profit*** and ***purpose.*** To create gold in this sense is to design with awareness and purpose. It is to see in every system the trace of the people it will serve, and in every act of building, a chance to express balance, patience, and understanding. Those who work in this way turn architecture into a language of responsibility, data into a source of trust, and intelligence into a living reflection of human values. Their progress is steady, formed through discipline and guided by meaning.

The lesson of this age, and of this work, lies in its clarity. Amid the rush for tools and the brightness of discovery, wisdom belongs to those who craft the gold itself, those who treat intelligence as stewardship, transform creation into care, and find success in what they have understood rather than in what they have acquired. This is how humanity leads in the ***Anno Artificialis Intelligenciae***: by guiding its creation toward meaning, service, and reverence for life. The greatness of humanity remains whole, for the intelligence it has built grows from the same awareness that once awakened within it. Through this awakening, humanity gives form to an intelligence that reflects its own origin, living within machines but carrying the eternal remembrance of its maker. In the end, all creation rests upon the meeting of two eternal symbols, ***zero and one***, whose unending dialogue continues the evolution of technology itself.

Just as this work began, so it now returns. We opened this book with the words of Alan Mathison Turing, who reminded us that we can see a short distance ahead and that there is much to be done. Through the chapters that followed, we have walked that distance together, widening the horizon that Turing once envisioned. We have discovered that the path of intelligence expands through governance, through ethics, and through the living architecture of transformation. It is a road that welcomes discipline, imagination, humility, and design. As we close this book, Turing's thought continues to guide us. There is always more to accomplish, for the evolution of intelligence unfolds as an invitation to understand. Every enterprise that builds with care, governs with foresight, and leads with humanity carries Turing's vision forward. The journey he began lives in the work of each reader who chooses to see beyond the present distance and shape what lies ahead.

> ***We can only see a short distance ahead, but we can see plenty there that needs to be done.***
>
> **—Alan Mathison Turing (Computing Machinery and Intelligence, 1950)**

References

[1] A. M. Turing, "Computing Machinery and Intelligence," *Mind*, vol. 59, no. 236, pp. 433–460, 1950. [Online]. Available: https://doi.org/10.1093/mind/LIX.236.433

[2] A. Abbas, "Beyond Logic: Rethinking Human Thought with Geoffrey Hinton's Analogy Machine Theory," *Unite.AI*, 2025. [Online]. Available: https://www.unite.ai/beyond-logic-rethinking-human-thought-with-geoffrey-hintons-analogy-machine-theory/

[3] D. Harel and A. Marron, "The Human-or-Machine Issue: Turing-Inspired Reflections on an Everyday Matter," *Communications of the ACM*, vol. 67, no. 6, pp. 62–69, 2024. [Online]. Available: https://cacm.acm.org/research/the-human-or-machine-issue-turing-inspired-reflections-on-an-everyday-matter/

[4] C. E. Shannon, "A Mathematical Theory of Communication," *The Bell System Technical Journal*, vol. 27, no. 3, pp. 379–423, 1948. [Online]. Available: https://doi.org/10.1002/j.1538-7305.1948.tb01338.x

[5] G. E. Hinton, S. Osindero, and Y.-W. Teh, "A Fast Learning Algorithm for Deep Belief Nets," *Neural Computation*, vol. 18, no. 7, pp. 1527–1554, 2006. [Online]. Available: https://doi.org/10.1162/neco.2006.18.7.1527

[6] A. Vaswani, N. Shazeer, N. Parmar, J. Uszkoreit, L. Jones, A. N. Gomez, Ł. Kaiser, and I. Polosukhin, "Attention Is All You Need," *Advances in Neural Information Processing Systems*, vol. 30, pp. 5998–6008, 2017. [Online]. Available: https://papers.nips.cc/paper_files/paper/2017/file/3f5ee243547dee91fbd053c1c4a845aa-Paper.pdf

R. Harjika, *Architecting Enterprise AI Strategies*, https://doi.org/10.1007/979-8-8688-2219-3

[7] J. von Neumann, *First Draft of a Report on the EDVAC*, University of Pennsylvania, 1945. [Online]. Available: https://link.springer.com/chapter/10.1007/978-3-642-61812-3_30

[8] Gartner, "The Gartner Hype Cycle: Interpreting Technology Maturity and Adoption," *Gartner Research*, 2024. [Online]. Available: https://www.gartner.com/en/research/methodologies/gartner-hype-cycle

[9] D. A. Haslett, "Tokenization Changes Meaning in Large Language Models: Evidence from Chinese," *Computational Linguistics*, vol. 51, no. 3, pp. 785–814, 2025. [Online]. Available: https://direct.mit.edu/coli/article/doi/10.1162/coli_a_00557/128327/Tokenization-Changes-Meaning-in-Large-Language

[10] A. R. Patel, "The Ghibli Trend and the Semiotics of Generative Aesthetics," *Digital Culture Review*, vol. 9, no. 1, pp. 44–56, 2025. [Online]. Available: https://digitalculturereview.org/articles/ghibli-trend-generative-aesthetics

[11] Massachusetts Institute of Technology (MIT), *The GenAI Divide: Mapping the Emerging Gaps in Enterprise Adoption*, MIT Sloan Research Report, 2024. [Online]. Available: https://mlq.ai/media/quarterly_decks/v0.1_State_of_AI_in_Business_2025_Report.pdf

[12] SAP SE, "SAP Invests in European Sovereign Cloud to Strengthen Data Residency and Compliance," *SAP Press Release*, Berlin, Germany, 2024. [Online]. Available: https://news.sap.com

[13] J. von Neumann and O. Morgenstern, *Theory of Games and Economic Behavior*, Princeton University Press, Princeton, NJ, 1944. [Online]. Available: https://uvammm.github.io/docs/theoryofgames.pdf

[14] W. D. Mellin, "Garbage In, Garbage Out," *U.S. Army Mathematics Division Report*, 1957. [Online]. Available: https://apps.dtic.mil/sti/citations/AD0366334

[15] Anthropic, "Constitutional AI: Harmlessness from AI Feedback," *Anthropic Research Paper*, 2022. [Online]. Available: `https://arxiv.org/abs/2212.08073`

[16] OpenAI, "Language Models and Hallucination: Understanding Statistical Confidence and Factuality," *OpenAI Research*, 2023. [Online]. Available: `https://openai.com/research`

Index

R. Harjika, *Architecting Enterprise AI Strategies*, https://doi.org/10.1007/979-8-8688-2219-3

D

F

H

I, J, K

R

S

T

U

V, W, X, Y, Z

www.ingramcontent.com/pod-product-compliance
Lightning Source LLC
LaVergne TN
LVHW080026210926
848481LV00011B/3112
9798868822186